"OUR HOUSE
IS HELL"

"OUR HOUSE IS HELL"

Shakespeare's Troubled Families

MAX H. JAMES

Contributions to the Study of World Literature, Number 31

GREENWOOD PRESS

New York · Westport, Connecticut · London

Library of Congress Cataloging in Publication Data

James, Max H.
  "Our house is hell"

  (Contributions to the study of world literature,
ISSN 0738–9345 ; no. 31)
  Bibliography: p.
  Includes index.
  1. Shakespeare, William, 1564–1616—Criticism and
interpretation.   2. Family in literature.   3. Parent and
child in literature.   I. Title.   II. Series.
PR3069.F35J3   1989   822.3'3   88–34735
ISBN 0–313–26040–6 (lib. bdg. : alk. paper)

British Library Cataloguing in Publication Data is available.

Library of Congress Catalog Card Number: 88–34735
ISBN: 0-313-26040–6
ISSN: 0738–9345

First published in 1989

Greenwood Press, Inc.
88 Post Road West, Westport, Connecticut 06881

Printed in the United States of America

The paper used in this book complies with the
Permanent Paper Standard issued by the National
Information Standards Organization (Z39.48–1984).

10 9 8 7 6 5 4 3 2 1

To my own most loving and much-loved immediate family,
having occasionally known a bit of "hell" of our own—
to Wanda,
to Teresa and Genaro with Marisa and Rachel,
to Jeremy and Mary with Stefanie

Contents

Preface

Dramatists present family situations because life, for most of us, begins that way. Shakespeare's dramas, however, portray an array of fragmented families, families divided and distressed. Happy families are hard to find in any of his many plays. That families are in trouble in the late twentieth century is a truism. Most of us seem to think that surely things were better back in the good old days, but literature as well as social history does not bear that out. Families have always been profoundly and pervasively troubled, and Shakespeare truthfully confronts his thinking audience with quarreling and fighting families, with family members hurting and being hurt, with single-parent families, with families who do not understand each other, and with others who understand each other, unhappily, only too well. Jessica, in *The Merchant of Venice*, speaks poignantly for almost all of Shakespeare's dramatic families: "Our house is hell."

This study takes as its primary audience undergraduate and first-year graduate students, nonspecialist teachers of Shakespeare, and interested lay readers and viewers of Shakespeare. It draws upon the proliferating studies of families in earlier ages, both sociological and historical, to gain a better perspective of Shakespeare's treatment of families. Thus, even specialists might, occasionally, gain a fresh view or two. It also heavily uses primary materials written in the sixteenth and early seventeenth centuries to help the inexperienced to bridge the gap between their own culture and the sociohistorical milieu of Shakespeare's plays and to reach interpretive conclusions. Many of the very issues concerning his troubled families about which Shakespeare seems deliberately to provoke thought remain relevant even today, contributing to the perennial freshness of his plays.

During the past ten years or so, many specialists have written about some of the same features dealt with in this work. Some who come immediately to mind, and not in any particular order, are Marilyn L. Williamson, Leonard Tennenhouse, Richard Helgerson, Louis Adrian Montrose, Coppélia Kahn, W. Thomas MacCary, Peter Erickson, Murray M. Schwartz, Janet Adelman, Stephen Greenblatt, Joel Fineman, Lisa Jardine, Jonathan Goldberg—and there are others who will forgive their unintentional lack of mention here. All of these have made valuable contributions, some subtle and intricately complex, all with considerable intellection. To do full justice to their varied ideas would require a book or two for that purpose alone, and even to attempt substantively to include their ideas here would possibly double the length of this work. The interested should go directly, without the limitation of mediation, to their writings to encounter their treatments of these issues. Many of these persons will be quoted in this work—but admittedly very minimally and never with the intent to explicate their various approaches.

Most of the primary materials upon which this study rests are familiar to specialists in the Tudor and Stuart periods of English history and social life. The less experienced would find their spellings strange, and actual print in those works of some four hundred years ago is even more difficult to read. The long *s* that looks much like the *f* cannot be easily reproduced in modern type, nor can modern computers readily place the tilde over the vowel to represent the following appropriate *n* or *m* sound. All quotations from Shakespeare's plays used in this work are from *The Riverside Shakespeare*, edited by G. Blakemore Evans (Boston: Houghton Mifflin, 1974), an excellent edition and one that usually modernized Shakespeare's actual spellings. It seemed only reasonable, therefore, to modernize all spellings, except in the titles of books, such as the interchangeable *v* and *u* and sometimes literally *vv* for *w* (that is, literally "double *u*") and also *i* for *j*. Typesetters often used makeshift devices and sometimes they simply made mistakes. Those features have been made regular and modern here, as far as it seemed reasonable and to the extent that no violence to the original resulted. These changes should result in greater ease in reading the quotations from those early texts, and in the titles one can still get a feel for the typography of Shakespeare's day.

One further note about *The Riverside Shakespeare* text will help. When the editors were forced to add a word so that the text would make sense, they placed that emendation in square brackets to warn the reader that the text is uncertain at that point. Because square brackets are used here to indicate material not in the original, the *Riverside* emendations that were in square brackets appear in this work in curly brackets.

The fresh contribution of this study rests not so much upon the discovery of many new materials as upon the bringing together for the less experienced considerable quantities of those early primary materials and in focusing them specifically upon family life in Shakespeare's age in order to contribute to interpretive observations. The interpretive suggestions are not at all exhaustive. Shakespeare is far too complex to be so easily explained. Yet the approach taken here, as obvious as it seems once undertaken, has not been done before in this manner, and so a very modest contribution to the rich field of Shakespeare studies results, genuinely helpful, perhaps, for the less experienced and not unpleasant or offensive, one might hope, to the specialist. And yet, as Puck pleads, "If we shadows have offended . . . ."

Acknowledgments

One's debts are always immeasurable. To my excellent graduate teachers at the University of Michigan and Claremont Graduate School and to all the great scholars of the past and present whose teachings have so permeated my own thinking as to become essentially indistinguishable from my own, I—along with countless others—am deeply indebted, and those who recognize familiar ideas here will know whence they entered into all our minds. Others, with further reading, will probably come to recognize them as proven friends.

Some debts should be specifically mentioned. Two graduate students, Margaret White and Theresa Thompson, searched for some materials for a chapter each. My colleagues at Northern Arizona University have been very helpful: James Bartell, whose brilliant ideas were always stimulating and whose own materials most useful, James Fitzmaurice, Greg Larkin, William Burke, and these administrators—Paul Ferlazzo, Karl Webb, Henry Hooper, Patsy Reed, and President Eugene M. Hughes, who wrote numerous letters to facilitate my access to materials.

The Department of English and American Literature and Language at Harvard University graciously extended "officer" status to make all Harvard materials freely available, and the excellent STC holdings in the Houghton Library there form the core of the sociohistorical materials used here. The personnel of the British Museum Library and the London Guildhall Library were also most cooperative.

Lawrence Stone kindly made specific suggestions for searching additional primary sources. However, my greatest single debt is to that omnificent scholar, that most gracious and generous of men, Harry Levin, and to his lovely wife, Elena. Harry Levin read all and made numerous helpful suggestions. I can only wish this were better still, for his sake, for he is certainly not in the least responsible for its shortcomings and flaws.

"OUR HOUSE
IS HELL"

1

Chastened Children: Family as Metaphor in *Romeo and Juliet*

Shakespeare's families are deeply troubled, with scarcely a single whole and healthy family to be found in the entire corpus of his plays. The swelling tide of historical and sociological studies of family life in earlier ages, including the sixteenth and early seventeenth centuries, forbids the simpleminded conclusion that the "crisis of the family" is only a late-twentieth-century phenomenon. Although their natures certainly vary from age to age, family problems are profound and pervasive in every age. In her poignant declaration, "Our house is hell," Shylock's daughter, Jessica, speaks painfully but appropriately for almost all of Shakespeare's families, including those of *Romeo and Juliet*, or, more precisely, including that of *Romeo and Juliet*, for ultimately the play forces one to see family as metaphor: the entire populace of Verona as one family, all as unruly children—not merely the impetuous young lovers, but the parents and their relatives and friends, and the Prince—all requiring chastisement in love.

THE BODY POLITIC AS FAMILY

The family was undergoing significant change in Shakespeare's day. Although practically every assertion is met with a counterassertion in the increasingly controversial sociohistorical family studies, a growth industry in its own right, all agree on the fact of change in western-European families between 1500 and 1700, including those of England. The debate over the nature of the extended family versus the nuclear family as a part of that change is not relevant here, but the fresh enhancement of the power of patriarchy, reinforced by both church and state, is central to many of the family problems in Shakespeare's plays and especially pertinent to *Romeo and Juliet*. Patriarchalism was certainly not a new concept in Shakespeare's age; it was not unique to the Reformation, not even to Christianity, nor, for that matter, to the western world.

Patriarchalism has been a human phenomenon for centuries, in both east and west, unquestionably reinforced by both Judaism and Christianity as the Judeo-Christian culture emerged in the west. Nevertheless, patriarchy received powerful fresh impetus in the sixteenth and seventeenth centuries from both the rise of the national state and the Reformation. The authoritarian state articulated by the Tudors and the Stuarts delighted to parallel the role of the ruler, on the one hand to that of God, and on the other to that of a father. Shakespeare was but citing standard doctrine when he has Gaunt say:

> God's is the quarrel, for God's substitute,
> His deputy anointed in his sight,
> Hath caus'd his death, the which if wrongfully,
> Let heaven revenge, for I may never lift
> An angry arm against His minister.
> (*Richard II*, I.ii.37–41)

So was James I when, in a statement to Parliament on 21 March 1610, he declared that kings "are not only GODS Lieutenants upon earth, and sit upon GODS throne, but even by GOD himself they are called GODS," and "Kings are also compared to Fathers of families: for a King is truly *Parens Patriae*, the politic father of his people" (cited by Bergeron, who retained original spellings, 28). In commenting upon Robert Filmer's *Patriarcha*, Jonathan Goldberg remarks, "For him [Filmer], the king is quite literally the father of his country, for parents are 'natural magistrates' and children are 'natural subjects' . . . and kings simply act within the 'natural law of a Father' . . . in making their absolute claims to obedience" (85).

Similarly, the Reformation reinforced the patriarchal power of those in authority in several ways, but chiefly two. First, although the Roman Catholic Church unquestionably stressed the authority of the father and other authority figures, it also taught that the highest calling was celibacy, not married life, and, therefore, many thought the family was fundamentally a concession to human weakness. The Protestants stressed the centrality of the married state; the role of the father was not weakened by any implied inherently second-class condition of spirituality. Second, although the Reformation taught the priesthood of all believers, each having no ultimate mediator between God and man save Jesus Christ, yet fathers had a peculiarly heavy responsibility to act as the "priest" for those in their households, especially for women and children. The Reformation attempted to eliminate the demarcation between sacred and secular callings by declaring all callings sacred, and now responsibility rested not upon the church as an institution but upon individual believers; yet, within the "natural" patterns of authority set forth in the Bible—kings, fathers, husbands, masters—the power that had formerly been ministered through the church was to be administered throughout all segments of society by authority figures. When, in *God and the King*, Richard Mocket declared all subjects were children of the king and were thus ordered by the Fifth Commandment to honor and obey him, "James I was so delighted with this book that he ordered it to be studied in schools and universities and bought by all householders, thus ensuring it a very wide sale" (Stone, *Family* 152). Children learned in their catechism that the Fifth Commandment applied to authority figures in society as well as to their actual parents:

Teacher: Show therefore in the first place who are meant by these titles of father and mother.

Student: First our natural parents, by whom as the instruments of God, we have received our being and life. And then also all those which in any respect are in stead of parents unto us for the preservation, direction, and comfort of life.

Teacher: Who are they, whom we ought to account to be to us in stead of parents, according to this commandment of God?

Student: First, civil Magistrates in the commonwealth, such as are sovereign Kings and Princes, with their Judges and Justices, and in all public office under them. Secondly, Pastors and teachers of the word in the Church of God, with all that have government and charge of souls, together with them according to the same holy word. Thirdly, schoolmasters and teachers of the tongues, and other liberal Arts, as also such as have the wardship & government of fatherless children: and likewise masters of manual trades and occupations. (Allen 120)

In these ways did both church and state drastically reinforce patriarchalism and force the people of Shakespeare's day, and Shakespeare himself, to think of the body politic as a family.

"CIVIL BRAWLS," A FAMILY AFFAIR

The family, therefore, is a natural metaphor for all of Verona in *Romeo and Juliet*, and that Shakespeare encourages that concept can be seen both early and late. It is not necessary to argue that Shakespeare consciously knew the fact that "civil" ultimately derives from a Proto-Indo-European word meaning "to rest" and from that, "home," for one to see that "civil" is a key word in many Shakespearean plays, including *Romeo and Juliet*, where it occurs five times, more than in any other play except *2 Henry IV*, where it also occurs five times. In the entire corpus of Shakespearean drama, the word appears fifty-one times, thirteen times meaning something like "well-mannered" or "well-behaved," four times meaning "serious" or "grave" or "decorous," and thirty-four times usually referring something very painful to contemplate: conflict, strife, or war where harmony and peace ought to reign. Thus it is used in the Prologue to *Romeo and Juliet*: "Where civil blood makes civil hands unclean" (4). On occasions, the "civil war" is within the same individual, as in Sonnet 35, where "to thy sensual fault I bring in sense— / Thy adverse party is thy advocate— / And 'gainst myself a lawful plea commence, / Such civil war is in my love and hate" (9–12). So it is also in *King John* when Pandulph hears that King Philip of France has "deep-sworn faith, peace, amity, true love" between his kingdom and that of John: "So mak'st thou faith an enemy to faith, / And like a civil war set'st oath to oath, / Thy tongue against thy tongue" (III.i.263–265). Within the entity of the individual, there should be unity, harmony, and peace, not strife. But strife too frequently prevails, destroying the "rest" of home; the place where peace should reign is itself the battlefield, as Venus argues with the reluctant Adonis: "So in thyself art made away, / A mischief worse than civil home-bred strife, / Or theirs whose desperate hands themselves do slay, / Or butcher sire that reaves his son of life" ("Venus and Adonis" 763–766).

Again and again, Shakespeare's characters lament "civil wounds" or "civil broil" or "civil brawls," as in this play, or "civil war" as the curse of the community made up of "kindred," the extended body politic, the extended family. And thus in "fair Verona," because two households refuse to recognize that they are really one, the parents, pouting and quarreling, bring chastisement upon themselves and the entire city. They are, despite themselves, made one and forced to recognize their sibling relationship inside the larger family of the city. The foolish and wicked "parents' strife" from "parents' rage" has to be disciplined in and through their children, for the "iniquity of the fathers" will be visited upon the children. Romeo and Juliet, the intensely sweet young lovers whose love seems purer than driven snow, are impetuous and headstrong, consciously rebellious against the will of their parents, and, indeed, suffer the dire consequences of their hot-blooded rash rebellion, but they are simultaneously the very instruments through which the wise "heaven," like a loving father, chastises the rash rebellion of their parents. "For whom the Lord loveth, he chasteneth: & he scourgeth every son that he receiveth. . . . Now no chastising for the present seemeth to be joyous, but grievous: but afterwards, it bringeth the quiet fruit of righteousness, unto them which are thereby exercised" (Hebrews 12:6 and 11, Geneva Bible). And so all Verona finally comes to recognize its one-family set of relationships as "All are punish'd" (V.iii.295).

THE CHASTENING OF CHILDREN: "ALL ARE PUNISH'D"

The chastisement of children was a major feature of child-rearing during the sixteenth and seventeenth centuries. Both severity and frequency increased during this period, resulting from the enlarged power of coercion residing in the authority of fathers in particular and of other authority figures in general. Jean-Louis Flandrin cites the jurist Pierre Ayrault concerning the power of fathers: "domestic discipline, in which the father is like a dictator, has decreed that from his voice shall depend all that is subject to him" (130). Flandrin quotes Guillaume de Vair, the Guardian of the Seals, as writing "we should consider fathers as gods on earth," and he declares that Jean Bodin carried that same concept only to its ultimate logical end by demanding that fathers of families be restored the power of life and death which had been theirs until abolished in late antiquity by Christian emperors (130). Aristotle viewed a household as "all persons subject to the authority of its chief—slaves and servants as well as spouse and blood relatives" (Herlihy 2). The Latin *familia* "designates everything and everybody under the authority (*patria potestas*) of the household head. *Familia* in classical usage is often synonymous with patrimony" (Herlihy 2).

Children were considered naturally stubborn and full of pride that had to be broken down. "During the period from 1540 to 1660 there is a great deal of evidence especially from Puritans, of a fierce determination to break the will of the child, and to enforce his utter subjection to the authority of his elders and superiors, and most especially of his parents" (Stone, *Family* 162). Flogging became the substitute for fines in the fifteenth century for the poor who were unable to pay their fines and, anyway, who were considered socially suitable for physical punishment. From the early sixteenth century, flogging became the standard punishment for academic shortcomings. Stone thinks the "greater evidence of brutality in the sixteenth-century home and school is a reflection of a harsher reality, not merely of a larger and more revealing body of written records" (164).

Beatings were usually of two forms—with a bundle of birches on the naked buttocks until the blood flowed, or with a ferula, a pear-shaped piece of wood with a hole in it, on hand or mouth, raising a painful blister. Punishment in the schools sometimes reached sadistic proportions, as apparently it did with Dr. Busby of Westminster School and with Dr. Gill of St. Paul's. Floggings were so much a part of university education that by the sixteenth century even the deans and tutors, not merely the college head, had authority to administer physical punishment. So much was flogging a part of education that "the characteristic equipment of the schoolmaster was not so much a book as a rod or a bundle of birch twigs" (Stone, *Family* 163). Masters regularly beat their servants and apprentices. On one occasion a female apprentice, stripped naked and strung up by her thumbs, was striped with twenty-one lashes (Smith, "Apprentices" 152), and on another, a boy was flogged until he bled, then salted, and finally held naked near a fire (Beattie 62).

In the home, beatings were usually applied by the women—nurses, governesses, or mothers—but also frequently by fathers as well. Robert Burton in the *Anatomy of Melancholy* complained that parents were often too harsh, too frequently chiding, striking, or whipping their children, causing the children to become cowed, unable to enjoy a single hour free from fear. In Shakespeare's lifetime, the severe chastisement of children was a matter of course, applied freely by parents, schoolmasters, and masters or heads of households. Although in *Romeo and Juliet* no actual flogging takes place, there is a strong hint that Capulet can scarcely restrain himself from flogging Juliet, when, in his extreme exasperation at her refusal to marry Paris, he cries out:

> Hang thee, young baggage! disobedient wretch!
> I tell thee what: get thee to church a' Thursday,
> Or never after look me in the face.
> Speak not, reply not, do not answer me!
> My fingers itch. (III.v.160–164)

The entire cultural setting conditioned Shakespeare and the viewers of his plays to accept severe chastisement as an essential part of life and to expect authority figures, each in his own sphere, to administer discipline and chastisement for correction. Physical chastenings were harsh and frequent. Escalus, Prince of Verona, utters his first words in the play as the authority figure administering discipline: "Rebellious subjects, enemies to peace, / Profaners of this neighbor-stained steel / . . . / If ever you disturb our streets again / Your lives shall pay the forfeit of the peace" (I.i.81–82, 96–97). And, just as Capulet is indifferent to the tears and pleadings of his child, Juliet, so is the Prince utterly unresponsive to the tears of his "children" at the banishment of Romeo: "Nor tears nor prayers shall purchase out abuses; / Therefore use none . . . . / Mercy but murders, pardoning those that kill" (III.i.193–194, 197). The Prince seems willing enough to play the father and to chasten his children/subjects, yet at the end of the play, he takes his own place as a whipped child for not being more consistently a disciplinarian, "for winking at your discords," and of the family of Verona he declares, "All are punish'd" (V.iii.294–295). Moreover, the Prince also insists that the feuding Capulets and Montagues see the loss of their children as chastisement for continuing the "ancient grudge": "See what a scourge is laid upon your hate" (V.iii.292).

THE VERONA FEUD: A FAMILY FIGHT

The sixteenth century was one of habitual violence, and "both feuding among kin factions and personal hostility of one individual towards another were . . . intense" (Stone, *Family* 94). Formal blood feuds among the aristocracy in England had been virtually eliminated by the thirteenth century, but blood feuds continued unabated in Italy and Germany and were endemic among Scottish nobility until virtually Shakespeare's own day. "For example, in the year 1478 there were serious feuds going on between the earl of Buchan and the earl of Atholl, between the master of Crawford and the lord of Glamis, and between the lord of Caerlaverock and the lord of Drumlanrick. There was also a lesser feud going on that involved the lords of Cathness, Ross, and Sutherland" (Given 73–74).

Violence, often ending in homicides, in homes and ale houses and frequently in the streets, characterized English life for centuries, through the Elizabethan era.

Although the formal, institutionalized blood feud had ceased to be a feature of English society by the thirteenth century, kinsmen on occasion still exacted revenge for the death of one of their relatives. In the second quarter of the century William of Radwell was hanged in Wiltshire on the accusation of William of Bowden Hill. If the suspicions of the jurors are to be believed, William of Radwell's kin came one night to William of Bowden's house and in retaliation killed both him and his son. . . . Simon Whetebred and Nicholas de Rede, both from Helmdon in Northhamptonshire, fought over a debt that Nicholas owed Simon. Simon fatally wounded Nicholas with a stick. When Nicholas' wife Isolda tried to raise the hue and cry to have Simon arrested, his sister Matilda enabled him to escape by throttling Isolda. (Given 44–45)

The hot-blooded rashness of old Capulet and old Montague is as childish as the hot-blooded rashness of Romeo and Juliet. Shakespeare found a feud in his source, Arthur Brooke's *The Tragicall Historye of Romeus and Juliet,* but bitterness, suspicion, distrust, lesser feuds, and violence were an ongoing part of English social behavior during Shakespeare's lifetime. Stone recounts the conflict between Oxford, the father of an illegitimate son by Anne Vavasour, and Thomas Knyvett, her patron. These were men important in Elizabeth's court, both having or having had immediate access to the Queen. In the early months of 1582, rumors flew about Oxford's intention to kill Knyvett. They fought a duel in March and both were wounded. One of Oxford's men was killed. The followers of the two powerful figures met in Lambeth Marsh in June, and again some of Oxford's men were wounded. As Knyvett was disembarking on the slippery Blackfriars stairs, someone tried to kill him. In July, in a fresh outbreak, Knyvett slew an Oxford follower. In February of 1583, another Oxford follower died, apparently killed by a Knyvett man. In the next month, Oxford supporters killed Long Tom, a former follower of Oxford who had become a Knyvett man, and so the quarrel continued (*Crisis* 233).

The remarkably candid records of Simon Forman include many accounts of bitter conflicts, particularly his persecution by doctors. When he saw Shakespeare's plays, Forman kept notes for his own edification, for "practical use." After viewing *Richard II* on 30 April 1611, Forman made this note for future reference, apparently about a passage no longer included as a part of the play:

Remember therein how Jack Straw by his overmuch boldness, not being politic or suspecting anything, was suddenly at Smithfield Bar stabbed by Walworth, the mayor of London, and so he and his whole army was overthrown. Therefore, in such a case or the like, never admit any party without a bar between; for a man cannot be too wise, nor keep himself too safe. (Rowse 14)

Even trivial incidents could easily be turned into real battles between two families and their respective friends:

William of Bucknell, his brother Geoffrey, and William Swete took part in a penitential procession in Kent. As they passed the house of Richard of Brennesham, John Ruckling, one of their companions, shot an arrow at Richard's dog. Richard and his brother immediately rushed out of the house. They and some of their neighbors pursued the penitents into Littlebourne and wounded them. William of Bucknell died of his wounds three days later, and Richard of Brennesham and his brother promptly fled. (Given 45–46)

The fanatic pursuit of Catholic recusants in Warwickshire by John Whitgift, Bishop of Worcester—recusants that included Shakespeare's father, John—must have been traumatic enough to seem somewhat like a feud to William, who was an impressionable twelve-year-old when the Grand Commission Ecclesiastical was appointed in 1576 to investigate infractions of the Supremacy Act. "Shakespeare's father had also private enemies, for in Trinity term (June 15–July 4), 1582, he petitioned the court of Queen's Bench for sureties of the peace against Ralph Cawdrey, William Russell, Thomas Logginge, and Robert Young, 'for fear of death and mutilation of his limbs'" (Eccles 31). The religiosity of the sixteenth century did not diminish the sickening violence nor exclude the persistence of feuding attitudes, even when no blood was actually shed. According to Stone, John Gilpin discovered that many parishioners in the border area of Northumberland refused to enter a church where members of a family with whom they were feuding entered. Separately, they would listen to his preaching, but they would not worship together (*Family* 94).

The ferocious intensity of the feud impinging upon the young lovers in *Romeo and Juliet* does not come from Arthur Brooke's boring poem but from the persistent, pernicious freshness with which such enmities continued to afflict English life in Shakespeare's own day. The feud between the house of Montague and that of Capulet, in the conclusion of the play, turns out to be a family fight, somewhat like that of Cain and Abel, hence an "ancient grudge" and "ancient quarrel," for when they have been chastened, Capulet cries out, "O brother Montague, give me thy hand" (V.iii.296).

DISTANCE AND DEFERENCE IN PARENT/CHILD RELATIONSHIPS

The parents of Romeo and Juliet, like most other parents in Shakespeare's works, display an astounding ignorance of their children as persons, reflecting the lack of in-depth communication between parents and children characteristic of the sixteenth and seventeenth centuries. Both families show some affection for their children, yet both sets of parents reveal an utter inability to communicate with their respective children. Montague remarks to Benvolio about Romeo's solitary behavior. When Benvolio asks, "do you know the cause?" Montague replies, "I neither know it, nor can learn of him," and when Benvolio pursues further, "Have you importun'd him by any means?" Montague confesses complete failure, "Both by myself and many other friends" (I.i.143–146).

One might dismiss that single incident as being unique, the result of Romeo's infatuation with Rosaline—until the Capulets' quarrel with Juliet. There it is clear that parents try to talk *to* their children but not *with* them. Then, if one but recalls Baptista's ignorance of Bianca and Kate, Shylock's of Jessica, Brabantio's of Desdemona, and Lear's of all his daughters, to name only the most glaring examples, one sees a recurring pattern of a profound problem persisting throughout Shakespeare's many troubled families. Once more, the best understanding of the problem derives from the culture at large, from an examination of parent/child relationships. There one sees that distance and deference are the key words—distance, both physical and psychological, of parents from children and deference of children towards parents.

Children were physically separated from their parents when they were placed, often at early infancy, with a wet-nurse. Most frequently, the wet-nurse was not like Juliet's nurse, a live-in, but rather one who took the baby into her own home. The usual period of separation was about eighteen months, but Sir Robert Sibbald seems almost to boast that he nursed until he was more than two years old and was able to run up and down the streets, apparently having an indulgent country woman as his wet-nurse (Stone, *Family* 430). Another period of separation came at about the seventh year of the child:

"The want of affection in the English is strongly manifested toward their children," wrote an Italian observer at the beginning of the sixteenth century, "for having kept them at home till they arrive at the age of seven or nine years at the utmost, they put them out, both males and females, to hard service in the houses of other people, binding them generally for another seven or nine years. And these are called apprentices, and during that time they perform all the most menial offices; and few are born who are exempted from this fate, for everyone, however rich he may be, sends away his children to the houses of others, whilst he in return, receives those of strangers into his own. And on inquiring their reason for this severity, they answered that they did it in order that their children might have better manners. But I, for my part, believe they do it because they like to enjoy all their comforts themselves, and that they are better served by strangers than they would be by their own children." (Pinchbeck and Hewitt 1:25)

Once this education period ended, the child was about ready to enter life on its own, and if the family were wealthy, perhaps to marry. If not, the child first might have to earn his or her own marriage portion.

The system of child-rearing itself caused extended periods of physical separation of parents from their children, but there was a deliberate psychological distance as well. Parents were warned by religious leaders against "being too fond of your children and too familiar with them at sometimes at least, and not keeping constantly your due distance: such fondness and familiarity breed contempt and irreverency in children" (Cobbett 219–220). Although Lawrence Stone observes that the psychological distance of parents from children was also a defense mechanism in an age of extremely high infant mortality, and that unconscious defense was no doubt present, the conscious reason parents insisted on psychological distance was to avoid "cockering" them, overly indulging them, and to bring them up in the discipline and instruction in the Lord exhorted by Paul in Ephesians 6:4 and by nearly all preachers and religious teachers. Deliberate psychological distancing resulted in a shocking lack of intimacy between parent and child. Richard Helgerson comments on the contents of a letter from Sir Henry Sidney to his twelve-year-old son, Philip: "One cannot help being struck by the impersonality of these precepts. We take up the letter expecting to penetrate the intimacies of sixteenth-century family life and find that there is no intimacy to be penetrated" (17).

It was essential that children be obedient and display due reverence toward their parents at all times; therefore, profound deference was expected of children, even after they had become adults. Juliet, appropriately deferential, addresses her mother with "Madam, I am here, what is your will?" (I.iii.5), and again, "Madam, I am not well" (III.v.68). Cobbett, and many other religious teachers, insisted that children must demonstrate their honor for their parents by actions of great respect—going to meet their parents when they approach, bowing to them, always speaking reverently to them, confessing faults and showing shame when rebuked by them, confessing unworthiness when corrected by them, never sitting in the presence of parents, or talking unless invited to speak, much less laughing, in their parents' presence, and certainly, therefore, never interrupting them when their parents were speaking. Many adult children, like Elizabeth Tanfield, Lady Falkland, knelt continuously when speaking to parents, even if the conversation continued for an hour or more, regardless of pain to legs (Pinchbeck and Hewitt 19).

Even though the Montagues cannot communicate with Romeo, worse devastation results from the Capulets' utter ignorance of Juliet as a person; they neither know her nor understand her, and she finds herself powerless to communicate with them. She tries to get the ear of her parents. Kneeling before her father, she pleads, "Good father, I beseech you on my knees, / Hear me with patience but to speak a word" (III.v.158–159). Capulet is implacable. She turns desperately to her mother, "O sweet my mother, cast me not away!" but her mother will not communicate: "Talk not to me, for I'll not speak a word" (III.v.198, 202). Their ignorance of their daughter and their inability to communicate with her lead to such a rupture of relationships that their emotional distance allows them to reject her totally: "Graze where you will," threatens Capulet, shaking with rage, "you shall not house with me. . . . hang, beg, starve, die in the streets, / For, by my soul, I'll ne'er acknowledge thee, / Nor what is mine shall never do thee good," and Lady Capulet, with a cold finality that is even more frightening, announces flatly, "Do as thou wilt, for I have done with thee" (III.v.188, 192–194, 203).

PARENTAL CONSENT A REQUISITE FOR MARRIAGE

The central family conflict in *Romeo and Juliet* is rebellion, or, to use an only slightly milder term, disobedience. Both children knowingly rebel against the will of their parents, constantly conscious as they are of the bitter feud between the two families, but in the case of Juliet, it is a matter of direct rebellion against the authority of her father, who had made known his will for her to marry Paris. The play thus focuses on a growing cultural conflict between the traditional family-arrranged marriage and individual choice. Lawrence Stone traces four stages in the gradual shifts of attitude towards marriage: (1) marriages entirely arranged by the parents with little or no involvement of the children; (2) marriages arranged by parents, but with the children able to veto; (3) marriage choices made by the children but with parents having the power of veto; and (4) most recently, in this century, children making their own choices with little or no parental involvement, although some indirect parental influence often attempted (*Crisis* 670).

In the sixteenth and seventeenth centuries, the gradual trend was from stage one to stage two, a trend that is evident within this very play, for in the initial discussion with Paris, Capulet makes it clear that Juliet herself is to have a say: "But woo her, gentle Paris, get her heart, / My will to her consent is but a part; / And she agreed, within her scope of choice / Lies my consent and fair according voice" (I.ii.16–19). Moreover, when Lady Capulet first approaches the subject of marriage with Juliet, she does so to encourage Juliet to examine Paris at the upcoming feast as a prospective husband. She cannot wait; soon after announcing, "The valiant Paris seeks you for his love," she asks, "What say you? can you love the gentleman?" and urges Juliet to "Examine every married lineament, / And see how one another lends content;/ And what obscur'd in this fair volume lies / Find written in the margent of his eyes" (I.iii.74, 79, 83–86). It is not surprising, therefore, that Juliet expects to have some say in her marriage choice: "I wonder at this haste, that I must wed / Ere he that should be husband comes to woo" (III.v.118–119). Juliet has been denied any input whatsoever, not that she wanted any in the Paris arrangements, except the right of veto.

Even though she had earlier been allowed to think she was to have some voice in her marriage choice, Juliet learns to her shocked dismay that old modes of thought are not easily altered. She is allowed no part in the decision. The somewhat plaintive but matter-of-fact memoirs of Anne, Lady Halkett, illustrate how jealously parents guarded marriage choices for their children. Anne was born in 1623, the year her father died, and, until she was twenty-one years old, she relates:

I may truly say all my converse was so innocent that my own heart cannot challenge me with any immodesty, either in thought or behavior, or an act of disobedience to my mother, to whom I was so observant that as long as she lived [her mother died in 1647] I do not remember that I made a visit to the nearest neighbor or went any where without her liberty. (*Memoirs* 11)

The brother of a friend and son of "Lord H." of France, to her own surprise, fell in love with Anne and, before she knew what was happening, spoke to her of marriage, something her mother had strictly forbidden. Anne found his passion violent, but she thought it would not last long, especially if not resisted ("a seeming complaisance might lessen it"), and so she promised him that she would not marry anyone until he married, a promise she found easy to make because she was not at that time inclined to marry anyone.

She was mistaken; his passion increased, and he urged that they marry secretly. She firmly resisted his overtures and

told him he need never expect I would marry him without his father's and my mother's consent. If that could be obtained, I should willingly give him the satisfaction he desired, but without that I could not expect God's blessing neither upon him nor me, and I would do nothing that was so certain a way to bring ruin upon us both. (14)

When the parents were approached through a third party, unsurprisingly, they both objected, most particularly Anne's mother, even though the marriage would have been advantageous to Anne. The memoirs explain that Anne understood her mother's reasoning. It seemed dishonorable to allow Anne to win the affections of the son to her own advantage. Lord H. needed a marriage arrangement for this son that would bring in a considerable marriage portion, far more than Anne's mother could manage. The more it seemed that Anne might be manipulating the affections of the young man, the more strenuously the mother objected, and the more angry she became with Anne, even though Anne was wholly innocent of any wrongdoing.

The young man persisted, making it necessary for Lord H. to leave, taking his son with him. Now the mother was so angry with Anne that nothing could pacify her wrath. "After she had called for me and said as many bitter things as passion could dictate . . . , she discharged me to *see* him and did solemnly vow that if she should hear I did *see* Mr.

H. she would turn me out of her doors and never own me again" (15, emphasis added). Obviously, Anne's mother, like old Capulet, reached the ultimate threat of disowning the child very quickly. Although Anne's lover persuaded his father to convince Anne's mother to allow a final farewell visit, once the mother thought they had returned to France, she upbraided Anne for causing all to think that Lord H. had been forced to whisk away his son to save him from Anne. In actual fact, the lover escaped his father's guard and once more returned secretly to Anne's home, insisting upon seeing her again. Perplexed beyond measure what to do, that night as she was passing through her brother's bedroom in order to reach her own, she laid her hand upon her eyes as was her custom when passing through his room while he was in bed, and suddenly she realized the answer to her dilemma: "If I blindfolded my eyes that would secure me from *seeing* him, and so I did not transgress against my mother" (18, emphasis added). Thus, Anne was faithfully obedient to the very letter of her mother's law, and, anyway, was the wholly innocent party in this painful affair, but she nevertheless was not spared her mother's ire. Her mother's anger increased to the extent that for fourteen months she refused her parental blessing and never spoke to Anne without additional words of reproach, "and one day said with much bitterness she did hate to see me" (20).

Against such deeply entrenched attitudes about the sanctity of total parental control over marriage arrangements, Juliet could not hope to prevail. The modern audience is shocked by the immediate violence of Capulet's wrath against Juliet. His anger springs from several sources simultaneously. First, he is as fond of Juliet as Lear is of Cordelia and is equally disbelieving of her response. He is completely surprised and taken aback that she is not elated, "proud," and full of joyful gratitude, her grief over the death of her cousin Tybalt thus assuaged. Second, he cannot believe his ears that she dare, even momentarily, challenge his authority by so much as hesitation. He is almost as vehement in putting Tybalt in his place when Tybalt fails to give prompt and total compliance to his will to tolerate Romeo's presence at the feast. Capulet puts words in Juliet's mouth, words actually reflecting some of his own earlier concerns for her: "I'll not wed, I cannot love; / I am too young, I pray you pardon me," and then picking up on his own word, "pardon," meaning to give freely or thoroughly, he threatens to give her more freedom than she ever dreamed—total freedom, in fact: "Graze where you will, you shall not house with me" (III.v. 185–186, 188). The absolute authority of fathers was to be entirely unchallenged, even when they were wrong or when the child had greater wisdom. John Stockwood, in 1589, makes that abundantly clear in his pamphlet with the daunting title, *A Bartholomew Fairing for Parentes . . . shewing that children are not to marie without the consent of their parentes, in whose power and choice it lieth to provide wives and husbondes for their sonnes and daughters.* He emphatically asserts:

> The question here is not, what children in regard either of age or wit are able for to do but what God hath thought meet & expedient. . . . For there are many children found sometimes far to exceed their fathers in wit and wisdom, yea in all other gifts both of mind & body, yet is this not good reason that they should take upon them their father's authority." (82)

To rebel against the father's authority in the matter of marriage, regardless of the age or wisdom of the child is rebellion against God as well. Third, Juliet's father is angry because he has already given his word to Paris, and he simply will "not be forsworn" (III.v.195). It is a matter of honor and integrity, similar to that of the mother of Anne, Lady Halkett. Finally, there is a fourth reason for Capulet's outrage toward Juliet, outrage he declares that

> makes me mad!
> Day, night, work, play,
> Alone, in company, still my care hath been
> To have her match'd; and having now provided
> A gentleman of noble parentage,
> Of fair demesnes, youthful and nobly {lien'd},
> Stuff'd, as they say, with honorable parts,
> Proportion'd as one thought would wish a man. (III.v.176–182)

His outrage continues. Part of it represents his disgust with Juliet's ingratitude for all his concerned efforts on her behalf. Yet embedded in it, too, is the primary reason for arranging marriages in the sixteenth and seventeenth centuries: for the improvement of status ("of noble parentage") and for material gain ("of fair demesnes").

The crassness with which people of Shakespeare's time considered children chattels and arranged marriages as a matter of buying and selling is virtually beyond belief today. Nevertheless, that view of children had the full weight of religion behind it. John Stockwood stresses that as a major reason why children must not marry without their parents' consent: "The children are worthily to be reckoned among the good and substance of their fathers, and that by a more especial right than anything else, the which belongeth unto their possession," and children simply must not arrange their own marriages "for it standeth with great reason, that the owner dispose of the goods, and not contrariwise the goods of the owner, which were in deed a thing very absurd and contrary to all reason" (21–22).

Nowadays, the sympathy of the audience is entirely with Romeo and Juliet, but "in Tudor England the prevailing conception of marriage was practical rather than romantic, and . . . the insistence on the duty of the children to obey their parents contributed to the conception" (Pinchbeck and Hewitt 1:48). When John Stockwood wrote *A Bartholomew Fairing* in 1589, he believed the plague England had just experienced was the judgment of God upon England because so many children had disobediently married without their parents' consent. The powerfully appealing love affair and marriage of Romeo and Juliet was so effectively portrayed by Shakespeare as, perhaps, to help change societal attitudes in later years, but at the time the Tudor audience would have viewed their actions quite ambivalently. The disobedience of children, in their minds, deserved punishment.

CONTRASTED RASH REBELLIONS AND THEIR PUNISHMENTS

The rebellion or disobedience of children deserves punishment, even when they are adults, for a part of the ambivalent response to Romeo and Juliet results from the fact that their disobedience is young and virtually innocent compared to the "ancient grudge" and "cank'red hate" of their parents, outbreaks of enmity continued in utter disobedience to and rebellion against their "father," the Prince. The antitheses in the play between youth and age, love and hate, eros and thanatos have not gone unnoticed, but the particular contrast between the rash rebellion of the parents in continuing the feud and the rash rebellion of the children in marrying without parental consent needs further treatment.

So much stress is laid upon the ancient nature of the quarrel as to make it seem almost primordial. It is in relation to the feud that both Montague and Capulet are described as being "old," and, since friends as well as relatives are drawn into feuds, that the feud has continued from virtual antiquity is underscored by the fact that "Verona's *ancient* citizens" have had to "Cast by their grave beseeming ornaments / To wield *old* partisans, in hands as *old*" (I.i.92–93, emphasis added). The constant ringing of the word "old" adds a hoary aura to their hate, as though their bitter enmity springs from and perpetuates the malignant malice theologically termed original sin, the malice that sadly characterizes many human relationships in all ages, not merely the age of Shakespeare.

The original cause of the feud is unknown, perhaps very slight if "bred of an airy word" refers to the initial source rather than to the most recent "three civil brawls." In the sixteenth century, as Stone observes, people quarreled over "prestige and property," causing bloodshed over status as surely as over money (*Crisis* 223). Honor, and its closely related concept of reputation, was a cherished cultural value; the impulsive readiness to repay a real or imaginary injury was thought a sign of spirit, and loyalty to family or friend in a quarrel a moral duty regardless of the worthiness of the cause. Poor diet and ill health produced constant irritability; men and, among the lower classes, women all carried weapons and were ready to the point of eagerness to use them—perhaps as a release from the frustration, tedium, and boredom of their daily lives. Sampson's opening swagger, "we'll not carry coals," suggests an eagerness to interpret the slightest "airy word" as an insult. The pettiness of the thumb-biting attempt to provoke a quarrel is not in the least beneath the childishness to which even nobility were willing to stoop in Shakespeare's day. The Earl of Lincoln, during a quarrel with a neighbor, placed a load of human waste on the windward side of his neighbor. Henry Howard, later to become the second Vicount Bindon, repeatedly galloped by the Sheriff of Dorset in order to splash him with mud and finally deliberately knocked his hat into the mud puddles (Stone, *Crisis* 224–225). Childishness in quarrels was not at all uncommon.

Moreover, one should remember that the play opens with an emphasis upon the breaking out of the "ancient grudge" into "new mutiny," with at least two "civil brawls" occurring prior to the one on the streets of Verona with which the play begins, for "Three civil brawls . . . By thee, old Capulet, and Montague / Have thrice disturb'd the quiet of our streets" (I.i.89–91). It is also not surprising that Mercutio, "kinsman to the Prince," is involved in the feud. Stone comments on the feuds, during the reign of Elizabeth, between the Stanhopes and the Markhams, between the Fiennes and the Dymocks, between the Danvers and the Longs, between the Muschampes and the Collingwoods, and between the Mansells and the Heydons. All of these, Stone says, pulled in, through family alliances, many other important people (*Crisis* 229). Queen Elizabeth tolerated a great deal of violence of that sort and even deliberately manipulated violent factions among the aristocracy in such a fashion that they acted as checks, each upon the other. When some special interest of the state was threatened, however, Elizabeth could act vigorously enough, as she did when the religious loyalty of the Earl of Shrewsbury was called into question (236).

In *Romeo and Juliet*, the fresh outbreak of the "ancient grudge" is termed "mutiny," with the Prince as outraged as Capulet was with Juliet when the brawls continue, and the fighting is not immediately halted, even in his own presence. His term for them is "Rebellious subjects," and his exasperation increases as the conflict continues. Although it is Tybalt who hates the word "peace" as "I hate Hell," one cannot escape the conclusion that he but reflects the intensity of the hatred of the heads of these two families. The impetuous rashness with which they have at each other on the street, and the cold calculating determination of Lady Capulet to "send one to Mantua" to poison Romeo, even though the Prince has already administered justice, manifest the deep-seated disobedience to the fatherly authority of the Prince. Their continued rebellion deserves a more severe chastisement than the almost incidental disobedience of Romeo and Juliet resulting from their love for each other. Moreover, if the bypassing of parental consent by the young people were rebellion against God, as Shakespeare's audience would have felt, how much more would an audience that heard in church nearly every Sunday the Homily on Obedience of 1547 view the continued rebellion of the two families against the authority of the Prince as rebellion also against God. "The power of kings in their realms was likened unto God in the universe; of corporal heads over the other limbs of the human body; and of fathers over families. . . . Order and obedience were indivisible. And just as order was the principle by which God's will was manifest, so were disobedience and rebellion the manifestation of disorder and defiance of God's will" (Ashton 35–36).

Just as David's rebellion against God in the matter of adultery with Bathsheba and the murder of her husband Uriah was mirrored in the rebellion of Absalom against both David and God, so was the rebellion of Romeo and Juliet but a dim reflection of the more culpable mutiny of the parents. The exquisite beauty of the love of Romeo and Juliet for each other, in sharp contrast to the "cank'red hate" of their parents, practically purifies their actions, especially since they receive the blessing of Friar Lawrence. The modern audience, however, imbued with the myth that romantic love is self-justifying, feels that contrast more keenly than one in Shakespeare's time would have done. Stone quotes Bacon about the mischief done by passionate love acting sometimes like a Siren and sometimes like a Fury. Since passionate love is a human phenomenon, as Stone says, "like influenza," Bacon warned that if one catches it, he should at the least keep that passion separated from the serious business of life. Stone also quotes the brother of Dorothy Osborne who says in effect that since passions cause more trouble than they provide satisfactions, one should minimize them if he wishes to be happy (*Crisis* 594). Even in this play, Juliet expresses distrust of "this contract," representing their impetuous passionate love: "It is too rash, too unadvis'd, too sudden, / Too like the lightning, which doth cease to be / Ere one can say it lightens" (II.ii.118–120). Yet, surely in any culture of any age, the play powerfully persuades one of the reality of their love, particularly in contrast to the artificiality of the infatuation Romeo formerly felt for Rosaline, another contrast of old and young, "old desire" versus "young affection."

Against the black enmity of their parents, their love, like Juliet herself "hangs upon the cheek of night / As a rich jewel in an Ethiop's ear— / Beauty too rich for use, for earth too dear!" (I.v.45–47). Their love is born in the festering charnel house of familial disobedience and ends literally in a tomb, surrounded by the bones of "buried ancestors" and Tybalt "fest'ring in his shroud." The "ancient grudge" comes to an end through the chastening of the forgivable rash disobedience of the young, for nothing less than their deaths could be sufficient chastening for the rash disobedience of the old, deaths so beautifully bright that they make "This vault a feasting presence full of light" (V.iii.86).

CONCLUSION

Like the slaughter of the innocents to assuage the rage of Herod, resulting in "mourning, and weeping, and great lamentation: Rachel weeping for her children" (Matthew 2:18, Geneva Bible), so Romeo and Juliet, albeit chastened for their own disobedience, become sacrificial lambs, taking away the deep-rooted and malignant hate of their parents, the very instruments through which the parents themselves are chastened—"Poor sacrifices of our enmity!" (V.ii.304). Shakespeare's plays are filled with troubled families about all of whom it may be said, "Our house is hell," but in *Romeo and Juliet*, Shakespeare uses the family as a metaphor to demonstrate how young and old alike are disobedient children requiring the correction of chastisement.

Prince: Where be these enemies? Capulet! Montague!
See what a scourge is laid upon your hate,
That heaven finds means to kill your joys with love.
And I for winking at your discords too
Have lost a brace of kinsmen. All are punish'd.
Capulet: O brother Montague, give me thy hand. (V.iii.291–296)

2

Conflicting Family Conceptions of Honor: *Titus Andronicus* and *Coriolanus*

It is scarcely possible to exaggerate the significance of honor as a cultural value during Shakespeare's lifetime. However, even this cherished value was undergoing change in several ways, resulting in conflicts adumbrated by Shakespeare's troubled families—especially, but not limited to, those in *Titus Andronicus* and *Coriolanus*. Honor was the foundation of the hierarchical conception of society and absolutely central to the relationship between parents and their children. Ideal conceptions of honor rejected revenge as a proper response to offended honor; nevertheless, revenge, pure and simple, remained a major cause of violent conflict between persons, parties, and nations. At the heart of such conflicts was not only a matter of right and wrong, but, so they thought, good and evil, and violence was often advocated as justice, the necessity of good to punish and overthrow evil.

"Virtue" was the door to honor in classical antiquity, and in Renaissance England that classical conception was retained, even as it was assimilated into Christian thought. Humanity has always had difficulty with abstractions: "right" versus "wrong," "good" versus "evil." Shakespeare was aware of conflicts resulting from differing cultural values, such as those of the Goths and Romans in *Titus Andronicus* and the Volsces and Romans in *Coriolanus*. Moreover, then as now, the generation gap often divided children from parents, and gradually changing conceptions of honor often set members of the same family into conflict with each other. Shakespeare seems to have grasped more clearly than many of his age that right and wrong or even good and evil are often a matter of relative perspective. Possibly, with his conscious mind, Shakespeare viewed good and evil as absolutes just as most in his period did, yet, artistically, he makes it clear that simple-minded either/or thinking does not at all do justice to the problems of society, both within and without the family. Rigid, inflexible, letter-of-the-law absolutism in matters of right and wrong is frequently challenged in his plays, such as *The Merchant of Venice* and *Measure for Measure*, and rigidly idealistic or absolutist views of honor are particularly addressed in *1 Henry IV*, yet nowhere are such views shown to be more disastrous than in *Titus Andronicus* and *Coriolanus*. In the entire Shakespearean canon, hardly any house is more overtly plunged into hell than that of the Andronici—but in a more terrifyingly subtle way, Shakespeare depicts a devouringly dominating woman in Volumnia, the mother of Coriolanus, and his ensuing hell results from the tangled snare of conflicting views of honor both within and without his family. Thus, in both *Titus Andronicus* and *Coriolanus*, Shakespeare confronts his audience with the confusions, contradictions, and hellish consequences of conflicting family conceptions of honor.

THE FOUNDATION OF HIERARCHY

Honor is the code defining the differing degrees in the social hierarchy and the deference deserved by each as well as the code of conduct controlling the interrelations of persons within and between societies. In an anonymous work devoted to a treatment of honor, printed in 1602, one reads the following:

And we in England do divide our men into five sorts: Gentlemen, Citizens, Yeomen, Artificers, and Laborers. Of Gentlemen, the first and principal is the King, Prince, Dukes, Marquesses, Earls, Vicounts, and Barons. These are the Nobility, and be called Lords, or Noblemen. Next to these be Knights, Esquirers, and simple Gentlemen, which last number may be called *Nobilitas* minor: for they in Parliament have no place among the Lords; therefore the Barons or degree of Lords do resemble the dignity of *Senatores* in Rome, and the title of our Nobilities is like unto *Patritij*, when *Patritij* did signify *Senatores aut Senatorum filij*. (*Honor* 51)

The writer makes it completely clear that honor distinguishes societal degrees and determines the behavior of each segment of society. He declares, "The scope and mark of each man's endeavor, is either profit or honor. The one proper to men in base or mean fortune, the other to persons of virtue and generous mind. But now we will in this work entreat only of the last: For as one man is more worthy than another, so ought he before others to be preferred and honored" (209). This writer, like others of his age, leaves nothing to chance; he presses his point from every possible angle:

Some are honored for their dignity, as Princes, Prelates, Officers, and other men of great place or title. Others are honored for their age or anciency.... To these, many other causes of Honor may be added, as subjects to honor their Prince, servants their masters, inferiors their superiors. And divers demonstrations of honor are also due by external countenance, words, and gestures; as by attentive hearing of him that speaketh, by rising to him that passeth &c. (211)

He describes in detail various behaviors that demonstrate deference. For example, one who sits receives honor from him who stands, except that "a man of dignity" should sit in the presence of judges and not stand "as common persons do, unless his own cause be pleaded." One who sits on the right receives more honor than the one sitting on the left. One who stands or walks in the midst of two or more receives the greater honor, as does one who walks next to a wall. At table, the one seated at the "chief end, or in the highest place of the table" is accorded the most honor. In these and many other specific details, the writer describes how honor determines the code of conduct for each individual in a hierarchical society. There was scarcely a moment, day or night, that a person could forget the claims of honor upon his life. It is not surprising, therefore, that honor plays a prominent role in many Shakespearean plays, and, because a conception as abstract yet all-pervasive as honor, despite the constant efforts to codify honorable behavior as exemplified above, was bound to cause many confusions and contradictions, it is also not surprising that Shakespeare, along with his other artistic objectives in *Titus Andronicus* and *Coriolanus*, should examine the painful consequences of those confusions and contradictions.

Modern British society, as democratic as it is, retains many vestiges of the hierarchical structure that dominated Shakespeare's age. The challenge of hierarchy had already begun, and Shakespeare is sensitive to the forces for social change at work. *Titus Andronicus* opens with a direct challenge to primogeniture. Saturninus pleads his "successive title" as his right to be named Emperor of Rome, the right of the firstborn son. Bassianus, his younger brother, argues his own right to be named Emperor on the basis of the best-man theory: "But let desert in pure election shine." The principle of primogeniture has never been fully displaced in Britain, but the loosening grip of this tenet central to the hierarchical system did not come about quickly or easily. In 1671, a small book emerged, the title of which sounds like a significant challenge to primogeniture: *The Yovnger Brother His Apologie or A Fathers Free Power disputed, for the*

disposition of his lands, or other his Fortunes to his Sonne, Sonnes, or any one
of them: as right Reason, the Lawes of God and Nature, the Civill, Canon and
Municipall Lawes of this Kingdom doe command. A title as assertive as that
suggests a major argument against traditional inheritance procedures,
but the anonymous writer turns out to be very tentative after all. With
many a cautious caveat permitting the continuation of traditional practices, he timidly concludes that "a Fathers freedom is such, that he may
Lawfully and *Religiously* give his Lands and Goods, or other his Fortunes
to any one of his Children" (3). Therefore, as late as 1671, the doctrine
of primogeniture still held such total sway that this writer, who says he
knows of no other work on this important subject, does not assert that
a father should ignore traditional procedures but only that he could:
"Only I mean to argue, whether a Father possessed in Fee-Taile, may in
law and equity, upon the former considerations, make any child which
he hath, his Heir, leaving to the rest a competency; and do an Act which
according to Equity & Religion may stand good and valuable" (3). Primogeniture, under attack in Shakespeare's day, an attack reflected in his
plays, only gradually relaxed its hold on inheritance practices.

The initial dramatic conflict of *Titus Andronicus* focuses upon this tenet so foundational to hierarchy that, when Richard II, in the play that
bears his name, seizes the inheritance of Bullingbrook, the Duke of
York protests that Richard is actually cutting out the ground from beneath his own feet: "For how art thou a king / But by fair sequence and
succession" (II.i.198-199). Indeed, the controversy between Saturninus
and Bassianus over this fundamental doctrine of inheritance sets in
motion all the other conflicts in *Titus Andronicus*. The unhesitating
choice of Titus, his reflexive response, commits him firmly to "create our emperor's eldest son, / . . . our Emperor!" (I.i.224, 229). For
Titus, the issue is not the least questionable; his rigid and unthinking
commitment to primogeniture as a principle of honor ignores "virtue,"
the basis of honor. The challenge of Bassianus is exactly that—namely,
that Saturninus is dishonorable, unworthy of the throne: "And suffer
not dishonor to approach / The imperial seat, to virtue consecrate, / To
justice, continence, and nobility" (I.i.13–15). His indictment proves valid;
Saturninus reveals himself to be a dishonorable scoundrel. The inheritance conflict in Rome, a conflict of honor as the basis of hierarchy versus
honor as the result of virtue, not only splits the brothers, Bassianus and
Saturninus, but because Titus yields to Saturninus not only "My sword,
my chariot, and my prisoners, / . . . Mine honor's ensigns humbled at
thy feet" (I.i.249, 252), but also his daughter Lavinia to become the wife
of Saturninus, the Andronici are thereby immediately split, the sons of
Titus taking sides against him along with their uncle, Marcus, because
apparently Lavinia had been earlier promised to Bassianus, and it is now
a matter of honor that the promise be kept. Conflicting conceptions of

honor split both families, and the bloody mess of this play, earlier set in motion by Titus' implacable insistence upon the sacrifice of Alarbus, the eldest son of Tamora, Queen of the Goths, now becomes still bloodier as Titus unhesitatingly kills his own son Mutius for seeking to oppose Titus' pursuit of Bassianus and Lavinia. C. L. Barber observes, "The Pandora's box of horrors opened in *Titus* centers on family relations, in blood ties and blood feud" (191). Honor, the foundation of hierarchy, both as primogeniture and as the unquestioned obedience due a father from his children, is an explosive issue blasting apart two Roman families in *Titus Andronicus* and *Coriolanus*.

Coriolanus opens with a different but equally serious challenge to hierarchy. A company of mutinous citizens demands social justice; they are hungry, they say, and they are rioting for grain. "What authority surfeits {on} would relieve us," they declare, but recognizing Coriolanus to be the supreme soldier enforcing patrician authority, as they resolve "rather to die than to famish," they call him the "chief enemy to the people," and conclude, "Let us kill him, and we'll have corn at our own price" (I.i.16, 5, 7, 10). Here is outright rebellion, a challenge to that great chain of being, the very foundation upon which the hierarchical conception of society rests: honor. The central conflict between the tribunes, Sicinus and Brutus, and Coriolanus—or Martius, as he is called before his astounding victory over the Corioles—is one of authority. Martius uncompromisingly asserts the traditional value of honor, the rule of the patricians over the plebeians. The masses, through rioting, succeed in gaining "Five tribunes to defend their vulgar wisdoms, / Of their own choice" (I.i.215–216). Martius is outraged. "The rabble should have first {unroof'd} the city / Ere so prevail'd with me; it will in time / Win upon power [that is, make further inroads upon traditional authority], and throw forth greater themes / For insurrection's arguing" (I.i.218–221).

Food riots were common in England in the late sixteenth and early seventeenth centuries. Buchanan Sharp, who has made a special study entitled *In Contempt of All Authority*, says that "there were between 1586 and 1631 at least forty [food riots], as well as two attempted insurrections and a considerable number of other riots and insurrections planned or rumored, all of which were related in some way to the state of the food market" (10). Indeed, Sharp asserts, "The most notable characteristic of artisans . . . was their readiness to engage in riot and insurrection" (3). Many of the riots were by nonagricultural workers, not only the artisans of whom Sharp writes, but the unskilled poor who constantly felt grinding poverty because their wages never caught up with rapidly inflating prices. Yet Shakespeare heightens the conflict by emphasizing the political power struggle, the exploitation of the mutable masses by the tribunes for the purpose of aggrandizing their own power. It is they who remind the people that

> when he [Martius] had no power,
> But was a petty servant to the state,
> He was your enemy, ever spake against
> Your liberties and the charters that you bear,
> I' the body of the weal. (II.iii.177–181)

And Martius, in return, recognizes the tribunes as the primary chal-
lengers to hierarchy and to the principle of honor upon which it
rests: "Behold, these are the tribunes of the people, / The tongues o'
the common mouth. I do despise them! / For they do prank them in
authority, / Against all noble sufferance" (III.i.21–24). He cries out to
the "reakless senators" to ask why they have given "Hydra," the many-
headed beast of the multitude, such officers to challenge their power:
"You are plebeians," he thunders at the senators:

> If they be senators; and they are not less,
> When, both your voices blended, the great'st taste,
> Most palates theirs . . . . when two authorities are up,
> Neither supreme, how soon confusion,
> May enter 'twixt the gap of both, and take
> The one by th' other. (III.i.101–104, 109–112).

The opportunistic and utterly unprincipled tribunes are able to exploit
the moral cowardice of the patricians as well as the personal weakness
of Coriolanus to rid themselves of him by driving him from Rome. The
shortage of food with which the play begins is but the initial challenge to
hierarchy; the central one is that of the tribunes, particularly Sicinus and
Brutus, in seizing the power of the masses so successfully that they are
allowed to reverse the election of Coriolanus and, as he rightly observes,
"To curb the will of the nobility" (III.i.39). Nowhere do the lower classes
more baldly set themselves into direct conflict with honor, the foundation of hierarchy, than in *Coriolanus*.

"VIRTUE," THE DOOR TO HONOR

Rome becomes almost a character in both *Titus Andronicus* and
Coriolanus, and what is at stake in both plays is the loss of virtue, the
degradation of honor. Titus declares Rome to be "a wilderness of tigers";
as Coriolanus banishes the tribunes after they attempt to banish him "As
enemy to the people and to his country," he rages, "Despising, / For you,
the city, thus I turn my back" (III.iii.118, 133). To men of honor, where
no virtue is, there is nothing more worth living for. As Francis Markham

said in 1625, "Therefore of all the Crowns which man's life can labor for, none is so precious as this of Honour; for that broken, all the rest are nothing but cinders" (12). Men of honor know that true honor is not in the externalities of great place and deference but springs from the heart and mind and manifests itself in acts of virtue. Markham says:

This Rare thing *Honor*, (which is now my Theme) is so excellent and worthy the pursuit of all men, that the *ancients* held it unvaluable, & not within the compass of any rate or price; & that it was to be acquired & sought of all men; & once attained, to be preferred before all earthly things how accomplished soever: for it is the reward of virtue, the witness of man's excellency, and the only friend and companion that walketh hand in hand with honesty. (1)

The only entrance to true honor is through the door of virtue:

Honor, saith Cicero, is the reward of virtue, and infamy the recompense of vice: whoso men then desireth to aspire unto Honor, it behooveth him to come therunto by the way of virtue, which the Romans covertly expressed in building the Temple of Honor, so as no man could pass therunto but first he was forced to go through the Church dedicated to virtue. (*Honor* 208)

The anonymous writer of *Honor* believed that too few were "well informed what Virtue meaneth," and so he presented his order and interpretation of the classical virtues. "Therefore to begin with that which of all others is most necessary for preservation of human society, I say that Justice is a virtue which informeth every man to rest contented with so much as to him appertaineth, and give to all others that which to them belongeth" (208). Justice is, indeed, a central concern in both *Titus Andronicus* and *Coriolanus*, for Titus in his borderline or actual madness is so obsessed with the loss of justice in Rome that he prepares messages attached to arrows "*Ad Jovem*," "*Ad Apollinem*," "*Ad Martem*," and others because, he raves, "Sith there's no justice in earth nor hell, / We will solicit heaven and move the gods / To send down Justice for to wreak our wrongs" (IV.iii.50-52). Similarly, Coriolanus, almost beside himself with outrage, inveighs against the honorless tribunes, "Your dishonor / Mangles true judgment, and bereaves the state / Of that integrity which should become't; / Not having the power to do the good it would, / For th' ill which doth control't" (III.i.157–161).

Justice, the leading virtue into the temple of honor, means resting contented with one's fair degree of reward on the one hand, and giving on the other, that fair degree of reward to others that rightly belongs to them. Thus, nothing is so monstrous as ingratitude. Titus and Coriolanus, both men of honor, find ingratitude to be as lacerating as does Lear. The third citizen in *Coriolanus* expresses Shakespeare's point: "Ingratitude is monstrous, and for the multitude to be ingrateful were to make a monster of the multitude; of the which we being members, should bring ourselves to be monstrous members" (II.iii.9–12). "Precisely," Coriolanus would have said had he heard that statement, for that is exactly what the unprincipled tribunes make of them—"monstrous members." Marcus, the brother of Titus, urges their kinsmen to "Join with the Goths, and with revengeful war / Take wreak on Rome for this ingratitude" (IV.iii.33–34). And Coriolanus asks Aufidius to "use . . . my revengeful services," for Coriolanus has determined to "fight / Against my cank'red country with the spleen / Of all the under fiends," and Aufidius gladly agrees to pour "war / Into the bowels of ungrateful Rome" (IV.v.89–92, 129–130). Ingratitude is a violation of justice, slamming shut the door of virtue with a consequent total denial of honor. With loss of honor, Rome becomes a jungle, barbarian and evil.

It is precisely the conflicting views of honor that distinguish honorable Rome from the barbarian Goths, on the one hand, and the barbarian Volsces, on the other. To the horror of both Titus and Coriolanus, Rome, considered now as a civic family, suffers civil war for the very reason that a portion of that civic family abandons honor, becoming as barbarian in behavior as either the Goths or Volsces, and as worthy of destruction. It is, in fact, the obligation of men of honor to fight against evil, for as Markham says, "this great Title and mark of Honor" has been

given unto man . . . as an Engine under which he ought continually to fight against all vice & wickedness. . . .
For as the Heart is in the Body, so is this matter of Honor in civil Government. If the Heart be sound and perfect, it giveth life to the whole Body, (for it is the Fountain of Blood and Spirits:) But if corrupt and diseased, then it brings Death and Dishonor to every member (17, 20).

Rome in both plays becomes a jungle, "a wilderness of tigers," as savagely unprincipled as the Goths or Volsces ever were, utterly lacking in honor, and totally unfit as a habitation for honorable persons.

When Rome was honorable, manifesting justice, temperance, fortitude, prudence, and the "Many other virtues [that] are fit to be found in every honorable personage, but among them, piety, liberality, mercy, and affability . . . excellent ornaments in every noble and generous mind" (*Honor* 209), it stood in noble contrast to the barbaric tribes around it. However, in *Titus Andronicus*, Saturninus readily accepts not only Tamora, the Goth Queen, but the Goth code of conduct as well—treachery, deceit, and completely ignoble and unfair practices.

Aaron, albeit a Moor, the epitome of Goth or barbaric code of behavior, celebrates Tamora's elevation as Rome's empress, exulting, "Upon her wit doth earthly honor wait, / And virtue stoops and trembles at her frown" (II.I.10–11); he is devoid of honor and ignorant of virtue as the essential ingredient of honor. "It is not therefore as ignorant persons and unskillful folk do surmise, that great riches, or titles of dignity, to make men honorable, unless they be accompanied with the virtues and perfections aforesaid: for riches (albeit they are a great ornament to illustrate virtue) yet are they not any efficient cause to make men honorable" (*Honor* 209). Similarly, in *Coriolanus*, the deceit, treachery, and ignobility of the tribunes parallel that of the barbaric Volsces; they, as surely as the barbaric Aufidius, cowardly manipulate others to destroy Coriolanus, for neither the barbaric tribunes nor barbaric Aufidius dare attempt it directly. Rome, a civic family, is divided against itself in both plays, for segments of that family abandon honor and embrace barbarism, exiting from the door of virtue.

"HONOR THY FATHER AND THY MOTHER"

The pervasive place accorded families in Shakespeare's plays reflects the dramatic magnification of the importance of family life emerging in Elizabethan and Jacobean society.

Between 1500 and 1700 the English family structure began a slow process of evolution in two related ways. Firstly, the importance of the surrounding kin declined; secondly, the importance of affective bonds tying the conjugal group together increased, and the economic functions of the family as a distributive mechanism for goods and services declined. . . . [together with the] decline of kinship as the main organizing principle of society; the rise of the modern state, with its take-over of some of the economic and social functions previously carried out by the family or kin, and the subordination of kin loyalties to the higher obligations of patriotism and obedience to the sovereign; and the missionary success of Protestantism, especially its Puritan wing, in bringing Christian morality to a majority of homes, and in some ways making the family serve as a substitute for the parish [contributed to family change]. (Stone, "Nuclear Family" 13)

All these factors help account for the emphasis on family in Shakespeare's plays. It is hardly possible to overemphasize the latter cause, the Puritan focus on family consequent to the weakening authority of the church in Protestantism. Puritan and other Protestant divines droned incessantly about the importance of the family, and sermons on "Honor Thy Father and Thy Mother" were almost numberless.

Cawdrey's teaching is representative:

As the Lord our God hath made and created children through their parents: so hath he cast and made them subject under the power and authority of their parents, to obey and serve them in his stead saying; *Honor thy Father and thy Mother*: which honor consisteth not in bowing the knee, or putting off the cap, or giving to their parents the upper hand only: but in this, that they love them with all their hearts, that they fear and dread them, that they cheerfully do their commandments, will and pleasure, that they seek their worship, credit, profit and preference in all things lawful; and if need require, that they give their lives for them: remembering that they are their parents goods and possessions, and that they owe to them even their selves & all that they are able to do, yea, and more than they are able. (342–343)

Equally insistent is William Gouge:

The *authority* of parents requireth *fear* in children: and their *affection*, love. So entire and so ardent is parents' *affection* towards their children, as it would make children too bold and insolent if there were not *authority* mixed therewith to work *fear*. . . .This *fear* in a child is an especial branch of that *honor* which the law requireth of children to their parents. (328, 330)

It is in the context of such interminable teachings that one should read all of Shakespeare's plays, especially *Titus Andronicus* and *Coriolanus*. Although Shakespeare, as Harry Levin wisely observes, "recognized the distance and the difference between the Romans and the Elizabethans" (34–35), it would have been asking far too much of his audience, and perhaps even of Shakespeare himself, to dehumidify their minds from the saturation of the Judeo-Christian teaching concerning parent/child relationships. Had they been able to do so, they would have known that "Honor thy father and thy mother," in the form to which they were accustomed, would not always pertain in the pagan culture of Rome in either *Titus Andronicus* or *Coriolanus*, even though pagan patriarchy, as it was practiced in Rome, was not drastically different from what they knew and practiced. Moreover, it would probably have been asking too much of them and perhaps even too much of Shakespeare to make and keep constantly in mind such cross-cultural distinctions while they were caught up in these plays.

The rebellion of the sons and the daughter of Titus against him was astounding, to Titus and to the audience of Shakespeare. For a son to lift up a sword against his father was equal to treason against the state and to satanic rebellion against God. Cawdrey warns:

Children have always to remember that whatsoever they do to their fathers and mothers (be it good or evil) they do it to God: when they please them, they please God: and when they disobey them, they disobey God: when their parents are justly angry with them, God is angry with them: neither can it be that they may come to have favor of God again (no, although all the Saints in heaven should entreat for them) until they have submitted themselves to their father and mother. . . . Take away the beam from the Sun, and it will not shine, the springs from the river, and it will dry up; the bough from the tree, and it will wither; the member from the body, and it will rot; and so take from children their duty to their parents, & they are no longer children, but brethren and companions with those unto whom Jesus Christ said: *Ye are the children of the devil.* (348, 344)

Children were repeatedly taught that they must be obedient to parents, even when the parents do wrong, just as citizens of the state, children in the civic family, must obey, even when the king does wrong. Thus when Lucius upbraids his father, "My lord, you are unjust, and more than so / In wrongful quarrel you have slain your son," Titus indignantly retorts, "Nor thou, nor he, are any sons of mine, / My sons would never so dishonor me" (I.i.292-295). Titus had done nothing more than exercise a father's right to marry his daughter to whomsoever he pleased, even to the breaking of a former promise she might have made, although the play does not make it altogether clear whether Titus even knows of the prior pledge of Lavinia to Bassianus. Everyone else seems to know; surely, Saturninus knew even when he declared, "Titus, to advance / Thy name and honorable family, / Lavinia will I make my empress" (I.i.238–240), and he possibly chose her not only for her sake or for the sake of Titus but to spite Bassianus, who had challenged his right to be emperor. But Titus has been out of the city, leaving Lavinia, probably, under the authority of Marcus. All the Andronici, save Titus himself, consider it dishonorable to break the "betrothed love" of Lavinia to Bassianus. Prior promise versus the father's right to dispose of his daughter in marriage as he pleases together with the children's obligation to obey him unquestioningly are the two conflicting conceptions of honor dividing this family in tragic ways. Against the unspeakably dishonorable Goths, including Saturninus who accepts their barbaric standards, the Andronici regroup, and ultimately Lucius prevails, leaving barbarized Rome some hope as Marcus, Lucius, and his little son remain to purge Rome of the evil of Aaron and Tamora, to "heal Rome's harms" (V.iii.148), and to return Rome to the ways of honor through the "last true duties of thy noble son" (V.iii.155).

The relationship of Coriolanus to Volumnia, his mother, is much more complex than that of the children of Titus to him, and what Shakespeare is saying to his thinking audience through them consequently more subtle and profound. Coriolanus has been berated both within and without the play for being so utterly devoted to the fundamental principle of honor, "Honor . . . thy mother," that he is, after all, nothing more than "his mother's puppet . . . a terrified little boy every time the two confront each other" (Campbell 211). Very early in *Coriolanus*, a citizen declares the heroic deeds of Coriolanus were "to please his mother" rather than "for his country." Coriolanus, had he heard, would wonder why anyone would want to make such a distinction. His mother, from his earliest childhood, had so inspired him to deeds of valor in war that pleasing her and fighting heroically for his country were inseparable in his mind. Volumnia herself explains this to her daughter-in-law, Virgilia: "I, considering how honor would become such a person [whose comeliness would pluck all gaze his way], that it was no better than picture-like to hang by th' wall, if renown made it not stir, was pleas'd to let him seek danger where he was like to find fame. To cruel war, I *sent him* from whence he return'd, his brows bound with oak" (I.iii.9–15, emphasis added). When Martius returns from his astounding solo entry into the city of the Corioles, for which deed he was named "Coriolanus," he protests to Lartius, "My mother, / Who has a charter to extol her blood, / When she does praise me grieves me. I have done / As you have done—that's what I can; induc'd / As you have been—that's for my country" (I.ix.13–17). Martius is saying, with more humility than he is usually given credit for, that he has merely done his duty to mother, country, and even the gods. The rightful honor of one is the honor of all.

Martius has honored his mother by internalizing her values and attitudes, unfortunately, to his harm as much as to his credit. His besetting sin is his uncontrollable anger; he is as hot-tempered as Lear, a noble failure, and one of which Volumnia is almost proud. "Anger is my meat," she veritably boasts to Virgilia; "Leave this faint puling, and lament as I do, / In anger, Juno-like" (IV.ii.50, 52–53). Any sensitive person poignantly feels for the son of Martius who is also internalizing his grandmother's uncontrollable anger. Valeria describes the boy's pursuit of a butterfly, but, perhaps because "his fall enrag'd him . . . he did so set his teeth and tear [the butterfly]. O, I warrant, how he mammock'd [shredded] it!" (I.iii.60–65). Even Valeria sees the resemblance, "the father's son" (57). Volumnia agrees, "One on 's father's moods" (66). The uncontrollable anger of Martius, justified in his own mind because of the outrageous violations of honor both by the tribunes and the plebs in Rome and by Aufidius and his co-conspirators in Corioles, results in his banishment and death.

Volumnia's class-conscious attitudes towards the plebeians become also largely those of Martius. However, he is particularly scornful of them because of their cowardice, laziness, and base desires. When they give any evidence of the courage of true Romans, he is generous in his praise of them: "If these shows be not outward, which of you / But is four Volsces? None of you but is / Able to bear against the great

Aufidius / A shield as hard as his" (I.vi.77–80). Yet, most of the time they deserve his scorn:

> What's the matter, you dissentious rogues . . . ?
> . . . What would you have, you curs,
> That like nor peace nor war? The one affrights you,
> The other makes you proud. He that trusts to you,
> Where he should find you lions, finds you hares;
> Where foxes, geese.
> . . . Your virtue is
> To make him worthy whose offense subdues him [him whose own flaws destroy himself],
> And curse that justice did it.
> (I.i.164, 168–172, 174–176)

They are corrupt and have not the Roman spirit. He is virtually beside himself when they flee before the Volsces in battle: "You shames of Rome! . . . You souls of geese, / That bear the shapes of men, how have you run / From slaves that apes would beat!" (I.iv.31, 34–36). Coriolanus despises the thought that he fights for pay, "A bribe to pay my sword," and when he sees the plebs busy about their looting, he is disgusted: "Cushions, leaden spoons, / Irons of a doit, doublets that hangmen would / Bury with those that wore them, these base slaves, / Ere yet the fight be done, pack up" (I.v.5–8). And their outrageous presumption to assert their wills against the authority of the patricians is such a rebellion as to keep his anger raging against the Senators as well as against the commoners for giving in to them:

> In soothing them we nourish 'gainst our Senate
> The cockle of rebellion, insolence, sedition,
> Which we ourselves have plough'd for, sow'd, and scatter'd,
> By mingling them with us, the honor'd number,
> Who lack not virtue, no, nor power, but that
> Which they have given to beggars. (III.1.69–74)

His sense of class superiority over the plebeians he has internalized from his mother, and he is surprised to find her shifting ground:

> I muse my mother
> Does not approve me further, who was wont
> To call them woolen vassals, things created
> To buy and sell with groats, to show bare heads
> In congregations, to yawn, be still, and wonder,

When one but of my ordinance stood up
To speak of peace or war. (III.ii.7–13)

Volumnia's hypocrisy toward the plebeians is the very conflicting conception of honor that divides this family, despite Coriolanus' deeply devoted determination to "Honor . . . [his] mother." He consistently and inflexibly maintains his attitude toward the degraded "mutable, rank-scented meiny": "Why do you wish me milder?" he asks her with surprise, "Would you have me / False to my nature? Rather say, I play / The man I am" (III.ii.14-16). She tries to teach him her hypocrisy under the guise of guile similar to that used in war:

If it be honor in your wars to seem
The same you are not, which, for your best ends,
You adopt your policy, how is it less or worse
That it shall hold companionship in peace
With honor, as in war, since that to both
It stands in like request? (III.ii.46–51)

The fallacy in her logic is that in war one is dealing with the enemy; in Rome, one should, at least, be dealing with fellow members of the civic family. Coriolanus honestly scolds the plebs for their lack of virtue; Volumnia, who still so despises them that when Martius says, "Let them hang!" she responds, "Ay, and burn too," now is willing for him to play the prostitute to gain their "voice," regardless of their moral condition. She urges: "My praises made thee first a soldier, so, / To have my praise for this, perform a part / Thou hast not done before" (III.ii.108-110).

One can call Martius a mamma's boy, as some both within and without the play have done, but the extraordinary stress of Shakespeare's age upon obedience, even of adult children, to demonstrate honor toward one's parents, father and mother, casts his otherwise apparent dependency in an altogether different light. "Well, I must do't. / Away, my disposition, and possess me / Some harlot's spirit!" he first responds, recognizing more clearly than Volumnia what is happening to their original principles, but the more he thinks about it, "I will not do't, / Lest I surcease to honor mine own truth, / And by my body's action teach my mind / A most inherent baseness" (III.ii.110–112, 120-122). Like Lady Macbeth, Volumnia plays unfairly. "To beg of thee, it is my more dishonor / Than thou of them," she veritably whines, and at that he acquiesces, "Pray be content. / Mother, . . . Chide me no more. I'll mountebank their loves" (III.ii.130–132). Yet one must not confuse Macbeth's violation of the chain of being in yielding to his wife with the decision of Martius to obey his mother. Markham teaches, "Honor is such a needful thing in the Chain of Order; that wheresoever it is broken, or taken away, there can nothing follow but *Contempt, Carelessness,* and *Negligence*; three such *Mutineers* in a Commonwealth, that like those at the Sack of Jerusalem, they produce nothing but Blood and Desolation" (19). Macbeth discovers that, but Martius is not guilty of Macbeth's breach; rather Martius is scrupulous in the rightful deference he renders his mother. On every occasion that Volumnia so violates the great chain of being as to place herself in the pleading role, later even kneeling to him, he immediately yields to her on the principle of "Honor . . . thy mother." Gouge teaches that adult children, even when "more wealthy or honorable" than their parents, must whenever possible render due reverence and honor: "The obedience of children doth most prove the authority of parents, and is the surest evidence of the honor a child giveth to his parent" (437, 441).

Volumnia destroys her son, not necessarily because she has too much tied him to her apron strings, but because he has so completely given himself to honor, including "Honor . . . thy mother," that he gives her the deference he believes he owes her, even when he knows more clearly than she that it will result in his harm. When Volumnia comes with Valeria, Virgilia, and young Martius to plead for Rome, Coriolanus kneels before her as an obedient son must do to show deference to his mother. She rather kneels to him, and he exclaims, aghast, "What's this? / Your knees to me? to your corrected son?" (V.iii.57–58). She pleads for the corrupt Rome he has come to scourge and purge, not that he spare Rome to destroy the Volsces, for that would now be "poisonous of your honor" but rather that he would reconcile the Romans and the Volsces. She knows the devotion Coriolanus has to honor her:

> . . . There's no man in the world
> More bound to 's mother.
> . . . the gods will plague thee
> That thou restraints' from me the duty which
> To a mother's part belongs. . . .
> Down, ladies; let us shame him with our knees. (V.iii.158–159, 166–169)

Her anger, her last resort, always devastates him—not, as many have suggested, because he is a mamma's boy, but because his rigid commitment to honor at all costs compels him to defer to her. He cannot abide her anger because, like Lady Halkett, even as an adult child, he thinks that a mother's anger represents a child's failure to honor her. He yields:

> . . . O mother, mother
> What have you done? Behold, the heavens do ope,

> The gods look down, and this unnatural scene
> They laugh at. O my mother, mother! O!
> You have won a happy victory to Rome;
> But, for your son, believe it—O believe it—
> Most dangerously you have with him prevail'd,
> If not most mortal to him. But let it come. (V.iii.183–189)

Coriolanus has so deeply internalized his duty to his mother, even as Cawdrey taught the people of England in Shakespeare's time, that properly obedient children, "if need require . . . give their lives for them." Thus, Coriolanus is willing to lay down his life for his mother, and, because of her, for corrupt Rome. Hence, the celebration by corrupt Rome about the triumph of this horrible woman over her son's determination to purge dishonor from Rome with fire, a harsh intent as shocking to modern audiences as Titus' unhesitating killing of "dishonorable" Mutius, is particularly ironic. She has triumphed precisely because of conflicting family conceptions of honor.

HONOR IN THE CONFLICT BETWEEN GOOD AND EVIL

Francis Markham, one of the innumerable writers of courtesy books in the Elizabethan and Jacobean periods, says:

That there is not anything . . . more necessary for man (in respect of worldly benefits) than the use & endowment of *Honor*, is diversely proved both by Divine and Human arguments, for besides the Omnipotency of the Eternal Majesty, who before the beginning of all Worlds hath created and placed in Heaven these several Ranks & Ranges of Honor, . . . also . . . it hath pleased him to take unto himself all the Attributes of Honor, whereby to express his perfection. . . . So likewise hath he from an Incomprehensible Bounty & Divine Liberality, distributed and given unto men this great Title and mark of *Honor*, as an Engine under which he ought continually to fight against all vice & wickedness. (17)

Those who are honorable persons, particularly those of "especial Ranks and Qualities," have an unceasing obligation to oppose vice and wickedness, within themselves and in society. Shakespeare is keenly aware of the over-simplified black-or-white absolutism that frequently contradicts itself. Nevertheless, he does not seem to doubt that profound wickedness exists and that to oppose it is imperative. In both *Titus Andronicus* and *Coriolanus*, evil is a viciously destructive force; honor must fight against it. Evil in both plays exists, unsurprisingly, in the barbarian Goths and Volsces, but both protagonists grieve most because evil has also infected Rome itself.

Once more, *Titus Andronicus* is the less complex play. Evil promulgated by the Goths, clumsily by Demetrius and Chiron but cunningly by Tamora and Aaron, almost prevails, essentially because of the gullibility and corruptibility of Saturninus, for it is virtually impossible for Titus with his inflexible adherence to the honor code to rebel against the Emperor. The rape and mutilation of Lavinia, to some extent represents the rape and mutilation of the civic family of Rome itself.

Mere revenge for its own sake is alien to the honor code, says Vincentio Saviolo, another of the courtesy book authors, even if someone has violated the chastity of one's own wife. However,

for adultery ought a man to combat, not as to revenge the wrong done to one particular person, but in regard of all, considering how holy and religious a bond matrimony is, being a lawful conjunction instituted and ordained by God, to the end that man and woman therin should not as two, but as one person, live together in such manner, that nothing except death only might separate and disjoin them. Wherefore perpending the dignity and worthiness hereof, and how that by adultery this divine ordinance and institution is violated, matrimony and all conjunction infringed, and lawful procreation corrupted, every Gentleman ought to undertake the combat, not so much to revenge himself, or his friends, or to chastise or punish the offenders, as to preserve and keep from violence a bond so sacred and inviolable, with sure hope, that God, who (as *S. Paul* saith) will judge the Adulterer, will by means thereof give most severe judgement. (Y4, verso and Z, recto)

Although one should never underestimate Shakespeare's ability to cross time and culture barriers, nevertheless such precepts of the honor code provided the substructure of the disparate teachings about honor in his day, both for himself and his audience. That is, for Titus to take revenge for the adultery forced upon Lavinia and for the murder of Bassianus simply to assuage his own wrath would be wrong; however, he not only can but should seek to eliminate this evil in the name of the greater good of society. For such an abominable deed as her rape and mutilation to occur in Rome is so horrible as to cause Titus to respond, "Give me a sword, I'll chop off my hands too, / For they have fought for Rome, and all in vain. / . . . 'Tis well, Lavinia, that thou hast no hands, / For hands to do Rome service is but vain" (III.i.72–73, 79–80).

The evil with which Titus must contend has corrupted Rome: "You heavy people," he vows when he has received the heads of his wrongfully executed sons, "circle me about, / That I may turn me to each of you, / And swear unto my soul to right your wrongs" (III.i.276–278).

Not for himself and his family alone, but for Rome will he seek "Revenge's cave." When Titus has succeeded in his ghoulish plan, not only to kill Chiron and Demetrius but to bake them in a pie "Whereof their mother daintily hath fed," when he has, like Virginius, slain his daughter to purge her shame and killed Tamora and been killed by Saturninus, Marcus asks, "what Sinon hath bewitch'd our ears, / Or who hath brought the fatal engine in / That gives our Troy, our Rome, the civil wound" (V.iii.85–88). The honor code requires nobility to fight against evil and restore good. Rome, corrupted by the Goths, including Aaron, who has not only done "a thousand dreadful things, / As willingly as one would kill a fly," but who also "grieves . . . that I cannot do ten thousand more" (V.i.141–144), and by "the traitor Saturnine," has received a deep "civil wound," but honor defeats evil, and Lucius, "son to old Andronicus, / Who threats, in the course of this revenge, to do / As much as ever Coriolanus did" (IV.iv.66–68), vows "To heal *Rome's* harms, and wipe away *her* woe!" (V.iii.148, emphasis added). Good defeats evil for the sake of the civic whole.

Likewise, Coriolanus determines to "fight / Against my cank'red country" (IV.v.90–91), corrupted and controlled by such lawlessness that the "dissentious rogues" can scarcely be kept from feeding on one another. So consistently does he articulate his rage against the plebeian presumption, egged on as they are by Sicinius and Brutus, to make "parties strong / And feebling such as stand not in their liking / Below their cobbled shoes" (I.i.194–196), their insurrection, dissention, being "such as cannot rule / Nor ever will be ruled," "rebellion, insolence, sedition," "mutinies and revolts" that one cannot fail to understand his perception that evil prevails in Rome. Therefore, the loves of such persons, he declares, "I prize / As the dead carcasses of unburied men / That do corrupt the air" (III.iii.121–123). Still, he is dedicated to the service of Rome and desires to rid it of its corruption. He seeks to explain to his mother that he would rather be the servant of the Roman people than to rule over them according to the humiliating custom of begging their "voices" or votes: "Know, good mother, I had rather be their servant in my way / Than sway with them in theirs" (II.i.203–205). Roman integrity is virtually an obsession with him.

Coriolanus is far more perceptive than any of the other patricians in recognizing the evil deceit of Sicinius and Brutus as they scheme to preserve and increase their political power: "You being their mouths, why rule you not their teeth? / Have you not set them on? . . . It is a purpos'd thing, and grows by plot" (III.i.36–37, 39). Even Cominius finally agrees that the people have been deceived and incited by trickery unbecoming to Rome: "The people are abus'd, set on. This palt'ring / Becomes not Rome" (III.i.58–59). To a true nobleman, to be charged with a lie required a duel, but the base tribunes, who have indeed taught the plebs to lie as they take back their voices or votes, are so intent on provoking Coriolanus to a reckless display of rage that they care not that he justly exclaims to Sicinius, "Thou liest." When Martius is face to face with Aufidius for the first time in the play, he says, "I do hate thee / Worse than a promise-breaker" (I.vii.2–3). A promise-breaker is one kind of liar, and the tribunes deliberately teach the plebs to become promise-breakers. Such evil has ruined Rome, Coriolanus believes; his declaration is worthy of restatement: "Your dishonor / Mangles true judgment, and bereaves the state / Of that integrity which should become't; / Not having the power to do the good it would, / For th' ill which doth controll't" (III.i.157–161). Evil rules Rome and robs it of the power to do good. Sensitive readers recognize that his egoism and vanity sometimes become confounded in his mind with honor; nevertheless, honor, as he sees it, requires Coriolanus to fight against evil for the sake of Rome itself.

Once engaged in the ageless struggle of the monomyth, good versus evil, humans often allow their own lower emotions to express themselves. One would be foolish not to recognize a personal desire for revenge emerging in both Titus and Coriolanus, but to these rigid men of honor, evil has triumphed over Rome, and for Rome's own sake, they must take drastic action. They have both risked their lives again and again for the common good of Rome. At one point a Senator says to Coriolanus, "No more words, we beseech you." Coriolanus retorts:

> How? no more?
> As for my country I have shed my blood,
> Not fearing outward force, so shall my lungs
> Coin words till their decay against those measles [leprosy]
> Which we disdain should tetter [infect] us, yet sought
> The very way to catch them. (III.i.75–80)

If he has been willing to shed his blood in fighting against Rome's external enemies, how much more is he willing to fight against her internal evil. Shakespeare forces his thinking audience to recognize the great irony of a Roman patriot of impeccable integrity failing to rid Rome of its internal evil, dying instead in ignominy and shame at the hands of a rabble of Volsces egged on by an ignoble Aufidius. Yet even the barbaric Aufidius has more nobility than Sicinius and Brutus. Coriolanus ultimately proved to be a prophet, not without honor save in his own country, for the Volsces in Corioles honor him in death, "Let him be regarded / As the most noble corse that ever herald / Did follow to his urn," a Volsce Lord commands, and even Aufidius, his envious rage gone now that Coriolanus is dead, orders, "Beat thou the drum, that it speak mournfully; / . . . Yet he shall have a noble memory" (V.vi.143–145, 149, 153).

Titus and Coriolanus, both men of inflexible honor, die because Rome departs from the way of honor. Both suffer from conflicting conceptions of honor within their own families. Coriolanus, in particular, lays down his life to honor his mother, even though he knows better than she that her compromises concerning honor will result in his death. The death of Titus is not in vain—Lucius will heal Rome and return her to the path of honor—but Coriolanus, fatally flawed by his mother, dies "Like to a lonely dragon," an idealistic champion of honor, who, for the sake of one kind of honor, was unable to heal his Rome of its rottenness and to restore Roman integrity.

3

Authority—Fathers Dominant from the Grave: *The Merchant of Venice, All's Well That Ends Well, Measure for Measure*, and *Hamlet*

Possibly no single word articulates Renaissance social relationships more forcefully than "authority." Authority is central to all social organizations, but hierarchical systems openly stress authority patterns more persistently than egalitarian systems generally do. Certainly, the question of where authority resides was recurrent before, during, and after Shakespeare's lifetime, and major changes were taking place. The Protestant Reformation replaced the locus of authority, taking it from the Church and placing it in the Bible, reversing the previous pattern. In the Roman Catholic system, the Church interpreted the Bible, exercising authority over it; Protestants subjected the Church organization to the Bible and required the Church to submit to the authority of the Bible, the supreme authority on earth for faith and practice. Therefore, the biblical patterns of authority were incessantly repeated: God, King and the nobility in their official roles, Ministers, Fathers and Masters who were often one and the same.

The linchpin or even the cornerstone of the entire system was the father. Francis Dillingham, in *Christian Oeconomy or Hovshold Government,* explains:

As it is meet that Commonwealths should be well governed, so it is meet that families should be well governed: . . . Fifthly are families called little worlds, as the world is God's family, so should every family be God's world: as God doeth order all things in the world to his own glory, so should Masters of families govern to the glory of God. (H 3, verso to H 4, verso)

The family was the basic social unit, the social microcosm, and the authority of the father was not merely considered axiomatic but was also taught and retaught throughout the land.

"YOUR FATHER . . . AS GOD"

In the Geneva Bible, Ephesians 3:13 and 14 read as follows: "For this cause I bow my knees unto the Father of our Lord Jesus Christ, (Of whom is named the whole family in heaven and in earth)." All mankind is a family; God is the father of that family; every family is a mirror of the concept of God as father and human beings as children. It is no surprise, therefore, that, in *A Midsummer Night's Dream*, Shakespeare has Theseus remind Hermia: "Be advis'd, fair maid. / To you your father should be as a god" (I.i.46–47). Children were thus catechized on all sides. John Dod, in *A Plaine and Familiar Exposition of the Ten Commandements, with a Methodicall short Catechisme*, writes, "This is the first reason, whereby God would move inferiors to obey, Because he is thy father. In that God makes this his reason, why the child should obey his father, because he is his father, we gather this doctrine" (186). Cawdry teaches: "Albeit the name of father belongeth properly unto God, as Jesus Christ said: 'You have but one father, even him that is in heaven.' Yet doth he so impart it to that have begotten us, that they being called fathers, do bear the title and image of God" (348). Robert Allen, in 1600, makes clear why subjection to the authority of fathers (and mothers, as Cawdry says, the "fellow helper" to the "Chief governor") is essential: "because child-like subjection is the entrance and preparation to all obedience and subjection" (120). Exactly so was the authority of fathers in the home the very cornerstone of the entire structure of society. "Father" was God's name for himself in relation to human beings. Beginning in the home where a child received his being, father was as God himself in authority to the child. If a child did not learn obedience and subjection in the home, he could not become a proper member of the social macrocosm, society at large. The pattern is clear: the child learns to submit to and obey the authority of the father, the "Chief governor" and his "fellow helper," the mother, in the home. Outward and upward, the lines of authority stream from the home into the rest of society right on up to the recognition of God's ultimate authority, because the very name "Father" means that.

Shakespeare's plays that present families as important to the dramatic activity, with the exception of *Coriolanus*, almost always focus on fathers. Mothers are often absent, hardly alluded to, and that is not particularly surprising because mothers frequently died in childbirth and if a father chose not to remarry, and many did not, the family consisted of the father and his motherless children. Although society obviously intended for the father to be the primary authority figure teaching subjection and obedience of the children to all properly constituted authority figures outside the home as well, fathers often failed in accomplishing that objective, toward themselves or others. Shakespeare's plays do not merely reflect the family problems in Renaissance society; Shakespeare's creative imagination embraces the given of his larger world and, in powerful ways, comments upon it, sometimes very critically, but often subtly and with the ambiguity of poetry. He makes fathers dominant, even dominant from the grave!

THE LETTER VERSUS THE SPIRIT OF THE LAW

Since the father was "as God" in the home, his will, his commands, were inseparable from the commands of God himself. Dod teaches, in his catechism:

Now the things wherein children must obey their parents are especially these. First, in doing the things they command. . . . for so soon as the father hath commanded it, being a thing lawful, God's stamp is set on it, and it carries the print of God's commandment: and he that thinks himself too good to do it, thinks himself too good to obey God. (191, 192)

Cawdry argues in the same vein:

Children have always to remember, that whatsoever they do to their fathers and mothers (be it good or evil) they do it to God: when they please them, they please God: and when they disobey them, they disobey God: when their parents are justly angry with them, God is angry with them: neither can it be, that they may come to have the favor of God again: (no although all the Saints in heaven should intreat for them) until they have submitted themselves to their father and mother. (348)

In *The Merchant of Venice*, Portia's dead father continues to impose his will upon her. It is his will that her husband be chosen through the device of the gold, silver, and lead chests. The fact that she has no choice in the matter disturbs her: "O me, the word choose! I may neither choose who I would, nor refuse who I dislike: so is the will of a living daughter curb'd by the will of a dead father" (I.ii.22–25). Nerissa seeks to console her by reminding her:

Your father was ever virtuous, and holy men at their death have good inspirations; therefore the lott'ry that he hath devis'd in these three chests of gold, silver, and lead, whereof who chooses his meaning chooses you, will no doubt never be chosen by any rightly but one who you shall rightly love. (I.ii.27–33)

To modern audiences, Portia is all the more to be admired, not only because she chafes at "the will of a living daughter curb'd by the will of a dead father" but also because she creatively finds ways to fulfill the spirit of her father's law while violating the letter of it. So determined is she not to marry the drunken German, "the Duke of Saxony's nephew," that she asks Nerissa to "set a deep glass of Rhenish wine on the contrary casket," for, she adds, "I will do anything, Nerissa, ere I will be married to a spunge" (I.ii.96–99). She and Nerissa obviously know which caskets are incorrect choices as well as the one committing her to marriage. Portia succeeds in enticing the sottish German to make a wrong choice, and she is equally creative in helping Bassanio, with whom she has fallen in love, to make the right choice. While Bassanio muses over the inscriptions of the caskets, Portia orders a song to be sung, and it is no accident that the most repetitive sounds of the song all rhyme with the metal of the right casket, the one of lead: "bred," "head," "nouri*shed*," "engen*d'red*," "fed." Modern audiences, certainly, recognize the subliminal help and rejoice in Portia's resourcefulness in thus asserting her own will and achieving a "right" marriage, after all.

However, it would be simplistic to think that Shakespeare was unaware of what he was doing or any less delighted with the inventiveness with which he endowed Portia, the work of his own creative imagination. In fact, the entire segment, by implication, criticizes curbing a living daughter's will in this fashion with the will of a dead father. At the least, even if one accepts Nerissa's pious statements about Portia's virtuous father as true, it certainly is clear that Shakespeare makes Portia act in the fashion that Carlisle urged upon Richard II, "The means that heavens yield must be embrac'd, / And not neglected, else heaven would / And we will not" (III.ii.29–31). Portia might have believed that somehow the "good inspirations" of her "holy" father would result in her "never be[ing] chosen by any rightly but one who [she should] rightly love," but she also was determined to do everything within her power to encourage an unwanted suitor to make a wrong choice and to enable Bassanio to make the right one. Shakespeare makes her flawed in a number of ways: She makes what might be a racist remark of satisfaction when the Black Prince of Morocco chooses incorrectly, "Let all of his complexion choose me so" (II.vii.79); she histrionically drags out the trial scene, having Antonio actually bare his chest, allowing Shylock virtually to indent the skin with the point of his knife before she does what she knows from the beginning she will do—stop Shylock cold; she takes advantage of her role as the delivering lawyer to extract her ring from Bassanio, tormenting him with uncertainty. Nevertheless, Portia is one of Shakespeare's most admirable creations, bearing, surely, his own stamp of approval, for even the histrionics and role-playing listed above as flaws also have their valuable uses. Shakespeare strongly suggests that

Portia's ingenious efforts to achieve her will while technically abiding by her dead father's will are also laudable.

The conflict between the letter of the law and the spirit of the law turns out to be a major theme in *The Merchant of Venice*. Portia's daring violation of the letter of her father's will in order to achieve the spirit of it suggests Shakespeare's awareness of and belief in Paul's statement, "the letter killeth, but the spirit giveth life" (II Corinthians 3:16, Geneva Bible). Shylock represents the "letter of the law," the unrelenting severity of the Old Testament. His incessant demands for "judgment" and "law" sound like a death knell for Antonio, and Shylock demands the very letter of the law: "Ay, his breast, / So says the bond, doth it not, noble judge? / 'Nearest his heart,' those are the very words" (252–254). But "the letter killeth," for it is the nature of the law to curse (Galatians 3:10), and Shylock discovers that his demands for the precise "letter" of the law hoist him with his own petar. His demands for judgment and the law give him exactly that, and nothing more, and the result is his death, figuratively, for he must become a Christian and lose most of his property, "my life," as he calls "the means whereby I live" (376–377).

Just as Portia achieves the spirit of her father's will by violating the letter of it, so must Shylock learn the painful lesson that the letter of the law, the old covenant, kills—that only the new, the spirit of the law, gives life. Not only do the casket motif and the bond motif teach that lesson, but so also does the ring motif. Bassanio certainly violates the letter of the agreement with Portia when he relinquishes her ring to the young lawyer, but his motive for doing so, gratitude for saving the life of his friend, fulfills the spirit of the agreement. Antonio, in the spirit of the new covenant, is willing to lay down his life for his friend; Bassanio, so the classical code of friendship teaches, could not adequately love his spouse had he not learned the principle of love in loving a friend. For the sake of Antonio and in response to Antonio's own plea that he give up the ring, Bassanio most painfully does so, and after all, fulfills the life-giving spirit of the law of the ring, thereby assuring Portia of his ability to love her. Thus, Shakespeare first establishes the principle of the essential nature of the inner essence or the spirit of the law, the new covenant, over the death-dealing nature of the outward form or letter of the law, the old covenant, in Portia's imaginative meshing of her spirit with her dead father's letter in the casket segment of the play. That achievement sets up a major theme recurring throughout *The Merchant of Venice*.

THE IMPERFECT IMAGE OF FATHERS

Of Domesticall Dvties by William Gouge is a storehouse of conventional ideas concerning domestic relationships in Shakespeare's general period.

He has several sections devoted to the duties of children after their parents are dead: to bury them decently, to pay their debts, to suppress evil reports against their parents, and to imitate their parents' good example in their own lives. He says:

Thus is a blessed memory of their parents kept fresh and green (as we speak) though their bodies be rotten. For when they who knew the parents behold the like good qualities and actions in their children, they will thereby be put in mind of the parties deceased and say, Oh how such parents yet live! behold a lively, and living Image of them. . . . There can be no better monument of a parent's piety, honesty, and virtue, than a child's lively representation of the same. (480)

Shakespeare takes this conventional idea of the image of the dead parents living in their children and, as usual, gives it an additional turn of the screw, most particularly presenting the imperfect images of dead fathers reproduced in their living children. In *All's Well That Ends Well*, there is a contrast of two children very much aware of the images of their dead fathers. Lafew, a good old lord, reminds Helena very early in the play that she should be a credit to her dead father (I.i.79). Helena is so much in love with Bertram that her immediate response is, "What was he like? I have forgot him" (81–82). However, when Bertram joins the king at his court in Paris, Helena promptly remembers her father's will. This time the will of a dead father brings a blessed bequest. Her father was poor, unable to leave her monetary riches, but he left her "some prescriptions / Of rare and prov'd effects" (I.iii.221–222). Among those prescriptions was one that Helena was sure would cure the king of his otherwise incurable disease. She journeys to Paris and presents herself to the king to offer him the most precious of those prescriptions left on her father's "bed of death" (II.i.104). When the king refuses her offer as hopelessly futile, since all "our most learned doctors . . . and / The congregated college have concluded" (116–117) that he is past help, Helena persists, and her father and "Him that all things knows" become blurred into one, and the cure she offers she says, in effect, is really God's cure being presented to the king. Finally, the king bursts out: "Methinks in thee some blessed spirit doth speak / His powerful sound within an organ weak;" and because Helena has offered to lay down her own life if the prescription fails to heal him, he continues:

Thy life is dear, for all that life can rate
Worth name of life in thee hath estimate:
Youth, beauty, wisdom, courage, all
That happiness and prime can happy call.
. . . Sweet practicer, thy physic I will try,
That ministers thine own death if I die. (175–186)

Helena has become the image of her father—indeed, actually transcends her father's image, demonstrating to all that she could "hold the credit of [her] father" (I.i.78). The authority of her father has been reproduced in her, his image in her.

Bertram, however, whose father is also dead, is a contrasting image. His mother, the Countess of Rossillion, blesses Bertram with these words, as much a prayer of petition as a blessing: "Be thou blest, Bertram, and succeed thy father / In manners as in shape!" (I.i.61–62). Unfortunately, her prayer is not immediately answered, and many interpreters of the play insist that her prayer is never answered. Clearly, Count Rossillion did not succeed in having his "monument" perpetuated in the "living Image" of himself in Bertram. Bertram reproduced his physical image, but no more than that, a very imperfect image of his noble and good father. Shakespeare makes this matter of the imperfect image of a dead father a repeated concern both in this play and in *Measure for Measure*. When the King of France welcomes Bertram to Paris, his first words are these: "Youth, thou bear'st thy father's face;/ Frank Nature, rather curious than in haste, / Hath well composed thee. Thy father's moral parts / Mayst thou inherit too!" (I.ii.19–22). He virtually repeats the prayer of Bertram's mother, that Bertram will reproduce not merely his father's physical image but his moral image, too. The king continues to praise Bertram's father, especially stressing at the conclusion of his encomium the father's democratic spirit:

> Who were below him
> He us'd as creatures of another place,
> And bow'd his eminent top to their low ranks,
> Making them proud of his humility,
> In their poor praise he humbled. (41–45)

And he concludes his warm approbation of that humble spirit in a genuine nobleman with a second statement of desire to see that image reproduced in Bertram: "Such a man / Might be a copy to these younger times; / Which followed well, would demonstrate them now / But goers backward" (45–48).

It is precisely in his failure to embody his father's democratic spirit that Bertram most mars the image of his father in his own life. Bertram is a mean-spirited, spiteful, ignoble, rebellious, elitist snob. In contrast to Helena, he does not reproduce the commanding image of his father. When the king has been miraculously cured through the prescription of Helena's father, he seeks to keep his part of their agreement by giving Helena the noble husband of her choice. Her choice, of course, is Bertram, but he immediately objects; he scorns her because she is "A poor physician's daughter." The king sermonizes Bertram concerning the nature of true honor: "Honors thrive, / When rather from our acts we them derive / Than our foregoers" (II.iii.135–137). Bertram's honor is in a mere title, his nobility only that external form of having been born into a noble family, and both in this scene and throughout the play, Bertram's ignobility most lamentably fails to reproduce his father's image.

Shakespeare never makes it fully clear whether the ignobility of Bertram results from the failure of Bertram's father, too much "cockering" or spoiling, perhaps, or simply the determined rebellion of a child against his father's authority. Once his father is dead, Bertram becomes the charge of the King of France, his surrogate father, and if one can judge by his outright disobedience and rebellion against the authority of the King of France, Bertram was ever a rebellious son, a flawed, imperfect image of his dead father.

SEVERITY VERSUS LENITY

Yet Shakespeare's interest in the reproduction of the image of the dead father in his offspring manifests itself in another play, *Measure for Measure*. Here both the ambiguity and the consequent complexity of this issue increase. Claudio has impregnated his beloved betrothed, Juliet. Sexual license of all kinds has reached such epidemic proportions in Vienna that the Duke, in effect, makes his escape, leaving the strict, "precise" Angelo to do the harsh and unpleasant work of cracking down, of closing the brothels and bringing under control the "liberty" that "plucks justice by the nose," for "The baby beats the nurse, and quite athwart / Goes all decorum" (I.iii.29–31). Angelo immediately shuts down the whorehouses, and, to make a public example, seizes the first offender who comes to his attention, Claudio, and sentences him to death, the penalty for fornication, although, before Angelo's rule, that penalty had not been enforced. That is the setting for another clash of contrasting images of a dead father, the father of Claudio and Isabella, but this contrast is not only more subtle and complex than that in *All's Well*, but it is also thematically more significant, the metaphor for the central problem of the play: severity versus lenity.

Shakespeare seems very much aware of the idealistic nature of conventional teaching concerning the role of fathers as "God" within their families, and of the family, under his authority, as the cornerstone of all society. Ever practical and truthful, Shakespeare could scarcely refrain from pointing out the contradictions and conflicts that arise from such idealistic expectations. In *All's Well*, the dead fathers of Helena and Bertram are presented as essentially idealized noble figures, and

the contrast results from the fact that Helena imaged forth her noble
dead father, whereas Bertram was only the physical image of his, falling
far short of his noble father's moral features. In *Measure for Measure*, the
contrast emerges in the two different images, both flawed and imperfect,
of the same dead father. Isabella images the strict, severe, demanding
holiness of life, cold and disciplined. Claudio images the warm, gentle,
loving, undisciplined indulgence, the celebration of this life rather than
life after death. Most earthly fathers are flawed and imperfect admix-
tures of contradictory principles, principles that have fragments of truth
in them but cannot be the whole truth. Any attempt to make a single
set of principles the whole truth, denying the truth in the contrasting
set, results in distortion and imperfection. The dead father of Isabella
and Claudio seems to have been just such an imperfect person—on the
one hand coldly austere and holy, and, on the other, warmly human
and indulgent. Isabella images forth, to an extreme degree, the first set
of features while Claudio images the second, both imperfect images of
the same imperfect father. Moreover, their family fight—severity versus
lenity—exactly mirrors the "family fight" in the macrocosmic family of
society at large in Vienna. Society perpetuates the imperfections of dead
fathers.

Claudio's failure is one of human weakness. He dearly loves Juliet,
and, since they are betrothed, when there is a delay concerning dowry, he indulges in sexual intercourse with her, resulting in her preg-
nancy—their sin of fornication thus coming to light. Gouge, a typical
voice of societal beliefs, warns against "two extremes" that often result
from the betrothal contract: "One of attributing too much to it: another of derogating too much from it. Many make it a very marriage, and
thereupon have a greater solemnity at their contract, than at their marriage: yea many take liberty after a contract to know their spouse, as
if they were married: an unwarrantable and dishonest practice" (202).
When Lucio encounters Claudio under arrest and on his way to prison
and asks, "whence comes this restraint," Claudio responds:

> From too much liberty, my Lucio, liberty:
> As surfeit is the father of much fast,
> So every scope by the immoderate use
> Turns to restraint. Our natures do pursue,
> Like rats that ravin [greedily devour] down their proper bane,
> A thirsty evil, and when we drink we die. (I.ii.124–130)

Claudio articulates the conflict succinctly: severity and lenity are at war
in human nature, each in its extreme leading to the other and back again
endlessly. Surfeit makes one want to fast, and liberty too much indulged

results in restraint, but conversely, too much restraint ultimately breaks forth into surfeiting and indulgence. Claudio's lack of discipline, his self-indulgence with Juliet in their "most mutual entertainment" (I.ii.154) is very much the problem in Vienna—license, most particularly manifested in sexual license. Just as Claudio's father, whom Escalus calls "a most noble father," surely had his austere and strictly disciplined qualities, so also Vienna has its "strict statutes and most biting laws" (I.iii.19). But too much restraint results in surfeiting as surely as over-indulgence makes one want to fast. Vienna's license has reached such proportions that "quite athwart / Goes all decorum" (I.iii.30 – 31).

If Claudio has embodied the warmly human and self-indulgent side of his father, Isabella has, to the nth degree, imaged forth his severity and austerity. Her very first words in the play inquire concerning the limits of privileges in the nunnery where she is, as yet, an unsworn "novice of this place." The nun, Francisca, asks, "Are not these large [generous or liberal] enough?" "Yes, truly," Isabella replies, "I speak not as desiring more, / But rather wishing a more strict restraint / Upon the sisterhood, the votarists of Saint Clare" (I.iv.2–5). The Order of Saint Clare had already perhaps the most severe and austere rule of any order in existence, but Isabella has as insatiable an appetite for severity as Claudio has for lenity. When she has been persuaded by Lucio to appeal personally to Angelo to spare Claudio's life, Isabella begins her appeal by admitting, "There is a vice that most I do abhor, / And most desire should meet the blow of justice" (II.ii.29–30), and as the play continues, her prudish abhorrence of sex, most explicitly illicit sex, becomes more clear. When Angelo states the obvious fact that laws against illicit sex have already condemned the act in general and that his role as law enforcement officer is to condemn the specific offender, Isabella readily agrees and is ready to abandon Claudio to his fate: "O just but severe law! / I had a brother then" (II.ii.41–42). Lucio objects, "You are too cold." That is precisely Shakespeare's word for such an extreme attitude toward sexual restraint: "cold." The extreme laws of Vienna against sexual license suit the early Angelo perfectly. He has never before been tempted by a woman; so cold and austere has been his life that Lucio says in one place his "blood / Is very snow-broth" (I.iv.57–58) and in another that he urinates icicles: "But it is certain that when he makes water his urine is congeal'd ice" (III.ii.109–111). Although Lucio shamelessly exaggerates, there is something delightfully appropriate about those two figures as they apply to Angelo's unnaturally severe and austere attitudes towards sex, and one tends to feel that Isabella is just as unnaturally cold. She has embodied, to an extreme degree, her dead father's austerity and severity.

The conflicting images of their dead father emerge in the family fight. Angelo, never previously attracted to a woman, recognizes in Isabella the same sort of insatiable appetite for austerity as he himself has. He suddenly, for the first time, is powerfully attracted to a woman sexually, to Isabella, her very purity being the point of attraction:

> O cunning enemy, that to catch a saint [like Isabella, he also has a rather high and congratulatory opinion of himself]
> With saints dost bait thy hook! Most dangerous
> Is that temptation that doth goad us on
> To sin in loving virtue [the very extreme Isabella seems to have].
> (II.ii.179–182)

He propositions her, and when she finally grasps his foul intent, she is predictably outraged. First, she threatens to blackmail him, to tell "with an outstretch'd throat . . . the world aloud / What man thou art" (II.iv.153–154). Her attempt to use force begets a greater force in opposition. Angelo taunts her, "Who will believe thee, Isabel?" and now demands that Isabella yield "up thy body to my will" or Claudio will not only die, but die a death drawn out "To ling'ring sufferance [suffering]" (II.iv.164–167). Isabella recognizes that he has successfully outpowered her, and she comforts herself that her brother, son of their noble father, will gladly die, even by torture, rather than allow her chastity to be violated:

> I'll to my brother.
> Though he hath fall'n by prompture of the blood,
> Yet hath he in him such a mind of honor
> That had he twenty heads to tender down
> On twenty bloody blocks, he'ld yield them up
> Before his sister should her body stoop
> To such abhorr'd pollution
> Then, Isabel, live chaste, and, brother, die;
> More than our brother is our chastity. (II.iv.177–185)

Meanwhile, the Duke, disguised as a friar, has been helping Claudio prepare for death by providing him with ideas similar to those in Boethius' *Consolation of Philosophy*. When Isabella arrives, he asks for hope; her reply is veiled, testing his reaction, and finally asking him outright, "Dar'st thou die?" He replies, "If I must die, / I will encounter darkness as a bride [a figure most appropriate for Claudio's love of sexual indulgence] / And hug it in mine arms" (III.i.76, 82–84). Ah, that was the answer Isabella sought. She bursts out in prideful approbation: "There spake *my* brother: there *my* father's grave / Did utter forth a voice" (III.i.85–86, emphasis added). Claudio's willingness to die for her was exactly the father's image for which she looked in him—self-discipline. She was able to ignore the rather intimate and warmly sexual figure Claudio used, for she heard his response in terms of her own austerity and severity.

However, Claudio's readiness to die is temporary; he is his father's warmly human and self-indulgent image; when Isabella exhorts him, "Be ready, Claudio, for your death tomorrow," Claudio soon responds, "Death is a fearful thing," and his abhorrence of death is eloquently articulated as only a man who loves this life far more than the next can word it:

> Ay, but to die, and go we know not where [he images his father's doubts as surely as Isabella images her father's faith];
> To lie in cold obstruction, and to rot [most abhorrent to a man who loves to hug warm bodies and cherishes warm flesh];
> This sensible warm motion to become
> A kneaded clod; and the delighted spirit
> To bathe in fiery floods, or to reside
> In thrilling [shivering] region of thick-ribbed ice [again reinforcing the contrast between cold and warmth];
> To be imprison'd in the viewless winds
> And blown with restless violence round about
> The pendant world; or to be worse than worst
> Of those that lawless and incertain thought
> Imagine howling—'tis too horrible! (III.i.117–127)

Unable to restrain his true emotions, he cries out most imploringly to Isabella: "Sweet sister, let me live" (133).

At that point, the family fight reaches its climax, the conflict between two equally imperfect images of an imperfect father: "O you beast!" Isabella bursts out, "O faithless coward! O dishonest wretch! / . . . Die, perish! Might but my bending down / Reprieve thee from thy fate, it should proceed. / I'll pray a thousand prayers for thy death, / No word to save thee" (III.i.135–146). The hell of this house has reached its nadir. In the midst of her not cold but boiling outrage, Isabella accuses those plaintive pleadings of Claudio to be so antithetical to the image of her father she has embodied that she must believe her mother had been unfaithful to her father, producing in Claudio a bastard, "For such a warped slip of wilderness / Ne'er issued from his blood" (III.i.140–142). Severity versus lenity—Isabella has reproduced the former image of her father, Claudio the latter.

Their family fight is precisely the fight in the larger family of Vienna—too much liberty versus too much authoritarian austerity.

The Duke, admitting having been too lax in the enforcement of the strict laws of Vienna, flees, reportedly to Poland but actually into disguise, because, he says:

> Sith 'twas my fault to give the people scope,
> 'Twould be my tyranny to strike and gall them
> For what I bid them do; for we bid this be done,
> When evil deeds have their permissive pass,
> And not the punishment. (I.iii.35–39)

The Duke, the "father" of the city, has the same imperfect admixture of lenity and severity as apparently the father of Claudio and Isabella had. He has been too indulgent, and now he turns to the most severe of his possible deputies, Angelo, to bring the city back into line. He places all his authority as father or governor of the city into the hands of the austere Angelo, and Angelo wields heavy-handed authority without mercy. "Thus can the demigod, Authority," Claudio too late philosophizes, "Make us pay down for our offense by weight / The words of heaven: on whom it will, it will / On whom it will not, so; yet still 'tis just" (I.ii.120–123). In this world, even heavenly justice is only imperfectly applied, seizing and punishing some while allowing others to escape unpunished. Angelo admits that "The jury, passing on the prisoner's life, / May in the sworn twelve have a thief or two / Guiltier than him they try" (II.i.19–21). Isabella, in her role as a pleader for mercy before Angelo, reminds him in effect that all have sinned and fallen short of God's expectations: "Why, all the souls that were were forfeit once, / And He that might the vantage best have took / Found out the remedy" (II.ii.73–75). When Angelo is unmoved, she excoriates him:

> but man, proud man,
> Dress'd in a little brief authority,
> Most ignorant of what he's most assured
> (His glassy essence), like an angry ape
> Plays such fantastic tricks before high heaven
> As makes the angels weep. (II.ii.117–122)

Angelo, human authority, is a bumbling apish imitator of true heavenly authority, so merciful that God himself "found out the remedy" for man's sin. However eloquent Isabella is in articulating the fact of God's mercy, effected through Christ's being "made sin" for humans, she herself cannot rise up to the heights of such mercy. Moses did, willing to be blotted out of God's book of life for the sinning Israelites; Paul did, willing to be accursed for his kinsmen according to the flesh; Christ did, being made sin for all human beings. Isabella cannot. She cannot rise up to such heights for sinning Claudio; instead, she authoritatively condemns him more severely than does Angelo.

Human authority, represented by mixed and imperfect fathers, dead or alive, in the microcosm of the home and in the macrocosm of the larger society, often seems unable to achieve a balance between liberty and restraint, between warm sexuality and cold austere holiness, between the love of this life and the love of the next. Imperfect fathers are imaged forth in imperfect children, in the home and in the city, and the conflicting contradictions of dead fathers perpetuate themselves.

FATHERS DOMINANT EVEN FROM THE GRAVE

In no play are fathers more dominant from the grave than in *Hamlet*. The hell of home, the microcosm and the macrocosm, in no play dominates the action more completely than in *Hamlet*. Shakespeare's sensitivity to words might very well have led him to name this play, focused on the corruption in the microcosmic and macrocosmic home, *Hamlet*, for "hamlet" derives from "hame," the earlier word for home. Dead fathers dominate the action of the play. Renaissance society echoed constantly with the authority of fathers. James Cleland, in *The Institution of a Young Noble Man*, voices the repeated theme:

The heathens themselves acknowledged the Law of Nature in permitting full, absolute & universal authority to all fathers to dispose at their own pleasure of their children's lives, honors, liberty and goods. . . . Whereby it appeareth evidently, (as also by many particular instances of sons, who submitted their necks willingly to their fathers' swords) that whosoever rebel, and refuse obedience unto their natural Parents, they are guilty of Leze-majesty against Nature herself. . . . And albeit neither the Law of Nature, nor of man exacted this duty of us, yet God's commandment (above them both) . . . should move us all to perform this duty . . . that we must honor them as half Gods, as they represent the Image of God invisible . . . acknowledging them to be the secondary causes and next authors unto God of your being & living, and in that point are like unto his Almighty Majesty. (126–128)

In *Hamlet*, the graves of three fathers "did utter forth a voice," and three sons feel compelled to respond. The cry from the grave, either implicitly or explicitly, to each of these three sons is "Revenge!" Young Hamlet's response controls the play, but Shakespeare deliberately contrasts the responses of Young Fortinbras and Laertes. The full impact of dead fathers dominating from the grave cannot be experienced without examining first the two foils of Hamlet, and how each of them responds to his felt duty to seek revenge.

The first is Young Fortinbras. Again it is impossible to be certain that Shakespeare intends the name to have significance, but it is too temptingly appropriate not to be observed as a possibility. "Fortinbras," most obviously, derives from the French, "fort-en-bras," or "strong arm." However, Shakespeare perhaps also intends a pun: "Strong [fort] in brass [bras, its original spelling]." "Brass" primarily refers, of course, to the hard alloy of copper and zinc or tin, but Shakespeare himself uses "brass" at least three times to mean "insensitivity" or "effrontery"—in *Love's Labor's Lost*, V.II.395, in Sonnet 120.4, and in this play, as a verb, meaning hardened into insensitivity, as Hamlet seeks to wring the heart of Gertrude, "for so I shall / . . . If damned custom have not brass'd it so / That it be proof and bulwark against sense" (III.iv.35–38). "Strong in Brass" is an appropriate name for Old Fortinbras, the father of Young Fortinbras. "Prick'd on by a most emulate pride" (I.i.83), he had the effrontery to challenge Old Hamlet, Hamlet's father, to combat, with the mutual agreement, "ratified by law and heraldry," that the winner would take possession of certain lands—for Norway, if Old Fortinbras won; for Denmark, if Old Hamlet won. Hamlet's father "Did slay this Fortinbras," and the lands in question became the rightful possession of Denmark.

Young Fortinbras is the image of his dead father, and he has, it seems, internalized his father's sins. William Cvpper, in *Certain Sermons Concerning Gods Late visitation in the citie of London* . . . , warns against the evil example of fathers before their children: "And so the proverb is fulfilled: an evil crow, an evil egg, like father, like son" (218). Young Fortinbras mirrors the insensitivity and effrontery of his father. Shakespeare's audiences would not only recognize the dishonorable illegality of his actions, but they would also hear echoes of countless exhortations about the sins of fathers being repeated in their sons. One of those voices they might have been hearing in their minds was John Dod's:

The use of all these duties to those whose parents are not alive, is, to look, that their sins be not alive after their parents' death. And therefore they must examine themselves, whether they have been faulty in any of these things: And if they have offended therein, let them repent for it, and crave pardon, else they be liable to two plagues. . . . Therefore such as be now fathers, and find that their children are stubborn against them, and unthankful and rebellious everyway, let them call themselves back, and see what children they were before, how they behaved themselves to their parents, whether they were not altogether faulty in this point. If it be so, let them confess their own sins have found them out, and are turned upon them: let them acknowledge that God is just, and hath given them their own measure into their bosoms, their own evil is fallen upon their own heads, they digged a pit in their youth, and now in their age are fallen into it. (197)

The point is that children must *not* repeat the sins of their dead fathers; otherwise, sin will repeat itself in their own children endlessly until thorough repentance takes place. The presumption of Old Fortinbras repeats itself in the presumption of Young Fortinbras. Thus Horatio explains to Marcellus and Barnardo:

> Now, sir, young Fortinbras,
> Of unimproved mettle hot and full,
> Hath . . . Shark'd up a list of lawless resolutes
> . . . to recover, by strong hand
> And terms compulsatory, those aforesaid lands
> So by his father lost. (I.i.95–104)

Young Fortinbras mirrors his father's brash effrontery; he also mirrors his insensitivity. Shakespeare makes him parallel Hamlet in that upon his father's death he does not ascend to the throne but rather his uncle does. Young Fortinbras has both the effrontery and insensitivity to attempt to invade Denmark without his uncle's knowledge because his uncle is "impotent and bedred, scarcely hears / Of this his nephew's purpose" (I.ii.29–30). Claudius sends Cornelius and Voltemand to Norway, asking "old Norway," the uncle of Fortinbras, to restrain the young man. The request succeeds, and the intended invasion terminates. Young Fortinbras, however, continues to feel pressure from his dead father; he still desires to revenge his father's lost honor. Full of the same pompous presumption, he marches instead toward Poland "to gain a little patch of ground / That hath no profit in it" (IV.iv.18–20). "Strong in brass," he is utterly insensitive to the absurdity of his objective. Twenty thousand ducats and two thousand souls will scarcely suffice to win this "straw" [worthless thing], but Fortinbras is insensitive to that unrealistically high cost. In fact, the "death of twenty thousand men" might result in the "fight for a plot" too small to serve as a burial ground "to hide the slain" (IV.iv.25–26, 60, 64–65). In one of his almost infinite ironies, Shakespeare has Hamlet refer to this brash and brassy Fortinbras as "a delicate and tender prince," "with divine ambition puff'd," because he is so presumptuously obsessed with honor and with his desire to revenge his father's honor that he will "find quarrel in a straw / When honor's at the stake" (IV.iv.55–56). Yet the very insensitivity of Young Fortinbras, ready to expose "what is mortal and unsure / To all that fortune, death, and danger dare, / Even for an egg-shell" (IV.iv.51–53) stands in deliberate contrast to the sensitivity of

Hamlet, even more compellingly forced to respond to his dead father's call for revenge.

Young Fortinbras is the first foil to Hamlet; Laertes is the second. To understand Hamlet's response to his dead father's "command" to revenge his murder, one should examine Laertes' thirst for revenge for the death of Polonius, his father. If Fortinbras is insensitive effrontery, Laertes is the sensitive, sentimental, yet secretively murderous avenger. He, too, images his dead father. Polonius has but one device for statecraft: eavesdropping, called, in Shakespeare's day, "noting." Shakespeare wrote a whole play about noting, *Much Ado About Nothing*, for in Elizabethan English, "nothing" was pronounced "noting," and the pun was intentional. *Much Ado* is very much about overhearing or eavesdropping. It is also about "nothing," often punned with "naught," a word meaning "wickedness." Polonius is not particularly a wicked man, but his veritable lust for eavesdropping suggests a secretive, cunning nature reproduced in Laertes. He literally eavesdrops himself to death. Hiding behind the arras, his favorite place for "noting," Polonius involuntarily cries out when Gertrude does. Hamlet whips out his rapier and stabs him, mistaking him for Claudius. Gazing upon the dead body of Polonius, in one of the classic understatements of the play, Hamlet observes, "Thou find'st to be too busy [prying or meddling] is some danger" (III.iv.33). Laertes' sentimental sensitivity loses itself in a cunning, hidden or secretive evil, resulting in his own death.

Laertes' sentimentality and sensitivity may be seen in a number of places, for in the second encounter with him in the play, when he is giving counsel to Ophelia, his words are rhetorically elegant: "A violet in the youth of primy nature, / Forward, not permanent, sweet, not lasting, / The perfume and suppliance of a minute— / No more" (I.iii.7–10). His concern for Ophelia seems genuine, and, from his perspective, seeking to protect her from hurt, sensible. Hamlet is a Prince, and his marriage is likely to be arranged for him despite his own personal preferences. When Polonius appears, although Laertes has already received one predeparture paternal blessing, he seems genuinely pleased to receive a second: "A double blessing is a double grace, / Occasion smiles upon a second leave" (53–54). He departs for France not to be heard from again until he returns in an excessive display of emotion seeking revenge upon Claudius for the death of Polonius. He has placed himself at the head of a riotous rabble, "And as the world were now but to begin, / Antiquity forgot, custom not known," he allows them to claim him as their king: "Choose we, Laertes shall be king! . . . Laertes shall be king, Laertes king!" (IV.v.102–109). His sentimentally excessive emotion he displays like a circus parade, and his rash rush into treason, even to breaking down the doors into the king's chambers, he justifies in the name of true sonship: "That drop

of blood that's calm proclaims me bastard, / Cries cuckold to my father, brands the harlot / Even here between the chaste unsmirched
brow / Of my true mother" (IV.v.118–121). Utterly throwing caution to
the wind, he virtually screams out of control: "To hell, allegiance! vows,
to the blackest devil! / Conscience and grace, to the profoundest pit! / I
dare damnation. . . . Let come what comes, only I'll be reveng'd / Most
throughly [thoroughly] for my father" (IV.v.132–137). If Fortinbras is
stolid insensitivity, Laertes is sensitivity heightened to its utmost degree
of sentimental excess, and he demonstrates the same sentimentality at
the funeral of Ophelia. At the moment when the first shovelful of dirt is
about to be thrown upon her, he impulsively leaps into the grave, shout-
ing, "Hold off the earth a while, / Till I have caught her once more in
mine arms," and then, hugging her corpse, he cries, "Now pile your
dust upon the quick [living] and dead" (V.i.249–251). That outrageous
display of histrionics is too much for Hamlet, who immediately seeks to
out-Herod Herod.

Laertes' rash excesses stand in contrast to both the insensitivity of
Fortinbras and the hesitant reasoning of Hamlet. Three sons have lost
their fathers, and all three feel the pressure of fathers dominant from
the grave, the duty to seek revenge, but their methods are different—deliberately, because Shakespeare surely wanted three different approaches to be contrasted. Fortinbras seeks "to find quarrel in a straw / When
honor's at the stake," insensitive to the absurd cost. Laertes, intoxicated
with excessive emotion, abandons "Conscience and grace" and stoops to
the lowest degree of wickedness, cunningly deliberate murder without
the slightest element of honor in it: "I'll anoint my sword. / I bought
an unction of a mounteback . . . So mortal that [nothing] . . . Under
the moon, can save the thing from death / That is but scratch'd with-
al" (IV.vii.140–146). Earlier, when Claudius had asked, "What would
you undertake / To show yourself indeed your father's son," Laertes
had unhesitatingly replied, "To cut his throat i' th' church" (124-126).
The secretive cunning of Polonius emerges a thousand times worse in
the secretive sellout by the son to an unmitigatedly dishonorable scheme
for coldblooded murder. Laertes' approach to revenge is the second foil
to Hamlet's.

FROM EARTHLY REVENGER TO HEAVENLY SCOURGE AND MINISTER

That Hamlet's father calls to him from beyond death for outright revenge is incontrovertible. When Hamlet follows the Ghost, he cries to it,
"Speak, I am bound [prepared] to hear," and the Ghost adds a second
meaning to "bound"—to be obligated or destined—when he replies, "So

art thou to revenge" (I.v.6–7). The obligation to seek revenge rests upon filial affection and duty, says the Ghost: "If thou didst ever thy dear father love— / . . . Revenge his foul and most unnatural murder" (23, 25). The call to revenge is clear and unequivocal. Hamlet's immediate response seems almost as rashly hasty and unquestioning as that of Laertes: "Haste me to know't, that I with wings as swift / As meditation or the thoughts of love, / May sweep to *my* revenge" (29-31, emphasis added).

Thirst for revenge has been a human characteristic in almost all cultures from earliest ages. Certainly, Anglo-Saxons had a tradition obligating kinsmen to seek revenge long before the Elizabethan period, and the tradition was far from dead during Shakespeare's lifetime. As late as 1607, William Wentword advised his son to remember that "Nothing but fear of revenge or suits can hold men back from doing wrong" (cited by Stone, *Family* 96). Although fear of revenge was a major deterrent to wrong, violence abounded, and the obsessive concern for "honor" made revenge obligatory in the minds of many. Saviolo teaches that "one should not duel for the sake of revenge" (Y4, verso) and that "every Gentleman ought to undertake the combat, not so much to revenge himself, or his friends, or to chastise or punish the offenders, as to [preserve the larger societal good]" (Z, recto). Nevertheless, even Saviolo declares, "But if the injury be such, that either murder be committed by treachery, or rape, or such like villanies, then it is necessary to proceed in revenging it" (P, verso).

Puritan preachers, particularly, in contrast to Saviolo's statement, constantly preached against revenge as a violation of the Scriptural truth, "Vengeance is mine, I will repay," as Paul teaches in Romans 12:19—alluding, no doubt, to Old Testament passages such as Leviticus 19:18, Deuteronomy 32:35, and similar prohibitions against private revenge. Gouge may again be cited as typical of this segment of societal beliefs. He has an entire section devoted to "the unlawfulness of children's seeking to revenge their parents' wrongs." He claims that the heathen require their children, after their parents' death, to "revenge such wrongs as have been done to them in their life time. And they press this so far upon their children, as they affright them with their parents' 'Ghost,' saying, that if they neglect to revenge their parents wrongs, their Ghost will follow them, and not suffer them to live in quiet, but molest them continually" (481). Gouge makes the usual Scriptural case against private revenge citing "such prohibitions [as] 'Resist not evil, Recompense to no man evil for evil. Avenge not yourselves' " (481).

As influential as the many ministerial voices against revenge no doubt were in Elizabethan and Jacobean England, there is no evidence that Shakespeare makes Hamlet's initial hesitation derive from such arguments. Hamlet seems to accept the duty of revenge laid on him by his father's ghost with enthusiasm and determination. He refers to the ghost's call to revenge as "thy commandement" (I.v.102), a term he continues to use during the ghost's last appearance in the play, in Gertrude's bedroom: "Th' important acting of your dread command." (III.iv.108). The reverence and respect with which Hamlet responds to the Ghost's appearance in his mother's bedroom seems appropriate both as awe toward this numinous figure, an awe Horatio earlier shared, and also as the proper respect and reverence one must show one's father. That Hamlet loved and revered his father is evident in his idealization of him, in contrast to Claudius, as he describes his father to Gertrude:

> See what a grace was seated on this brow:
> Hyperion's curls, the front of Jove himself,
> An eye like Mars, to threaten and command,
> A station [manner of standing or of deportment] like the herald
>   Mercury . . .
> Where every god did seem to set his seal
> To give the world assurance of a man. (III.iv.55–62)

In fact, in his first reference to his father, he declares to Horatio, " 'A was a man, take him for all in all, / I shall not look upon his like again" (I.ii.187–188). Hamlet, out of love, reverence, and obedience, unquestioningly accepts his dead father's call for revenge. He accepts it and identifies with it, and calls it "my revenge."

He does, nevertheless, hesitate. He hesitates partly because he is uncertain whether or not the ghost comes from Satan to damn him. Roland Frye speaks to this issue:

Ghosts were regarded as especially dangerous instigators of revenge, as various comments show. Sir Thomas Browne wrote that "those aparitions and ghosts of departed persons are not the wandering souls of men, but the unquiet walks of Devils, prompting and suggesting us unto mischief, blood, and villainy." King James I also "pictured the Devil as leading his victim on to guilt through desire of revenge, as appearing in the likeness of one dear to the victim in order to secure his attention, as taking advantage of the victim's despair to entice him to his own destruction." (23)

In his first speech of self-accusation for not hastening to revenge, Hamlet asks: "Am I a coward? . . . Prompted to my revenge [his second claim that the revenge he seeks is his own as well as that ordered by his father] by heaven and hell, / Must like a whore unpack my heart with words," (II.ii.571, 584-585), but he does not elaborate on just how both heaven and hell prompt him to revenge. In that same speech, he first articulates doubt about the origin of the ghost:

> The spirit I have seen
> May be a {dev'l}, and the {dev'l} hath power
> T' assume a pleasing shape, yea, and perhaps,
> Out of my weakness and my melancholy,
> As he is very potent with such spirits,
> Abuses me to damn me. (598–603)

Conventional teaching against revenge has at least that much hold on his thinking.

The success of "The Mousetrap" in startling Claudio into a guilty reaction elates Hamlet: "O good Horatio, I'll take the ghost's word for a thousand pound. Didst perceive? . . . Come, some music!" he cries with exuberance. His doubts about the nature of the ghost have disappeared. In a playful mood, he dispenses with Rosencrantz and Guildenstern and then with Polonius. Hamlet, alone, exclaims:

> 'Tis now the very witching time of night,
> When churchyards yawn and hell itself {breathes} out
> Contagion to this world. Now could I drink hot blood,
> And do such {bitter business as the} day
> Would quake to look on. (III.ii.388–392)

Once more, now that the suspicion of the devilish nature of the ghost has been cleared from his mind, he is hot for revenge. Only minutes later, he finds Claudius on his knees, and, although he speaks of revenge three times, including, "And am I then revenged . . . ?" once more speaking of the act of revenge as though it is for himself as much as for his father's ghost, he decides against it because Claudius might go directly to heaven, having just confessed his sins, as far as Hamlet knows.

Seeking to wring the heart of Gertrude, he suddenly sees the ghost for the last time. He immediately concludes the ghost has come to chide the "tardy son . . . That laps'd in time and passion, lets go by / Th' important acting of your dread command" (III.iv.106–108). He speaks of revenge just once more, castigating himself for the last time—at his encounter with the Norwegian troops when he learns from the Captain of the "egg-shell" objectives of Fortinbras: "How all occasions do inform against me, / And spur my dull revenge!" (IV.iv.32–33). Hamlet has struggled for an extended period with his dead father's call to revenge and his own earthy passion for revenge, too extensively both for the ghost and for himself. He has not spoken as sentimentally nor acted as hastily as Laertes; he has not directed his energies toward an unworthy "egg-shell" goal, insensitive to ridiculously high costs in human life, as Fortinbras does. As a Renaissance gentleman, full of admiration for "that man / That is not passion's slave," he has agonized with sensitivity over his filial duty and over his own human yearning for revenge, and has most assuredly avoided, except for the rash killing of Polonius, excessive haste. But the greatest difference between Hamlet and the two foils given him by Shakespeare lies in Hamlet's unique move from earthly revenger to heavenly "scourge and minister."

The move begins in his mother's bedroom, while he is trying to expunge from both their souls the absolute hell that has most tormented him since his return to Denmark: his mother's marriage—too hasty, but wrong whether hasty or not—to the murderous "king of shreds and patches," Claudius. When he determinedly forces his mother to sit down to hear him out, perhaps literally thrusting a looking glass before her at the same time, she cries out in fright, "What wilt thou do? Thou wilt not murder me?" Polonius, hiding behind the arras, also involuntarily cries out, "What ho, help!" At that moment, still seeking earthly revenge, Hamlet, believing and hoping the voice behind the arras to be that of Claudius, whips out his rapier and kills Polonius. As he continues with Gertrude, he achieves a measure of success, for she exclaims, "O Hamlet, speak no more! / Thou turn'st my {eyes into my very} soul, / And there I see such black and {grained} spots / As will {not} leave their tinct" (III.iv.88–91). Before he leaves her, he pleads for her to abandon the bed of Claudius, and he says good night with these words: "And when you are desirous to be blest, / I'll blessing beg of you" (171–172). Immediately, he observes, "For this same lord," referring to the dead Polonius, "I do repent; but heaven hath pleas'd it so / To punish me with this, and this with me, / That I must be their [that is, heaven's] scourge and minister" (172–175). He begins to recognize that earthly revenge leads to rash and bloody deeds, such as the unintended killing of Polonius, and yet, like heavenly justice itself, he also observes that "I must be cruel only to be kind" (178). His internalization of the need to move from his role of earthly revenger to heavenly minister is not without backsliding, at the encounter with the Norwegian army, but the wholly unpredictable deliverance at the hands of the pirates, returning him utterly unexpectedly to Denmark, remarkably advances his movement toward the heavenly rather than the earthly goal. He never speaks of revenge again, nor does he castigate himself again, even though much more time has passed without his having achieved the revenge his father called for. He seems no longer to be seeking revenge at all; in fact, he seems to be waiting for direction, not from his earthly father, who, indeed, does not appear again, but rather from Providence.

Hamlet could not help but know that the human father is but the earthly representation of God, the Heavenly Father; at least, both Shakespeare and his audience were well aware of that repeated teaching. Upon his return to Denmark, most miraculously returned there by "thieves of mercy" [that is, thieves full of mercy], Hamlet is not only a distinctly changed man, but he also talks with Horatio about the change he has experienced: "Sir, in my heart there *was* a kind of fighting / That would not let me sleep. . . . Rashly— / And prais'd be rashness for it—let us know / Our indiscretion sometime serves us well" (V.ii.4–8, emphasis added). To what does he refer? Almost certainly to the experience in his mother's bedroom, to his "rash and bloody deed" in the hasty attempt to achieve earthly revenge, resulting in the unintentional death of Polonius. Moreover, he interprets for Horatio why "all things work together for good," even human failures: "Our indiscretion sometime serves us well / When our deep plots do pall [lose effectiveness and appeal], and that should learn us [that is, teach us] / There's a divinity that shapes our ends, / Rough-hew them how we will" (8–11). The move from earthly revenger to heavenly scourge and minister is definitely under way.

As Hamlet explains how he changed the commission to England from his own death to that of the "sponges" Rosencrantz and Guildenstern, Horatio asks, "How was this seal'd?" Hamlet responds, "Why, even in that was heaven ordinant [that is, ordaining or controlling]" (V.ii.48). Osric comes to Hamlet and Horatio to arrange the contest between Laertes and Hamlet, the scheme Claudius and Laertes have concocted together to result in the murder of Hamlet. Horatio fears that Hamlet will lose the contest. Hamlet says, rather confidently, "I do not think so," but what concerns him more is the pain "about my heart—but it is no matter" (V.ii.212–213), he quickly adds. When Horatio protests, Hamlet laughs it off as only a slight misgiving "as would perhaps trouble a woman" (216). Horatio tries to persuade Hamlet to postpone indefinitely or at least delay the contest. "Not a whit," Hamlet insists, "we defy augury [referring, no doubt, to that prophetic misgiving that had just pained his heart]," and he now clearly articulates the complete shift from earthly revenger to heavenly scourge and minister: "There is special providence in the fall of a sparrow" (220), surely referring to Matthew 10:29, "Are not two sparrows sold for a farthing and one of them shall not fall on the ground without your Father?" (Geneva Bible). The authority of the earthly father has now been swallowed up by that higher source from which it derives; the voice of the earthly father has been replaced by that of the Heavenly Father. Hamlet no longer needs to chafe about accomplishing revenge; he need only to be ready, to allow whatever Providence brings about to happen: "If it be [now], 'tis not to come; if it be not to come, it will be now; if it be not now, yet it [will] come—the readiness is all. Since no man, of aught he leaves, knows what is't to leave betimes, let be" (221–224). That marvelously relaxed "let be" dramatically contrasts with the condition he earlier describes: "In my heart there *was* a kind of fighting" (V.ii.4, emphasis added). Hamlet no longer feels the strife of seeking to achieve an earthly revenge; he has no fear, even though he has a kind of presentiment that the end of the hell of his home is at hand, for he knows that he is of more value than many sparrows. He no longer curses "That ever I was born to set it right!" Although the end of his mother, Claudius, and himself, occurs suddenly and comes about in a way wholly beyond any possible anticipation on his part, because he has learned to "let be," to "hang loose" in the hands of Providence, he has achieved a higher state; he has learned that "the readiness is all."

Shakespeare confronts his audience with the contrasting responses of three sons who hear, figuratively and literally, their fathers' voices from beyond the grave. All three fathers call for revenge, at least as their sons understand the pressures from their dead fathers. Only one son allows the extremely earthy thirst for revenge to be replaced with a surrender to that source of all authority of human fathers, to be replaced with the heavenly call for justice that "if it be not now, yet it *will* come" to those who surrender themselves into the hands of the Father who does not allow so much as a single sparrow to fall to the ground without a loving purpose. That son is the one in whom Shakespeare is most interested. He calls him Hamlet, and "hamlet," whether Shakespeare deliberately intended it or not, does derive from "hame," from home.

4

A Jealous Obsession with Chastity: *Much Ado About Nothing*, *The Winter's Tale*, *Cymbeline*, and *Othello*

According to the Old Testament account, violence of one human being against another began in the home: Cain killed his brother Abel. No woman was involved in that domestic quarrel, but, even though the word is not used in the Genesis record, jealousy seems to have been the powerful human emotion provoking the first homicide. In the Anglo-Saxon cultures of England and America, even to this day, "our house" is often "hell." It has long been so. James Buchanan Given, in *Society and Homicide in Thirteenth-Century England*, says that prior to Shakespeare's age, homicides by relatives occurred with "fairly great regularity." He cites the domestic homicide rate in Philadelphia in 1952 as 1.4 per 100,000 per annum, but says that, in the middle ages, the counties of Kent, Warwick, and Oxford all exceeded that rate (56).

In England and America, for many generations, one has always been in greater danger of being killed by some family member than by any kind of outsider. Modern movies and television programs portray the theme of criminals seeking revenge against the prosecutors and/or judges who sent them to prison. In actual fact, lawyers and judges regularly stand in greater danger of revenge by those involved in divorce cases and other domestic quarrels than by ordinary thieves and thugs, even those clearly involved in organized crime. Violence, often resulting in homicides, is largely homegrown. The reasons are many and complex, far beyond the scope of this study; however, in all preceding ages as well as in the present one, the powerful emotion of jealousy has repeatedly been the explosive force in domestic violence, frequently homicidal violence. In cases far beyond any possibility of enumeration, jealousy on the rampage because of actual or imagined violation of chastity has been the motivation for murder. It cannot be a surprise to find that Shakespeare's terribly troubled dramatic families are often in "hell" because of a virtual obsession with chastity—and of the double anguish of accuser and accused when even only imagined loss of chastity occurred.

DISTINGUISHING BETWEEN VIRGINITY AND CHASTITY

Every culture in every age has its hierarchy of moral values, and in Renaissance England, chastity filled an extremely high place in the value system. Moralists and preachers spoke of it constantly, and, in the culture at large, maintaining or losing chastity virtually preoccupied the populace. However, in the Renaissance, an important distinction began to be made between virginity and chastity.

In the middle ages, and in the Roman Catholic Church right on through to modern times, virginity has been celebrated as the highest possible state. Of course, no one can remain a virgin who is at least not chaste in body. As Protestantism spread and a married clergy emerged in sharp distinction to the virgin state of the priests and nuns of the Roman Catholic Church, the celebration of married life brought about a shift of emphasis, urging purity of virgins until marriage but now using the term chastity to refer to those who kept their marriage vows inviolate after virginity was no longer an accurate term. Erasmus represents one example of this emerging distinction. His small treatise, entitled *The comparation of a vyrgin and a martyr* and published in English in London in 1537, was written in response to a request supported by a gift of sweetmeats from the Benedictine nuns of Cologne, whose Warden, Helias Marcaeus, was on friendly terms with Erasmus for some time. Erasmus wrote this little work in praise of the dedication of those nuns to the virgin state of life. He compares, as the title suggests, their chosen life of virginity with willing martyrdom, and he finds it difficult to decide which is the higher calling. He declares that Christ loves both martyrs and virgins, being each himself and is, therefore, "the very fountain" of both: "O what great purity is in this virgin, he the prince of virgins, and spouse and crown of virgins, was conceived of the heavenly spirit, and born of a virgin, the glorious beauty of virginity not broken. Of wives the husband is the glory, but of virgins Christ is the glory" (9, recto). He reminds them of Paul's warning that marriage is demanding, that, on the one hand, wives "must please their husbands, they must chide and brawl with their maids and servants, & chastise their children," while, on the other hand, "Our virgins, being free from all care and thought of this world, do nothing else, but in spiritual choirs, sing sweet hymns to their spouse. For they ascribe nothing to themselves, but give all the glory of their felicity to him, to whom only they owe all things" (12, verso; 13, recto). He asserts that "a monastery to a virgin that loveth her spouse, is not a prison . . . but it is a paradise" (38, verso). He concludes: "A true virgin doth differ very little from a martyr. A martyr suffereth the executioner to mangle his flesh: a virgin daily doth with good will mortify her flesh, she being in a manner a tormentor of her self" (27, recto). Later, Erasmus came to believe that virginity, as a way of life, is profitless and a waste, thus agreeing with most Renaissance humanists and Protestant preachers who taught that the life-long virgin neglects the natural and scriptural call to procreate.

The Protestant conviction that marriage is natural and scriptural, even for the clergy, did not eliminate their recognition that Paul taught that one would be freer to serve Christ in the unmarried state, although that particular calling was reserved for the very few. Again and again Protestant preachers proclaimed the scriptural teaching that it is better to marry than to burn with lust. A little work with a very long title, bearing no date inside but 1567 on the spine of the apparently rebound work, devotes itself to an elaborate expansion of its scriptural epigraph: "Let Matrimony be honorable in all persons, But fornicators and adulterers God shall judge. Hebre.xiii." The title virtually says it all:

A Defence of priestes mariages, stablyssed by the imperiall lawes of the Realme of Englande, against a Ciuilian, namyying hym selfe Thomas Martin doctour of the Ciuile lawes, goyying about to disproue the saide mariages, lawfull by the eternall worde of God, & by the hygh court of parliament, only forbydden by forayne lawes and canons of the Pope, coloured with the visour of the Churche. Whiche lawes & canons, were extynguyshed by the sayde parliament, and so abrograted by the conuocation in their Sinode by their subscriptions. Herewith is expressed, what moderations and dispensations haue ben vsed heretofore in the same cause, & other like, the canons of the Churche standyng in full force. Whereby is proued, these constitutions to be but positiue lawes of man temporall.

The sum of the work is this: Unmarried priests, often failing to maintain chastity, bring reproach upon the cause of Christ. Thomas Martin's work, the writer says, is dead wrong in trying to forbid marriage to priests. He accuses Martin of not understanding Latin very well, of misquoting and misrepresenting his sources, and of other equally serious failures in scholarship. Most of all, he concludes concerning all priests, "either let them marry, if they cannot keep themselves in chastity: or else let them keep themselves in chastity, if they will not marry" (208).

Protestants in support of a married clergy repeatedly stressed certain Biblical statements. Henry Smith asserts:

Now if marriage be a remedy against the sin of fornication, then unless Ministers may commit the sin of fornication, it seemes that they may use the remedy as well as other: for it is better for a man to marry than to burn, so it is better for all men to marry than to burn: and therefore Paul saith, *Marriage is honorable amongst all men.* And again, *For the avoiding of fornication let every man have his wife.* (15)

So the last bastion of virginity as a lifelong calling, for those called to the special service of God, crumbled before the Protestant celebration of marriage as the wholesome and proper state for almost all adults, approved by nature and by God.

Now it became necessary to shift the emphasis from chastity as a pure virgin, like Christ himself and the Virgin Mary, to chastity as a married person. "For this cause marriage is called Matrimony, which signifieth mothers, because it maketh them mothers which were virgins before" (Smith 13). That distinction was defined as early as 1580, if not before, when William Hergest, in *The Right Rvle of Christian Chastitie,* provided two distinct definitions:

Virginity or Maidenhood, is a virtue of the mind or soul, graunted unto some (especially to such as crave it, by continual prayer in Christ's name) by the gift of God, to bridle flesh lust, and to avoid all contaminations and defilings of the mind and body, whatsoever, that they may live the more godly, being chaste and pure both in body and mind, or soul, without polutions, unshamefast or filthy cogitations, speech or actions. . . .

Chastity, is a virtue of the seventh commandment, wherby a married woman, being lightened with faith in Christ the Mediator, knowledgeth the ordinance of God in marriage, loveth her Husband as her own flesh, keepeth the covenant of Marriage holy and inviolable, knoweth no man besides her Husband, and studieth to keep both her mind chaste, and her body pure and undefiled. And they that use this virtue, are chaste wedlockkeepers, and they that do not are adulterers or adulteresses. (2, 3)

Thus, virginity is the term for the unmarried who keep themselves pure, and chastity is now the term for married women who have sexual intercourse with no men other than their husbands. However, Hergest observes that chastity is the wider term and can still apply to either state he had previously so carefully distinguished: "Chastity, is either to live in single life without carnal knowledge of any person, without burning of sensual lust, and without any abuse of mind or body: or else in Marriage to keep the ordinance instituted of God" (4). Endless exhortations to chastity were addressed to both men and women, but most of them, like Hergest's definition above, "Chastity, is a virtue . . . whereby a married woman," were directed toward women.

CHASTITY FOR THE UNMARRIED

Plays in which families are portrayed by Shakespeare as plunged into hell because of doubts about chastity primarily present married couples—the anguish of husbands who believe their wives have been unfaithful and the anguish of wives who find themselves so accused. The most notable exception is *Much Ado About Nothing*. Much of the dramatic interest centers upon the battle of the sexes waged by Benedick and Beatrice, who fall in love, thanks to deliberately manipulated "notings"—statements about how each cares for the other being made in such a way that the other overhears. However, at the very heart of the meaning of "much ado about nothing" is the false accusation, the "nothing" causing all that ado, that Hero, the unmarried daughter of Leonato, Governor of Messina, has been wanton, resulting in the sudden rejection of her by Claudio at the moment of their intended marriage. Without an understanding of the extreme emphasis upon chastity for unmarried girls as well as for wives, one can scarcely comprehend the intensity of the hell that erupts. Don John, the bastard brother of Don Pedro, with the help of Borachio, who has won the heart and cooperation of Margaret, one of Hero's attendants, convinces Claudio and Don Pedro that the figure at Hero's window bidding Borachio "a thousand times good night" is, indeed, Hero, and "away went Claudio enrag'd; swore he would meet her as he was appointed next morning at the temple, and there, before the whole congregation, shame her with what he saw o'ernight, and send her home again without a husband" (III.iii.159–163). At the church, instead of accepting Hero as his wife, Claudio abruptly says to Leonato, "Take her back again. / Give not this rotten orange to your friend, / She's but the sign and semblance of her honor" (IV.i.31–33). Leonato and Hero are dumbfounded, but Don Pedro confirms what Claudio has said:

> . . . Upon mine honor
> Myself, my brother, and this grieved count
> Did see her, hear her, at that hour last night
> Talk with a ruffian at her chamber-window,
> Who hath indeed, most like a liberal villain,
> Confess'd the vile encounters they have had
> A thousand times in secret. (IV.i.88–94)

Claudio makes a melodramatic farewell: "But fare thee well, most foul, most fair! Farewell, / Thou pure impiety and impious purity!" (IV.i.103–104). Hero swoons. Beatrice thinks she is dead. Leonato hopes

she is: "O Fate! take not away thy heavy hand, / Death is the fairest cover
for her shame / That may be wish'd for" (115–117).

Modern audiences are shocked to hear a father so readily condemn his
daughter to death. Leonato cannot help but believe the three witnesses
against Hero: "Would the two princes lie and Claudio lie . . . ?" (152).
These are noblemen, he thinks, for at this point he has no reason to
consider Don John anything other than noble, as noble as Don Pedro,
Prince of Arragon, and Count Claudio. Noblemen always tell the truth,
always, "seeing when a man lieth he loseth the form and shape of a man,
& becometh a brute beast" (Cleland 187). Base or ignoble persons might
lie, but noblemen, never. Moreover, Hero, at this point, has not denied
the accusation; even if she had, her denial against three noble witnesses
would be futile. Leonato, in the hell of his anguish at having his only
child, so accused, cries out:

> Do not live, Hero, do not ope thine eyes;
> For did I think thou wouldst not quickly die,
> Thought I thy spirits were stronger than thy shames,
> Myself would, on the rearward of reproaches,
> Strike at thy life. (IV.i.123–127)

Leonato has many classical precedents of fathers who killed their daughters rather than let them live in shame. The pain of the shame of lost
chastity far exceeds the pain of death. "O she is fall'n," Leonato wails,
"Into a pit of ink, that wide sea / Hath drops too few to wash her clean
again, / And salt too little which may season give / To her foul tainted
flesh!" (139–143). Loss of chastity, for a woman, meant the loss of everything.

The proof of that statement may be found in innumerable declarations of preachers and moralists of the age. Cawdry insists:

For in a maid, the honesty and chastity is instead of all. . . . The which thing
only if a woman remember, it will cause her to take great heed unto, and be
more wary and careful keeper of her honesty, which alone being lost, though
all other things be never so well and safe, yet they perish together therewith,
because she that hath once lost her *Honesty*, should think there is nothing left.
Take from a maid or woman her beauty, take from her kindred, riches, comeliness, eloquence, sharpness of wit, cunning in her craft, and give her, *Chastity* and
you have given her all things. And on the other side, give her all these things, and
call her whore, or naughty pack: with that one word you have taken all from her,
and left her bare and foul. (351–352)

Printed in 1598, Cawdry's *A Godlye Form of Hovseholde Government* was
preceded by many years by the English translation of a work by "Lewes

Vives" (actually Juan Luis Vives), called *A very frvtefvl and pleasant booke called the Instruction of a christen woman*. Vives goes to considerable trouble to demonstrate why the loss of a woman's chastity is even worse than the loss of a man's chastity:

The same pain have wicked men, but women far sorer, because their offences be reckoned fouler, and they be more timorous of nature . . . . For as for a man needeth many things, as wisdom, eloquence, knowledge of things, with remembrance, some craft to live by, Justice, Liberality, lusty stomach, and other things more, that were too long to rehearse, and though some of these do lack, it is not to be disliked, so that many of them be had: but in a woman no man will look for eloquence, great wit, or prudence, or craft to live by, or ordering of the commonweal, justice or liberality: Finally no man will look for any other thing of a woman but her honesty [chastity]: the which only, if it be lacked, is like as in a man, if he lack all that he should have. For in a woman the honesty is instead of all. . . . Because she that hath once lost her honesty, should think there is nothing left. Take from a woman her beauty, take from her kindred, riches, comeliness, eloquence, sharpness of wit, cunning in her craft; give her chastity, and thou hast given her all things. And on that other side, give her all these things, and call her a naughty pack: with that one word thou hast taken all from her, and hast left her bare and foul. (F, verso, to Fii., recto)

Cawdry was obviously quoting, without giving credit, from the work by Vives. But the real point is this: again and again, moralists and preachers declared that a woman has but one "jewel," one single reason for being—namely, to be chaste. A man has many reasons for being, many responsibilities in addition to maintaining his chastity. A man may lack a little of this or a little of that and still be a man, for no man has total perfection, but a woman has but one supreme responsibility: to keep herself chaste. Hergest argues in the same vein: "It is more shame for a woman to commit this vice, than for a man, for the chief, and almost only virtue that above all things is required in a woman is Virginity and Chastity, which being once lost, her credit is cracked, especially among the wise and godly" (35).

There were a few voices against the double standard. In a work translated out of French "as near as our English phrase will permit, by H. VV. Gentleman" but otherwise anonymous, and entitled, *A courtlie controuersie of Cupids Cautels. . .* , the Gentlewoman, the hostess of the group of three gentlemen and two gentlewomen, mildly protests: "The occasion wherefore ancient decrees have licenced this crime in men, & so straightly forbidden it in women, the same is, because the Laws have been ordained and established by men" (30). But such feeble voices against the double standard were drowned out by the incessant tintinnabulations of those ding-donging about the *one* "pearl of great price" belonging to a woman being her chastity. The writer of *A moral Methode of Ciuile Policie* explains:

The true ornaments of women are Modesty, chastity, shamefastness and praise, which cannot be purchased, with any gold, pearls, or precious stones; but seeing it is so, that all these cannot be seen in any one good woman, although very honest: Chastity yet is that only ornament, which may supply whatsoever lacketh in the others: for this enlargeth the dowry when it is not of it self sufficient, it not only adorneth and maketh comely that which is deformed, but also reduceth a woman to the similitude of beauty itself, it enobleth ignobility, and finally fulfilleth all things, which in any part may otherwise be wanting. (Patricius 41–42)

Chastity in a woman is the be-all and end-all of her existence. Take from a woman her chastity, and she has lost all. Simply *call* her whore or naughty pack, and "with that one word thou hast taken all from her, and hast left her bare and foul."

Leonato's readiness to kill his own daughter but follows the many examples provided by Vives:

Puplius Attilius Philiseus slew his daughter because she defouled herself in adultery. In the same city, Lucius Virgineus the Centurion because he had leaver lose his daughter, and see her die a good maid, than have her deflowered, slew with a sword his wellbeloved and only daughter Virgina, when he could find none other means, lest she should be compelled to be at the lust of the judge. (E.iiii, verso)

The mere charge of wantonness against Hero is sufficient, although Leonato cannot help but believe the charges true. Yet a part of Shakespeare's apparent purpose is to call attention to the power of a "report." The play rings constantly around the word "nothing." "Noting" or overhearing is at the core of the play. Almost all the action results from overhearing. Don Pedro and Claudio are deceived by overhearing the conversation between Borachio and Margaret, the latter of whom they take to be Hero. The power of gossip, of reports, true or false, has concerned writers of all times; Chaucer's "The House of Fame" deals with it, and Shakespeare frequently refers to the impoverishment that results from the loss of "reputation," the loss of a good name. Just as honor for a man is more to be desired than life, "being that *Gem* which is most precious amongst all the Jewels of external benefits" (Markham 1), so is chastity to a woman. Any hint of the loss of her reputation is the greatest possible evil. Therefore, it may be said of a woman, as of a man's concern about his honor, "he is ever accounted cruel to himself, that is careless of his *Reputation*; It is an interest above all Interests, and no benefit of Fortune (how pleasant soever) bringeth with the loss half the grief, that the fear doth of a spotted *Reputation*; for dishonor is more to be feared than death, and *Honor* more to be desired than life" (1). The analogy with the loss of a man's honor is apparent in Leonato's lament for Hero's lost reputation as he cries out from the depths of his hell:

> . . . Griev'd I, I had but one?
> Chid I for that at frugal nature's frame?
> O, one too much by thee! Why had I one?
> . . . Why had I not with charitable hand
> Took up a beggar's issue at my gates,
> Who smirched thus and mir'd with infamy,
> I might have said, "No part of it is mine;
> This shame derives itself from unknown loins?" (IV.i.127–135)

Whereas before Leonato had grieved to have only one child, now he feels that one was one too many. He laments that he had not taken a beggar's issue, so that, now that such besmirching infamy and shame has been brought to his house, he could say, "This is not my child; this shame derives itself from loins other than mine, from unknown loins." Slander has done its dirty work; Hero's chastity has been impugned; the tongue, a fire, a world of evil and set on fire by hell (James 3:6) has effected its hell in the house of Leonato and Hero.

The Friar expresses confidence in Hero's innocence, and certainly Beatrice does, but because Hero has not yet actually denied the charges, Leonato still believes the two princes and Claudio. Hero arouses to protest:

> . . . If I know more of any man alive
> Than that which maiden modesty doth warrant,
> Let all my sins lack mercy! O my father,
> Prove you that any man with me convers'd
> At hours unmeet [improper], or that I yesternight
> Maintain'd the change of words with any creature,
> Refuse me, hate me, torture me to death! (178–184)

The Friar, totally convinced that she has been wronged, proposes a plan: that is, since Don Pedro, Don John, and Claudio departed thinking that Hero is dead, let them continue to think that. In time, "slander" might change to "remorse," and, even if that failed, belief that Hero died "best benefits her wounded reputation . . . / Out of all eyes, tongues, minds, and injuries" (211, 241–243). The Friar's plan works; in time, the evil plot of Don John is uncovered; Borachio confesses; Don John flees. Leonato, not yet revealing to Claudio that Hero is still alive, sets up another wedding, supposedly between Claudio and Leonato's niece, "Almost the copy of my child that's dead" (V.i.289). At the wedding, Hero, to Claudio and Don Pedro, returns from the dead. "One Hero died defil'd, but I do live," Hero declares to Claudio, "And surely as I live, I am a maid" (V.iv.63–64). Slander, gossip, loss of reputation concerning her chastity had "killed" her, but now, her good name cleared, she lives. As Leonato proclaims to Claudio, "She died, my lord, but [only] whiles her slander liv'd" (66). Merely the apparent loss of chastity brought disaster to the home of Leonato and Hero; she could not live while her slander lived. When it died, she revived, "for dishonor is more to be feared than death, and *Honor* more to be desired than life, being that *Gem* which is the most precious amongst all the Jewells of external benefits." For an unmarried woman, a maid, like Hero, "call her a naughty pack: with that one word thou hast taken *all* from her, and hast left her bare and foul" (Vives, F.ii, recto, emphasis added).

JEALOUSY, UNJUST BUT UNALLAYED

The jealous obsession with chastity plunging three other Shakespearean families into hell bursts like a pus-filled abscess in the minds of three husbands, each convinced of his wife's unfaithfulness. Two of those husbands are victims of deliberate Machiavellian deceit, one attempting and the other completing the murder of his wife. However, the third husband, Leontes of *The Winter's Tale*, finds himself suddenly inflamed with jealousy, overwhelmed with anguished doubts about the chastity of Hermione. His doubts have absolutely no foundation in fact, but Shakespeare did not need to wait for modern psychologists to discover that perceptions, even utterly mistaken perceptions, have a reality of their own.

Modern psychologists have anatomized the powerful emotion of jealousy. They declare that it is a highly possessive emotion, a powerful desire to dominate.

There is no such thing as a little jealousy; it is an all-out effort to destroy the object of its envy. Like the Trojan horse, it attacks the part as an excuse to destroy the whole. Numberless marriage partners are affected this way. They usually make the mistake of believing that this is sexual interest or sexual jealousy. They almost never see the coherence of the total behavior of the mate. (Beecher 83)

Shakespeare, that sharp observer of life, able to penetrate to the innermost core of human motivations, whether he actually took conscious thought of such ideas or not, portrays obsessive jealous behavior with convincing clarity. Jealousy arises from a sense of competition, of rivalry, and musters intense emotional energy to squash the opposition, to seize total control. "The word 'jealous' is defined as 'deeply resentful of successful rivalry; intolerant of all but exclusive worship and love' " (Beecher, 175-176). Exactly that sense of rivalry sparks and feeds the fire of Leontes' entirely unjust jealous accusations against Hermione.

Leontes, King of Sicilia, and Polixenes, King of Bohemia, have perfectly exemplified the classical code of friendship, in childhood inseparable, and even as adults, when the duties of maturity have kept them apart, through a constant "interchange of gifts, letters, loving embassies, . . . they have seem'd to be together, though absent" (I.i.28–29). So profound is their mutual love of friendship that Archidamus observes, "I think there is not in the world either malice or matter to alter it" (32–33). Polixenes has been visiting Sicilia for nine months and has determined to return to the duties of his throne. Leontes seeks to persuade him to stay longer, even if it is only a week longer. Polixenes assures him, "There is no tongue that moves, none, none i' the world, / So soon as yours could win me" (I.ii.20–21); however, he is adamant; he must return home "to-morrow." Leontes turns to Hermione, commanding her to help persuade Polixenes to stay longer. She responds, observing that Leontes has been pleading "too coldly." She reminds Polixenes that she will allow her husband, the next time he visits Bohemia, an extra month beyond the intended limit, even though, she assures Leontes, "I love thee not a jar o' the clock behind / What lady she her lord" (43–44) That is, she loves Leontes not as much as one tick of the clock less than any lady who has ever loved her lord. Finally, she playfully insists that Polixenes *will* stay, either as a prisoner or as a guest. At that, Polixenes gives in and agrees to stay as "Your guest then, madam. / To be your prisoner should import offending, / Which is for me less easy to commit / Than you to punish" (56–59). As often happens in Shakespeare, a little line is uttered that seems to be entirely appropriate and even insignificant at the moment of utterance but later its great significance emerges. Leontes observes, while commending Hermione for never having spoken "to better purpose" (89), "At *my* request he would not" (87, emphasis added). In retrospect, one can see that Leontes' first hint of jealousy unconsciously slips out, unnoticed at the time by himself or anyone else—rivalry with Hermione: "At *my* request he would not."

His jealousy soon flares up like a flash fire in his mind. Hermione, pleased for her husband's sake that Polixenes is staying a while longer, gives her hand to Polixenes. At that moment, Leontes exclaims to himself, "Too hot, too hot! / To mingle friendship far is mingling bloods. / I have 'tremor cordis' [a sudden palpitation of the heart] on me; my heart dances, / But not for joy, not joy" (108–111). Irene G. Dash comments on

Hermione's success, "Ironically, her success as wife and hostess leads to her personal failure in these roles. For, employing coquetry, charm, and the familiar skills expected of a woman, she convinces Polixenes—but loses Leontes" (139). Hermione has succeeded in persuading Polixenes to stay longer when Leontes had failed. He immediately sees that unconscious rivalry in terms of sexual interest. So stricken is Leontes with jealousy that he promptly questions the paternity of his son: "Mamillius, / Art thou *my* boy?" (119–120, emphasis added). The bliss of home, the joy of friendship with Polixenes with whom he has been as frolicsome "as twinn'd lambs," his own sense of manhood—all have been shattered by this explosion of hellish jealousy. Once more he challenges Mamillius, "Art thou *my* calf?" (127, emphasis added) as though Mamillius would know who sired him. "Yes, if you will, my lord," Mamillius replies, not understanding the implications of these questions. "Thou want'st a rough pash [head] and the shoots [branches, but implying here the cuckold's horns] that I have," Leontes declares, too pointedly for Mamillius to grasp, for he is too young to know about the shame or, perhaps, if one can believe it, the boast of cuckoldry. Coppélia Kahn explains:

Virile animals, such as bulls, stags, and the traditionally lecherous goat have horns and are associated with cuckoldry. Horns would thus seem inappropriate for the cuckold who has not been able to keep his wife in his own bed; not he, but the sexually successful cuckolder should wear them. The cuckold's horns *are* his virility, however; or rather, as I will show, they are the mockery made of it by marriage. Regarded endopsychically, from the cuckold's point of view, horns are a defense formed through denial, compensation, and upward displacement. They say, "It's not that I can't keep my wife because I don't have enough of a penis. I have two of them, in fact, right up where everyone can see them." (122)

But Mamillius is much too young to understand anything like that. Probably taking the boy's face between both his hands, though stage directions for that do not appear, Leontes peers into the eyes of Mamillius: "Come, sir page, / Look on me with your welkin [blue as the sky] eye. Sweet villain! / Most dear'st! My collop [that is, flesh of my flesh]! Can thy dam—may't be?" (135-137), he cries with poignant agony. The hell he feels "stabs at the centre" of his innermost being, and yet, at this point, he is rational enough to admit that the power of "affection," in his case this intense jealousy, is such as to make things that are not appear as though they are, "to the infection of my brains / And hard'ning of my brows" (145–146). Later, jealousy so overwhelms him that he convinces himself that not only is Mamillius, who is almost a carbon copy of Leontes, a bastard, the offspring of illicit sex between Polixenes and Hermione, but also that the child she is now carrying in her womb is a bastard as a result of exactly the same cuckoldry. Jealousy, indeed, has power to make things that are not seem as though they are.

Shakespeare, of course, was not the only person during the Elizabethan era who observed the devilish power of jealousy. Many teachers of conventional morality wrote about it. Vives declares:

Cicero, calleth Jealousy after the opinion of the stoic Philosophers, a care of a man's mind, lest another should have as well as he, that thing, which he himself would enjoy alone. It is called also a fear, lest another man should have in common with him that thing, which he would have to be several his own. What words so ever they expound it with, verily it is a sore vexation and agony, and a very cruel tyranny, which as long as it reigneth and rageth in the husband's heart, let the wife never hope to have grace. It were better for them both to be dead, than any of them to fall into Jealousy, but specially the man. (Aa.iiii, recto)

The raging fire of jealousy within Leontes flames out in his words: "Say that she were gone, / Given to the fire, a moi'ty [fragment] of my rest / Might come to me again" (II.iii.7–9). When the new baby is born, a lovely little girl, Perdita, Leontes blasts from the furnace of his blazing heart: "This brat is none of mine, / It is the issue of Polixenes, / Hence with it, and together with the dam / Commit them to the fire!" (II.iii.93–96). Paulina insists that it is his child. Leontes, like a dragon, promptly flares out at her: "A gross hag! . . . I'll ha' thee burnt" (108, 114). Paulina remarks, "It is an heretic that makes the fire, / Not she which burns in't" (115–116), and she departs. Leontes, still raging with jealousy, now turns upon Antigonus, "Even thou, that hast / A heart so tender o'er it, take it hence, / And see it instantly consum'd with fire / . . . Go, take it to the fire" (132–134, 141). Vives and other moralists recognized what a hellish fire jealousy is, but Shakespeare's many references to fire make Leontes' raging internal inferno intensely real.

The moralists explicitly and Shakespeare implicitly all suggest that the wife—in this case, Hermione—must bear more responsibility for the husband's jealousy, now out of control in Leontes, than most modern audiences are able or willing to recognize. Vives warns:

What pains or torment can be compared, both for him that is vexed with the unquietness of Jealousy, and her of whom the fear is? Thereof riseth groaning, complaining, crying, with hate both of himself and other, and perpetual suspicion of harm, and chiding, brawling, frighting, yea and also murder. For we have both read and heard tell of many, that have slain their wives, moved only with jealousy. The which affection doeth also rage in wild beasts: the Lion, if he take her in adultery. And I my self with many other more, have seen the Cock swan kill his hen, because she followed another cock. Therefore let the woman labor with all her power, lest this fantasy come upon her husband: or if it come upon him, to get him out of it, and cause him to leave it. (Aa.iiii, verso)

Vives not only vividly describes the hell that jealousy brings to a home, he clearly says that it is the wife who must see to it that her husband does not fall into the pit of jealousy, and, if he does, to get him out.

The unfairness of this burden placed upon wives is patent. Vives is not wholly unaware of that complaint:

Peradventure thou [speaking to an imaginary wife] wilt say, that this is an hard thing. For who can rule other men's suspiciousness? Yes, many ways, first if thou live chastely, and that is the readiest way. For time, ever bringeth forth the truth, and time causeth the falsehood to fade and vanish away, and confirmeth and strengtheth the truth. If thou be good, and have a jealous husband, yet mayest thou hope that he will put away that unquietness of mind. But and [if] thou be naught, be sure, that that fantasy shall never go from him, but rather increase daily. . . . Therefore shalt thou both love thine husband, and labor that he may perceive himself loved. (Aa.iiii, verso) Let her show herself not only to love no man so well as her husband but also to love none other at all but him. If she love any other, let it be but for her husband's sake. . . . For there be many men, that can be well content and thereto very glad, to have all other things in common with their wives except friends. (Bb, recto)

Women have the greater obligation to keep themselves chaste than do men; they also have the responsibility to keep themselves from all appearance of evil and so completely love their husbands as to make it impossible for them to fall into jealousy. Vives is explicit about this.

Shakespeare only implies that Hermione is a little too careless about touching and being touched by Polixenes. When she has persuaded Polixenes to stay a little longer after Leontes could not do so and gives her hand to Polixenes, Leontes bursts out with his first jealous explosion: "Too hot, too hot!" From that moment, he keenly observes their every action together, commenting frequently upon their "paddling palms and pinching fingers [seeing more in his infected brain, no doubt, than is really there], / As now they are, and making practic'd smiles, / As in a looking-glass; and then sigh, as 'twere / The mort [the florish blown on the horn at the death of the deer] o' th' deer" (I.ii.115–118). Later in the same vein, he complains, "How she holds up the neb [the bill of a bird, i.e., her mouth]! the bill to him! / And arms her [engages her arms with his] with the boldness of a wife / To her allowing husband!" (183–185). As deeply filled with suspicion of their actions as he is, Leontes encourages the two of them to walk into the garden without him and Mamillius, but as soon as they leave he exclaims: "Gone already! / Inch-thick, knee-deep, o'er head and ears a fork'd one!" (185–186). Their very departure without him, even at his encouragement, appears to him to be too hasty. But by the time he charges Hermione to be a wanton woman, "a {hobby}-horse," to Camillo, her behavior has become exaggerated and distorted in his mind:

> Is whispering nothing?
> Is leaning cheek to cheek? is meeting noses?
> Kissing with inside lip? stopping the career
> Of laughter with a sigh (a note infallible
> Of breaking honesty)? horsing foot on foot?
> Skulking in corners? wishing clocks more swift?
> Hours, minutes? noon, midnight? and all eyes
> Blind with the pin and web [filmed over with cataracts] but theirs only
> That would unseen be wicked? Is this nothing? (284–292)

Although most of that behavior exists only in Leontes' inflamed mind, Hermione's giving of her hand to Polixenes a little too freely invites misinterpretation—so says Vives explicitly and Shakespeare implicitly.

If Shakespeare most mildly and covertly criticizes Hermione, in terms of conventional convictions that a wife should behave in such a careful way as to avoid giving the slightest cause to arouse her husband's jealousy, his criticism of Leontes is overt and explicit. However much conventional society would like to blame wives for the jealousy of their husbands, Leontes' jealousy erupts as the volcanic fire from deep within Leontes himself. Leontes is a competitive person, and he must win in every imaginable way. The play opens with a discussion of the extravagant entertainment provided by Leontes for Polixenes and his entourage from Bohemia. The "great difference betwixt our Bohemia and Sicilia," explains Archidamus to Camillo, is that "we cannot with such magnificence" reciprocate when Leontes and his lords visit the country of Polixenes. Shakespeare possibly never gave any conscious thought to the extravagant munificence of Leontes' behavior, but modern psychologists describe such behaviors as an effort to control, a manifestation of the competitive urge for "one-up-manship." The deep insecurities of the Leonteses of this world cause them to want to outgive, to exert control by making the recipients of such largesse admit defeat, much as Ruth Benedict describes the ruinous competitive giving, the incredible burning up of oil, blankets, and other precious possessions at the potlatches of the American Indians in the Northwest (189–199).

That Leontes unconsciously places himself in competition with his wife is also nowadays clearer than it might have been to either Shakespeare or his audience. Shakespeare repeatedly presents competition between the

sexes, but usually before marriage. At marriage, so conventional morality taught, a wife must consciously and consistently recognize her inferior role and always be in complete subservience to her husband. That
Shakespeare often indirectly challenges conventional morality about
man/woman and husband/wife relationships is apparent in many plays,
but regularly and openly, he portrays the prevailing conventional roles.
William Whately describes the wife's role:

The wife's special duty may fitly be referred to two heads: first, she must acknowledge her inferiority: secondly, she must carry herself as an inferior. First
then, every good woman must suffer herself to be convinced in judgement, that
she is not her husband's equal (yea, that her husband is her better by far), without
which it is not possible there should be any contentment, either in her heart, or in
her house. . . . let her set down this conclusion within her soul: Mine husband is
my superior, my better: he hath authority and rule over me, nature hath given
it him . . . God hath given it him . . . His will I see to be made by God the tie
and tedder, not of mine actions alone, but of my desires and wishes also. I will
not strive against God and nature: though my sin have made my place tedious,
yet will I sure confess and hold the truth: Mine husband is my superior, my better. (190)

Hermione innocently believes herself subservient to Leontes, but he
interprets her success in persuading Polixenes to extend his visit as a
victory over him, and that reminded him of the fact that she had kept
him waiting to accept his proffered love, that "Three crabbed months
had sour'd themselves to death, / Ere I could make thee open thy white
hand, / {And} clap thyself my love [pledge her faith by joining hands]"
(I.ii.102–104). But nowhere is their contest more clearly evident than in
the judgment scene, and there Shakespeare's criticism of Leontes is most
evident.

Leontes "wins," but only tyrannically, and that despite his avowed
intent: "Let us be clear'd / Of being tyrannous, since we so openly / Proceed in justice" (III.ii.4–6). An officer reads the indictment
against Hermione. Whately stresses the fact that a wife mistreated by
her husband must take it quietly, for she should say to herself, "yea,
if he strike me causelessly, and in mere passion, I will take it quietly,
and not suffer myself to break forth into rebellious and contemptuous
words and gestures" (211). He stresses that the Bible teaches a woman
must "bear them [unjust "reproofs or chastisements"] meekly and quietly . . . [and] remember that Saint *Peter* saith, *A woman of meek and quiet
spirit is most set by of God*: and that meekness and quietness is not worthy
the name of meekness and quietness, which can only then be quiet, when
no cause is offered unto it of unquietness, by hard and unjust usage"
(212). Hermione is not "quiet." She is not loud and boisterous, but she

is not quiet. Her response to the indictment is eloquent. She pleads not for life but only to allow her honor to be exonerated for the sake of their children. She trusts the "pow'rs divine" will somehow enable "innocence . . . [to] make / False accusation blush, and tyranny tremble at patience" (III.ii.28–32). She declares that her love for Polixenes was only

> . . . as in honor he requir'd;
> With such a kind of love as might become
> A lady like me; with a love even such,
> So, and no other, as yourself commanded;
> Which not to have done I think had been in me
> Both disobedience and ingratitude." (63–68)

In the minds of all, save for the infected and inflamed brain of Leontes, she wins this contest also. Leontes has sent to the oracle of Delphos, and even that declares her innocence: "Hermione is chaste," but Leontes tyrannically exclaims, "There is not truth at all i' th' oracle. / The sessions shall proceed; this is mere falsehood" (140–141). Leontes "wins," but his "victory" is horrible. Mamillius dies; Hermione swoons and is taken away believed to be dead; his whole court shares the sentiments of Paulina toward him, "O thou tyrant! / . . . betake thee / To nothing but despair" (207–210). Beecher declares that "the deep tragedy of jealous competition is that the jealous person's enemy does not destroy him; the jealous person destroys himself" (179). Nearly four hundred years ago, Shakespeare recognized the destructive power of jealousy arising from deep within the individual.

JEALOUS HOMICIDE ATTEMPTED

The jealous obsession with chastity turns into such hell in two more dramatic families portrayed by Shakespeare that each husband attempts to murder his wife; one fails while the other succeeds. Each husband is deceived by an Italian Machiavel into believing his wife unfaithful. Describing life in England in a period prior to Shakespeare's, Barbara Hanawalt observes: "Jealousy and infidelity also brought discord to family and community. Robert Mannyng urged men and women not to indulge in jealousy, for it was sure to cause strife. . . . Sexual infidelities are a classic scenario for murder" (209). So valuable is a wife's chastity to her husband, so painful the loss of honor (hers and his), so violated the sense of justice at thinking what was to have been wholly his has been given to another, so out of control the volcanic eruption of jealousy, that cold and calculated murder results merely from the belief that a wife has committed adultery.

Preachers and moralists of the sixteenth and seventeenth centuries were seldom more eloquent than when inveighing against adultery. In 1633, Matthew Griffith declares that a "general duty common to man and wife is *Loyalty*: for their bodies, and marriage-beds must be kept *chaste* and *undefiled*" (297). As Griffith warms to his subject, he exclaims:

Adultery is forbidden between the commandments of *killing* and *stealing* . . . For they that commit *Adultery*, do both *kill* and *steal*: yea of all *thieves* and *murderers* whatsoever, they are the worst. . . . the *Adulterer* steals away from a man that which God himself hath made most near; and all good men that have ever lived, accounted most dear unto them, *viz.* The use (and so the *right*) of his wife. (298)

Much earlier, Hergest defines the sin:

Adultery, is a wicked and mischievous deed, committed against the seventh commandment, that springeth of carnal security, & lack of the love and fear of God, and from contempt of his judgements, whereby a married person breaketh the covenant of marriage, and defileth his or her body by following of strange flesh: they that commit this sin are adulterers or adulteresses. (7)

One should remember that Hergest insists that

it is more shame for a woman to commit this vice, than for a man, for the chief, and almost the only virtue that above all things is required in a woman is Virginity and Chastity [and it is Hergest who most clearly distinguishes the two terms], which being once lost, her credit is cracked. (35)

And Vives pontificates that "A married woman ought to be of greater chastity than an unmarried," for "with one wicked deed: How many revengers thou shalt provoke against thee," and he lists Almighty God, "next unto God . . . thine husband," the church, father and mother, sisters and brothers, kinsfolk, alliances, friends, children—indeed, all ages both spiritual and temporal. A woman, Vives says, who relinquishes her chastity gives up that which is not hers, for it was given to her husband. Finally, Hergest appropriately sums up the common attitude and belief that the violation of the seventh commandment springs from

the lack of the love and fear of God, and from contempt of his judgements and punishments, whereby persons not joined together in Matrimony, have carnal knowledge one of another's body, and so defile and pollute the same, contrary to God's commandment, will, and ordinance, and therefore deserve the wrath

of God, and eternal damnation. And they that commit this sin . . . are commonly . . . called Whores and Strumpets. (7)

Interestingly enough, Shakespeare portrays the intensity of the jealous
reaction of the husband who believes his wife an adulteress focused not
upon the male adulterer with her, but upon his own wife. He attempts
or completes the murder, not of the man believed to be the adulterer,
but of his wife.

The first, the attempted murder, occurs in *Cymbeline*. Posthumus has
won the heart of the lovely Imogen, daughter of Cymbeline, and has
married her without her father's consent. For that, he is exiled, while
Cymbeline and his Queen, not the mother of Imogen but a second
wife, seek to prevail upon Imogen to marry Cloten, the Queen's son
by a former husband. In Rome, Posthumus proclaims Imogen "more
fair, virtuous, wise, chaste, constant, qualified [well gifted], and less
attemptable [susceptible to seduction] than any" (I.iv.59–61). Jachimo
unequivocally declares, "That lady is not now living" (62). Posthumus,
step by step, enters into a foolish contest with Jachimo, and finally blurts
out: "My mistress exceeds in goodness the hugeness of your unworthy
thinking. I dare you to this match: here's my ring [the ring Imogen
gave him at his departure into exile]" (144–146). Posthumus reserves
the right to kill Jachimo, "If she remain unseduc'd, you not making it
appear otherwise, for your ill opinion and th' assault you have made to
her chastity, you shall answer me with your sword" (160–163).

However, "making it appear otherwise" is precisely what Jachimo
does. He travels to Britain, lies to Imogen about the loose behavior of
Posthumus in Rome with prostitutes, and offers himself to her as her
means of revenge. When he offers himself, she is outraged and knows
that he has been lying. Seeing that he has failed, Jachimo admits that he
lied and asserts that he was merely testing her for the sake of making
Posthumus feel good to learn how pure and chaste she remains. He
requests but one small favor: that she safely stow a trunk of treas-
ures for the night. She agrees, "I will keep them / In my bedchamber"
(I.vi.195-196). That night, when she has gone to sleep, Jachimo steals
out of the trunk, makes a mental note of the furnishings of her bedroom, even discovers "On her left breast / A mole cinque-spotted [of
five spots]" (II.ii.37–38), and steals the bracelet from her wrist—the
bracelet Posthumus gave her when he left Britain. He can now make
a very convincing case, by making the truth "appear otherwise" than it
actually was, that he had successfully seduced Imogen.

Posthumus is furious. Imogen had been so chaste as to urge forbearance in their copulation. When she did, she was but being a good, chaste
wife. Wives were urged not to arouse their husbands, in dress, word, or
deed. Whately teaches:

The married must not provoke desires for pleasures sake, but allay desires, when they provoke themselves. They must not strive by words and gestures, to enflame their passions, when were it not for such enforcements, they would be cool enough. But when such passions are of themselves moved, then must they take the benefit of their estate and assuage them, that for want of just satisfaction, they may not be troublesome to them in the duties of religion, and of their callings. In a word, marriage must be used as seldom and sparingly, as may stand with the need of the persons married: for excess this way doth weaken the body, and shorten life: but a sparing enjoyment would help the health, and preserve the body from divers diseases in some constitutions. Excessiveness inflameth lust, and disposeth the persons so offending to adultery. Moderation kills lust, and is a great furtherance to purity. Excessiveness breeds satiety, and makes them each weary of the other, desirous of strangers; moderation endeareth them each to the other, and breeds contentment in themselves. (19)

Imogen, in urging the "forbearance" of moderation, was simply being the chaste wife, and, until he comes to believe her otherwise, that is how Posthumus accepted her forbearance, for, he says, she "did it with / A pudency [modesty] so rosy the sweet view on't / Might well have warm'd old Saturn; that I thought her / As chaste as unsunn'd snow" (II.v.10–13). But now, convinced that she has committed adultery, his rage is not against Jachimo, the supposed adulterer, but against Imogen: "O vengeance, vengeance!" he cries in his anguish, and then bitterly inveighs against the "women's part in me"—

> . . . be it lying, note it,
> The woman's; flattering, hers; deceiving, hers;
> Lust and rank thoughts, hers, hers; revenges, hers;
> Ambitions, covetings, change of prides, disdain,
> Nice longing, slanders, mutability,
> All faults that name, nay, that hell knows,
> Why, hers, in part or all; but rather, all;
> For even to vice
> They are not constant, but are changing still;
> One vice but of a minute old, for one
> Not half so old as that. I'll write against them,
> Detest them, curse them; yet 'tis greater skill
> In a true hate, to pray they have their will:
> The very devils cannot plague them better. (II.v.22–35)

He writes to his servant Pisanio in Britain of Imogen's adultery and orders him to kill her.

As far as Posthumus is concerned, he has murdered his wife. Later, when he has slipped back into Britain, Posthumus repents that he ordered her murdered. "You married ones, / If each of you should take this course, how many / Must murther wives much better than themselves / For wrying [swerving or straying] but a little!" (V.i.2–5). He accuses Pisanio of failing as a good servant for obeying his command: "Every good servant does not all commands; / No bond, but to do just ones" (6–7). In actual fact, Pisanio is exactly that sort of good servant. He has not murdered Imogen, and in the end, Jachimo confesses his lies; he restores first the ring to Posthumus and then the bracelet he had stolen from "the truest princess / That ever swore her faith" (V.v.416-417). In effect, Posthumus receives his faithful wife, like Hero, as though resurrected from the dead, the light of life restored.

JEALOUS HOMICIDE COMPLETED

Othello (and Shakespeare's audience), however, knows that there is no "Promethean heat / That can [Desdemona's] light relume" (V.ii.12–13). The inevitability of Othello's murder of pure Desdemona makes their tragedy perhaps the most painful of all the tragedies Shakespeare wrote, one of the most painful of any in the world. As in all of his dramas, particularly his mature ones, Shakespeare weaves the threads of many disparate themes into an intricate whole. *Othello*, like *Much Ado About Nothing*, *The Winter's Tale*, and *Cymbeline*, for that matter, is an extremely complex play and cannot adequately be accounted for, any more than the others can, simply in terms of the jealous obsession with chastity in the Elizabethan and Jacobean eras. Nevertheless, just as the homes of the other three plays were plunged into hell by that cultural feature, so is the home of Othello and Desdemona, yet with a supreme difference: in *Othello*, it is as though Shakespeare so perfectly balances and then mixes the hell of jealousy in the mind of Othello with the extremity of Desdemona's purity and chastity as to maximize the injustice and the consequent pain for his audience who must suffer the hell of this home, as though there is a distillation of these two cultural features resulting in the tremendously explosive power of two volatile forces. All the other characters—the quintessential Machiavellian villain, Iago; the incorrigible and unreconcilable racist, Brabantio; the "gull'd" Roderigo and the "honorable" but manipulated Cassio; the earthy foil to Desdemona, level-headed Emilia, and all the others—serve but to sharpen the focus upon Desdemona's chastity and Othello's blindingly white-hot jealousy.

In all of literature, one can scarcely find a purer heroine than Desdemona. For all her purity and gentility, Shakespeare takes pains to portray her as no insipid milk-toast. Invited to the home of Brabantio often, Othello told of his many "disastrous chances," "moving accidents," "hair-breadth scapes," and many other strange and wonderful adventures of this most noble and accomplished general, this man of war, this successful leader of men. Desdemona, during those sessions, would hastily dispatch her household responsibilities in order to "come again, and with a greedy ear / Devour up [his] discourse" (I.iii.149–150). And with that delightful Shakespearean efficiency for making a phrase serve more than one purpose, he has Othello report:

> . . . My story being done,
> She gave me for my pains a world of {sighs};
> She swore, in faith 'twas strange, 'twas passing strange;
> 'Twas pitiful, 'twas wondrous pitiful.
> She wish'd she had not heard it, yet she wish'd
> *That Heaven had made her such a man.* (158–163, emphasis added)

The double meaning was surely intended—namely, that Desdemona would have liked to be just such a man as Othello, and that Desdemona would like for Othello to be the man made for her. She gives him enough hints about how stories of fearful adventures so attracted her that, in Othello's words:

> . . . if I had a friend that lov'd her
> I should but teach him how to tell my story,
> And that would woo her. Upon this hint I spake:
> She lov'd me for the dangers I had pass'd,
> And I lov'd her that she did pity them. (164 –168)

Desdemona's spirit was as adventuresome and warlike as the spirit of Othello; matched in nobility of spirit, and compatible in outlook on life, Othello and Desdemona exemplify as ideally as any couple in Shakespeare the love-match of companionate marriage—more mature than Romeo and Juliet, less exploitative of each other than Antony and Cleopatra, so magnificent in mind and heart as to make matches outside the tragedies seem unworthy of comparison and almost trivial—Rosalind and Orlando, Portia and Bassanio, Ferdinand and Miranda, even Benedick and Beatrice, with, perhaps, depending upon one's reading, Petruchio and Kate slightly of a pair but too remotely distant to be meaningfully compared. Their perfect compatibility finds its best expression, perhaps, in Othello's exclamation as they meet in Cyprus: "O my fair warrior!" Their expressions of mutual delight in each other are as exquisite and convincing as any love talk between any Shakespearean lovers. Shakespeare's audience might shift uncomfortably to hear such passion between lovers, but only those so coldly cloddish as never to have loved could not identify with the love of Othello and Desdemona for each other. Shakespeare, as perfectly as any writer who ever wrote, could express the sense of passionate love, that the man is the original Adam, the woman the first Eve, and the two the first Lord and Lady of a universe newly made for them alone. Desdemona is no insipid milk toast; she is the perfect match for this man among men, Othello.

More purely in comparison with Angelo's sudden attraction to Isabella, Othello, a man of chaste mind and heart himself, is attracted to the purity and chastity of Desdemona. Shakespeare stresses the meeting of their minds, higher than mere physical attraction. "I saw Othello's visage in his mind" (I.iii.252), Desdemona says, and Othello tells the Duke and the Senate that he would like Desdemona to accompany him to Cyprus, not "To please the palate of my appetite . . . But to be free and bounteous to her mind" (262, 265). Othello's conception of the universe emphasizes its purity and chastity. When he has finally been convinced of Desdemona's unfaithfulness, he thinks adultery to be so vile that "Heaven stops the nose at it, and the moon winks; / The bawdy wind, that kisses all it meets, / Is hush'd within the hollow mine of earth / And will not hear't" (IV.ii.77–80). About to murder Desdemona, he exclaims, "Let me not name it [the cause] to you, you chaste stars" (V.ii.2). Like Cardinal Bembo in *The Book of the Courtier* (309), Othello believes purity of soul and outward beauty have a natural affinity. Like Desdemona herself, Othello loves chastity; it seems quite apparent that the very intensity of his abhorrence of her believed unfaithfulness arises, in part, from his own purity of soul and devotion to chastity. Othello and Desdemona begin their marriage with exemplary compatibility of mind about chastity.

In all of Shakespeare, perhaps in all of literature, nobody is purer of mind and soul than Desdemona. She is all that the moralists and preachers could ever desire as the very epitome of chastity. She cannot understand Othello's disturbed state of mind nor comprehend his meaning when he uses increasingly foul figures of speech and allusions, and she is stunned more than she was by his sudden physical blow (IV.i.240) when he finally uses the unspeakable word, "whore," and actually declares to her, "I took you for that cunning whore of Venice / That married with Othello" (IV.ii.89–90). So pure of mind is Desdemona—and Shakespeare makes her convincingly honest in this respect—that she cannot bring herself to utter the word "whore." Like Ophelia in her madness, from the depths of her agony, Desdemona sings a song of madness, the "Willow" song of poor Barbary, but she seems not to be thinking about the words of the song, merely singing it absent-mindedly out of her identity with the depths of despair felt by deserted Barbary. What she is really thinking about soon comes out: "Dost thou in conscience think—tell me, Emilia— / That there be women do abuse their husbands / In such gross kind [still unable to name the sin]?" (IV.iii.61–63). The wholesomely earthy and equally honest Emilia admits she might commit adultery not "by this heavenly light" but perhaps "i' th' dark" and would "make her husband a cuckold to make him a monarch," another twist upon Desdemona's words that she cannot believe Emilia would "do such a deed for all the world" (65–67). Anyone can recognize Emilia as a realistic inhabitant of this dirty world, and her remarks against the double standard stir the souls of sensitive advocates of minority rights in all generations as surely as Shylock's "Hath not a Jew eyes?" speech, although Shakespeare's contemporary audiences would have had ambivalent responses to both. However, Emilia's earthy statements, amusing and poignant as they are, heighten the other-worldly quality of Desdemona's purity. The hell of this house, felt so keenly by all audiences, arises in large part from the utter injustice of the accusations against the chastity of Desdemona. The charges are absurd to a rational mind.

That is precisely Othello's problem; once aroused by Iago's clever deceptions, he no longer thinks rationally; his judgment has become darkened. Perhaps the most completely evil of all Shakespearean characters, Iago is the consummately clever Italian Machiavel, intelligent and opportunistic, cunningly deceitful, coldly manipulative, and viciously selfish. Other vice figures, like Aaron in *Titus Andronicus* and Jachimo in *Cymbeline*, have slight redemptive features, but in Iago there is none. His rationalizations for his determined destructive efforts—namely, that he, the experienced soldier, has been passed over for promotion to lieutenant in favor of Cassio, utterly inexperienced in "soldiership" but socially adept in Venice, and that it has been absurdly rumored that Othello, "'twixt my sheets," has been intimate with Emilia—are sufficient justifications for his wickedness only in his own mind. Shakespeare more convincingly provides the real motivation for Iago's evil in a comment Iago makes about Cassio: "He hath a daily beauty in his life / That makes me ugly" (V.i.19–20). That is, he simply cannot stand people who live beautiful, noble lives, and if that is true of Cassio, how much more true it is of Othello and Desdemona. Like the child in Wordsworth's poem, "Nutting," Iago responds to natural beauty with veritable lust to spoil it, much the way children, looking out on the smooth, white beauty of a fresh snowfall, can scarcely wait to plunge into it and in a few minutes completely ruin it. Iago hates the beauty of chastity in Desdemona and of nobility in Othello. Extremely intelligent though he is, Iago's extraordinary intelligence is completely at the service of his coldly calculating evil spirit. It is not without reason that Dante pictures Satan embedded in ice in the bottommost point in hell; not only is ice for destruction "also great," as Robert Frost's poem asserts, it is worse than fire because it is not merely hot emotions devoted to wrong, but the highest human quality—intelligence, reason—devoted to evil. Iago's clever scheming plays upon Othello's weaknesses, arouses his powerful emotions, and saps Othello's ability to make rational judgments.

Shakespeare, ever insightful into human nature, vividly portrays Othello's vulnerability to the clever manipulations of Iago. Othello, the successful general, the leader of the Venetian armed forces, at home on the battlefield, is out of his element in time of peace. He is, after all, an alien in Venice. Although of royal descent, he is an outsider in Venice, unaccustomed to Venetian etiquette and social behavior. No doubt, even though Cassio is a Florentine, he is educated, "bookish," and skilled in etiquette, able to guide Othello through the social pitfalls of dinners such as those at Brabantio's house. Othello is advanced in years and yet has never married. If Milton felt his inexperience with women left him vulnerable, Shakespeare, as he often does, anticipates that sort of vulnerability. Desdemona, aggressive as she is, takes the first step in establishing their personal relationship. There is even a hint of Othello's possible sexual impotence—"the young affects / In {me} defunct" (I.iii.263-264). Othello is a black, not a brown, Moor. His blackness was no cause for stumbling for Brabantio so long as Othello came as General Othello to his dinners, providing free entertainment for the other guests with the stories of his adventures. But although Brabantio might have boasted that he had a black friend in Othello, he certainly did not want his daughter to marry a black man. He cannot believe that his daughter, "a maid so . . . fair," unless enchanted and enslaved in "chains of magic," would risk the "general mock" by running "to the sooty bosom / Of such a thing as [Othello]" (I.ii.62–71). The Duke's assurances that "virtue" is beautiful and therefore that "Your son-in-law is far more fair than black" (290) do not comfort the racist Brabantio at all. His rejection of Desdemona for having married without his consent—and to a black, of all bad choices, at that—is not lost upon Othello. As Iago's lies begin their dirty work in Othello's pure mind, he articulates his own sense of vulnerability: "Haply for [perhaps because] I am black, / And have not those soft parts of conversation / That chamberers have, or for I am declin'd / Into the vale of years. . ." (III.iii.263–266).

Like any soldier, to whom winning is what fighting is all about and losing is the worst possible fate, Othello is intensely competitive. The insecurities he feels, despite his successes, prompt the possessiveness he admits:

> . . . O curse of marriage!
> That we can call these delicate creatures ours,
> And not their appetites! I had rather be a toad
> And live upon the vapor of a dungeon
> Than keep a corner in the thing I love
> For others' uses. (III.iii.268–273)

His sense of noble parentage, his past outstanding achievements—"My parts, my title, and my perfect soul / Shall manifest me rightly" (I.ii.30–32) —make him seem extremely confident, and he is. He has great pride, but modern psychologists, like Adler, have often observed that a superiority complex is a mask for an inferiority complex. However, in terms of the writings of the Renaissance preachers and moralists as well as modern psychologists, Othello is the quintessential candidate for jealous obsession, that "fear, lest an other man should have in common with him that thing, which he would have to be his several own. . . . For we have both read and heard tell of many, that have slain their wives, moved only with jealousy" (Vives, Aa.iiii, recto and verso). Othello's towering jealousy has become archetypal, the supreme example of jealousy of which all lesser cases are but faint shadows.

Othello's jealous obsession, once aroused, is supreme, and so is the hell he experiences. Iago, with Machiavellian cunning, exploits the given. Othello has won Desdemona's heart with the telling of his adventures, but, Iago reasons,

Her eye must be fed; and what delight shall she have to look on the devil? When the blood is made dull with the act of sport, there should be, {again} to inflame it and to give satiety a fresh appetite, loveliness in favor, sympathy in years, manners, and beauties [suggesting that Othello is physically ugly]—all which the Moor is defective in." (II.i.225–231)

In fact, Desdemona continues to love the handsomely noble inner Othello, and all those "reasons" mean absolutely nothing to her, but Othello himself begins to doubt for those reasons under the barrage of Iago's clever lies. The audience feels Othello's hell perhaps even more than he does, for the audience, as readily as Othello, falls in love with Desdemona. The unjust blackening of her reputation is intensely painful, more painful to the audience because the viewers all know how completely false the charges against her chastity are. Moreover, Othello is noble and pure; the audience, like Desdemona, loves him because he is worthy to be loved, regardless of external appearance. It is precisely at this level that Shakespeare is able to plunge the audience into the excruciating hell of this home to suffer intensest agony. Othello's jealousy, deceived as he is, is as great as he is; the greater the person, the greater the possibility for pain. Othello's pain results from his reluctant conviction that Desdemona has committed adultery with Cassio, but the pain of the audience is twofold: that Desdemona's chastity has been falsely impugned and that Othello's murderous rage against her is most unjust, exactly when he thinks it is only justice to hate and kill her. The greatest tragedy anyone can ever experience is being wrong without knowing one is wrong. Otherwise noble and lovable Othello is wrong, utterly wrong. His horrible hell is real, and the anguish he feels the audience shares, but the audience must also feel the greater pain of knowing that his jealousy is uncalled for, that lovely Desdemona, the purest of the pure, remains beautiful in her total chastity, and that what Othello calls justice is grossest injustice. Shakespeare's balancing of Othello's unjust jealousy and Desdemona's continuing perfect chastity extracts from his audience, culturally conditioned to its own jealous obsession with chastity, the utmost pain.

Although Vives observes that jealousy rages in wild beasts, Othello's tragedy is that he thinks he is heaven's scourge and minister when, most painfully, he is but the dupe of a Machiavellian villain. Othello's rage is towering because nothing more outrages any person than a sense of injustice, of violated justice. Othello approaches the murder of Desdemona, not like a wild beast, but like a carefully reasoning human being. Innocent Desdemona lies asleep on their bed, made afresh with their wedding sheets. Othello, convinced of her lost chastity, enters carrying a candle: "It is the cause, it is the cause, my soul; / Let me not name it to you, you chaste stars, / It is the cause" (V.ii.1–3). His love for her, even though he has completely accepted the idea of her guilt, which he hates, is exquisitely painful. Her guilt requires death; justice demands it: "Yet she must die, else she'll betray more men" (6). He is aware of the finality of the act he is about to commit:

> Put out the light [here the candle, so that he will not have to look upon her as he kills her], and then put out the light [of Desdemona's life]:
> If I quench thee, thou flaming minister [the candle],
> I can again thy former light restore,
> Should I repent me; but once put out thy light [now speaking directly to the sleeping Desdemona],
> Thou cunning'st pattern of excelling nature,
> I know not where is that Promethean heat
> That can thy light relume. When I have pluck'd thy rose,
> I cannot give it vital growth again,
> It needs must wither. (7–15)

Overwhelmed by his love for her, he kisses her, and experiences such sweetness that he exclaims, "O balmy breath, that dost almost persuade / Justice to break her sword!" (16–17). This is a moment of intense audience pain, for all know Desdemona's chastity to be absolute and Othello's act in the name of justice unspeakable injustice. She has been wronged; he has been wronged, and now he is about to commit the greatest wrong of all. He kisses her again, and again, and then "One more, and that's the last. / So sweet was ne'er so fatal.

I must weep. / . . . This sorrow's heavenly, / It strikes where it doth love" (19–22). Othello believes he is acting as heaven's scourge and minister. He compares himself to God the Father who loved God the Son, but, for the sake of humankind, struck him dead. When Desdemona awakens and insists on her innocence, he cries, "By heaven, I saw my handkerchief in's hand. / O perjur'd woman, thou dost stone my heart, / And {mak'st} me call what I intend to do / A murther, which I thought a sacrifice" (62–65), a sacrifice because she will bear away this sin that pollutes the universe, a death that will satisfy ultimate justice.

In four plays particularly, Shakespeare addresses the jealous obsession with chastity that afflicted his age. He challenges that obsession in a variety of ways, not finding fault with chastity per se, but with the various ways his culture foolishly wronged people in being controlled by it. Nowhere is his statement about the possibility for wrong resulting from the jealous obsession with chastity more powerful or more hellishly painful than in his portrayal of the chaste Desdemona and the deluded Othello, committing most horrible injustice in the name of justice.

5

Property and the Grasp of Greed: *The Merchant of Venice*, *King Lear*, and *Timon of Athens*

Family quarrels about money are commonplace nowadays, but they are not new. Family conflicts about property—i.e., possessions—are probably as old as humankind. The term "property" is closely related to "proper," meaning "one's own" or "belonging to one's self." Certainly, in English-speaking cultures, "mine" is one of the very early additions to a child's vocabulary, particularly when other children are present. After the biological urge to procreate and the natural affinity parents tend to feel toward their children, property becomes a major tie holding members of a family together, but, at the same time, it also frequently emerges as a primary bone of contention. The reasons are many. Property means power in most cultures, and it especially did in Shakespeare's England. Both family and individual identities are intimately related to possessions, defining who "we" are or who "I" am. The way one uses possessions expresses personality, and one's possessions become an extension of one's self. Western cultures have been extremely acquisitive for many generations, but acquisition is often both a form of and the result of aggression.

During the medieval period, extreme stress on the comparative superiority of "riches in heaven" over "riches on earth" often made poverty a positive value, many deliberately abandoning material possessions for lives of poverty. During the Renaissance, however, considerable emphasis on the fact that God created the earth and called it good and upon man's responsibilities to develop himself in this world provided ample rationalization and justification for acquiring wealth. Shakespeare's

England was caught up in the contradictions of the continuing medieval values of subordinating material gain to heavenly gain and the emerging modern values of economic self-interest and the accumulation of earthly wealth. Not only do Shakespeare's troubled families reflect these conflicts, but his dramas about families fighting over property also become his call to his serious audiences to think deeply about these changing values. The lament, "Our house is hell," is Jessica's description of that very conflict in *The Merchant of Venice*.

MERCHANT/USURER: TWO SIDES OF THE SAME COIN

Some people, not particularly familiar with the play, think Jessica's father, Shylock the Jew, is the merchant of Venice, and, curiously that confusion is possibly one of Shakespeare's major points. Portia's question in the context of the judgment scene is natural enough, "Which is the merchant here? and which the Jew?" (IV.i.174). She has seen neither before, and yet that question haunts one; Shakespeare seems to take pains to suggest, subtly and indirectly, yet persistently, that any fundamental difference between usurer and merchant is extremely difficult to discern and that beneath the skin all humans share a common humanity, all profoundly flawed, especially with reference to a virtual lust for property.

In writing about one of Elizabethan England's great merchants, Sir Thomas Gresham, Michael Foss observes, "It was a sentence of St. Jerome that 'the merchant can never please God,' and much of the economic thinking of the Middle Ages seemed to have been governed by this text" (107). In antiquity, merchants were despised; in the land of the Phaeacians, Euryalus deliberately insults Odysseus by calling him a master of merchantmen sailors. Even as late as 1589, Thomas Smith, in *The Common-vvelth of England*, lists the ranks of society from the dukes through the barons, on to the lesser gentlemen, and then to the yeomen, who "confess themselves to be no gentlemen" (31). Then he remarks,

The fourth sort or class amongst us is those of . . . day laborers, poor husbandmen, yea merchants, or retailers which have no free lands, copyholders, and all Artificers, as Tailors, Shoemakers, Carpenters, Brickmakers, Masons, &c. These have no voice nor authority in our Commonwealth, and no account is made of them but only to be ruled, not to rule other, and yet they be not altogether neglected. (34)

Despite Smith's snobbery about "merchants," great merchant companies had emerged from the earlier merchant adventurers: the "Mercers, Grocers, Drapers, Fishmongers, Goldsmiths, Skinners, Merchant

Taylors, Haberdashers, Salters, Ironmongers, Vintners and Cloth-workers . . . . Hardly any of these men practised the business of the Company they represented, but had acquired their wealth from foreign trade, mainly in wool, cloth and corn" (Cathcart 101). Merchant adventurers, the general term for those not associated with one of the great companies, also continued to go out from England into all the world in search of trade. In February 1583, Ralph Fitch set out as a part of the Turkey Company to Aleppo on a ship called *Tiger*; one might recall, "Her husband's to Aleppo gone, master o' the Tiger" (*Macbeth*, I.iii.7), although there is no necessary connection. His party traveled by land to Basra, and from there intended to go to India, but they were arrested as heretics by the Portuguese at Ormuz and sent by them to Goa where raged an Inquisition "more cruel and terrifying than the Inquisition of Spain" (Collis 9). They managed to flee, and Fitch, in September 1584, went on to Pegu in Burma. There he noted how weak they were by sea; he compiled a list of their chief goods and what foreign goods were likely to be desirable there. He visited Rangoon and other places. After eight years, he returned to England, and his report to the merchants of London ultimately resulted in the formation, nine years later, of the East India Company, the organization that, in 250 years, acquired almost all of the towns Fitch had visited (15). Merchant adventurer companies formed, dissolved, realigned, reorganized, in almost kaleidoscopic fashion, sometimes failing but often succeeding in making huge profits, and, although few merchants became quite so wealthy as Sir Thomas Gresham, a member of the Mercers' Company from 1543, merchants became some of the wealthiest men in England.

Modern audiences are often unaware of the fact that Shakespeare and his audiences knew thoroughly—namely, that most usurers in Elizabethan and early Jacobean years were not Jews but merchants. Jews had practiced usury in England, but in 1290, all Jews were expelled from England, and nearly 16,000 of them were forced to abandon homes and all outstanding I.O.U.s held by them. There were almost no Jews in England during Shakespeare's lifetime, and possibly not any practicing usury. Bronstein explains:

To begin with, Shakespeare's portrait of the Jew could not possibly derive from first-hand contact with Jews or with Jewish life. There had been almost no Jews in England for over three hundred years and no Jewish community life even of the most rudimentary form. Shakespeare's lack of knowledge of the Jews and of Jewish life is revealed repeatedly in the text of the play: the unlikely names of the Jews, Shylock, Tubal, Chus, Jessica, all probably derived from early chapters in Genesis; the various expletives in Shylock's mouth, "by Jacob's staff" (which was, by the way, a Christian oath), "by the Holy Sabbath," "my deeds upon my head," phrases that are not characteristically Jewish, the fact that nothing distinctively Jewish in the home of Shylock is manifest. (34–35)

English merchants, however, had excess liquidity, and many of them put those available resources to use. An act in 1487 prohibited usury, but in 1545 a new measure permitted loans and limited the interest rate to ten percent. Another act against usury in 1552 once more made usury illegal until 1571 when again it was permitted at a maximum rate of ten percent. Not all usurers in Shakespeare's England were merchants, but a great many of them were, including famous names like Sir Thomas Gresham and Sir John Spencer. The social and economic history of the period makes clear why Shakespeare sees the merchant and the usurer as two sides of the same coin.

That Shakespeare separated the usurer from the merchant in *The Merchant of Venice* and then gave them a covert intimacy bordering on identity is representative of the complexity of the play. Usury was highly controversial in his day. The Bible clearly teaches against usury, a fact that preachers expounded incessantly. One preacher in particular, Henry Smith, envisions the hell of the house built by usury. In a sermon, "The Examination of Usury," he takes Proverbs 23:8 as his text: "He which increaseth his riches by Usury gathereth for them which will be merciful to the poor" (106). Smith observes, "God saith, that he will smite the usurer with his fist [a reference to Ezekiel 22:13], not with the palm of his hand, but with his fist, which giveth a greater blow" (107). As Smith's imagination takes over, he declares:

But if you will hear their final sentence, David saith here, *That they shall not dwell in God's Temple, nor rest in his holy mountain* . . . . If he shall not rest in heaven, then he shall rest in hell, where no rest is. Then saith one, the Usurer shall cry unto his children, Cursed be you my Children, because you were the cause of these torments, for lest you should be poor, I was an Usurer and robbed other, to leave riches unto you. To whom the children shall reply again: nay cursed be you, father, for you were the cause of our torments, for if you had not left us other men's goods, we had not kept other men's goods. Thus when they are cursed of God, they shall curse one another: curse the Lord for condemning them, curse their sins for accusing them, curse their parents for begetting them, & curse themselves because they cannot help themselves. (107)

According to Smith, usury damns to hell not only the usurer but his entire household, and in hell they curse one another.

Despite all the sermons against usury, the practice spread. England was comparatively late in becoming sophisticated about international finance, Italy having developed letters of credit and other financial devices nearly four hundred years earlier and Antwerp well established as the trade center and international money market for northern Europe during much of Shakespeare's life. As England's international trade developed, her increased sophistication in monetary matters, including borrowing and lending at interest, became a necessity. Moreover, the English government frequently needed to borrow, and had "to pay 14 per cent and more at Antwerp" (Foss 108). Therefore, many treatises emerged, one by Thomas Wilson, *A Discourse upon Usury* (1572), another by Miles Mosse on *The Arraignment and Conviction of Vsvrie* (1595), still another by Robert Fenton, *A Treatise of Vsvrie* (1612), to mention only three—all carefully defining and redefining usury, making minute distinctions to justify certain kinds of usury and yet condemn others.

Nevertheless, preachers, like Henry Smith, argued that human law might allow usury because of human weakness, but God's law still prohibited it. Smith further argued that the law did not "allow ten in the hundred [a reference to the ten-percent maximum interest permitted by law], nor five in the hundred, nor one in the hundred, nor any usury at all" but only that the law punished those that exact "above ten in the hundred" (105 and 106). Similarly, Phillip Stubs reasons:

Although Civil laws (to the avoiding of further inconveniences) do permit certain sums of money, to be given, overplus beyond and above the principal, for the loans of money lent, yet are the Usurers no more discharged from the guilt of Usury before God thereby, than the Adulterous Jews were from Whoredom, because Moses gave them a permissive law for every one to put away his wife, that would, for any light offence. And yet the positive laws there give no liberty to commit Usury: but seeing how much rageth, lest it should exceed, rage further and overflow the banks of all reason and godliness (as Covetousness is a raging Sea, and a bottomless pit, never satisfied nor contented) they have limited it within certain meers [boundaries], and banks (to bridle the insatiable desires of covetous men) beyond the which, it is not lawful for any to go. (imprinted 74 but actually 72, recto and verso)

And yet, even though both Stubs and Smith declare that the government placed a cap on interest rates at ten percent maximum to restrain greed, in actual fact, ten percent was usually the minimum, and many devices were used to circumvent the law and to charge a much higher percentage rate, at twenty or twenty-five percent, or even higher (Foss 106). Phillip Stubs, in his rage against usurers, declares:

The Usurer killeth not one, but many, both Husband, Wife, Children, Servants, Family, and all, not sparing any. And if the poor man have not wherewith to pay, as well the Interest, as the principal: when soever this greedy Cormorant doth demand it, their suit is commenced against him out go Butterflies [a humorous or sarcastic designation for legal papers] and writs, as thick as Hail. So the poor man is apprehended, and . . . sentence proceedeth against him, compelling him to pay, as well the Usury and the loan of the money, as the money lent. (imprinted 76, actually 74, recto)

Stubs' figure of the "Cormorant" for the greedy person was one rather frequently used in Shakespeare's day, but some audiences do not recognize that Shakespeare's choice of the name, Shylock, for his usurer, probably results from the fact that *shalak* is the Hebrew word for that biblically unclean bird with a voracious appetite, the "cormorant."

In various ways, Shakespeare depicts Shylock as the hated usurer, a Jew, an alien, the outsider, the greedy cormorant, a veritable devil, and he depicts Antonio as the merchant, generous and even willing to lay down his life for his friend. Yet underlying all of this is the fact that most usurers were merchants, and that merchants were often criticized and excoriated as severely as usurers. Thomas Lodge recognizes their underlying identity and storms against the merchants *as* usurers in his work, *An Alarum against Vsurers*: "I mean the state of Merchants, who though to public commodity they bring in store of wealth from foreign Nations, yet such are their domestical practices, that not only they enrich themselves mightily by others misfortunes, but also eat our English Gentry out of house and home" (1, recto). He describes how a young gentleman is led into expensive riotous living and then exploited by the merchant/usurer who lends at high interest for the purpose of taking the property put up as security for the loan. Lodge waxes eloquent in his indignation against the merchant/usurer:

Nay, such they are, as will rather bind thee prentice with Satan, than exhort thee to eschew [flee] sin. They be the Caterpillers [a common term for those who eat away between the tree and its bark, destroying the tree] of a Commonweal, the sting of the Adder, nay, the privy foes of all Gentry, and such they be, that if they get, they care not how ungodly, and if they cousen [deceive], they care not how commonly: So that three vices have now taken hold of thee, first prodigality, the enemy to continency, next lasciviousnes, the enemy of sobriety, and thirdly, ill company, the decayers of thy honesty. (6, verso)

Stubs, like Lodge, inveighs against merchants: "The Merchant men by their untrue weights, and by their surprising [overpricing] of their wares, heap up infinite treasure" (imprinted 70, but actually 68, verso).

Moreover, in the play, Shylock and Antonio each confesses that property is his very life. In the court scene, when the severe judgment is handed down by the Duke, representing supposedly Christian mercy, sparing Shylock's life but laying claim to his property, half to Antonio and half to the state but with the possibility of reducing the latter portion to only a fine, Shylock bursts out, "Nay, take my life and all, pardon not that: / You take my house when you do take the prop / That doth sustain my house; you take my life / When you do take the means whereby I live" (IV.i.374–377). To Shylock, his property is his very life. It is surely

no accident that Shakespeare has Antonio make an almost identical declaration later in the play. When Portia gives him a letter in which Antonio
reads that "three of [his] argosies / Are richly come to harbor suddenly"
(V.i.276-277), Antonio bursts out effusively, "Sweet lady, you have given
me life and living" (286). For Antonio, as surely as for Shylock, property
and life are one and the same. Indeed, the merchant and the usurer are
but the two sides of the same coin.

GREEDY HOARDERS AND GREEDY WASTERS: WHERE EXTREMES MEET

"Our house is hell," declares Jessica of Shylock's lifestyle, "and thou,
a merry devil," she says to Launcelot, "Didst rob it of some taste of tediousness" (II.iii.2–3). Many teenagers feel their houses are hell and are
full of tediousness, regardless of their parents' lifestyles. However, the
anal-retentive tight-fistedness of Shylock's home is extreme. He wears
"Jewish gaberdine" (I.iii.112), a loose-fitting smock frock of such coarse,
poor material that beggars often wore it. Although Launcelot exaggerates and his testimony cannot be wholly trusted, the food in Shylock's
house probably was equally poor, for not only does Launcelot complain
to his father "I am famish'd in his service" (II.ii.106), but Shylock, keenly aware of food consumption in his household, contrastingly complains
that Launcelot has been "a huge feeder" (II.v.46). Clearly Shakespeare's
portrait of a miser, Shylock watches the expenditure of every doit, the
smallest piece of money. He is opposed to every frivolous activity. When
he learns the foolishly wasteful Christians are going to have a masque, he
orders Jessica:

> Lock up my doors, and when you hear the drum
> And the vile squealing of the wry-neck'd fife,
> Clamber not you up to the casements then,
> Nor thrust your head into the public street
> To gaze on Christian fools with varnish'd [painted or perhaps here,
> masked] faces;
> But stop my house's ears, I mean my casements;
> Let not the sound of shallow fopp'ry enter
> My sober house. (II.v.29–36)

Such singleminded avoidance of the slightest waste, including an intense focus upon severe sobriety unrelieved by any relaxed pleasures
or joys of life, sounds like a lifestyle somewhat similar to that of other Shakespearean caricatures, of Puritans. It certainly represents one
lifestyle, portrayed here as Jewish, of dull, gray stinginess—in attitude

toward life itself as well in the handling of material goods. Small wonder that Jessica complains, "Our house is hell."

Shylock is a hoarder who dreams of money-bags, as ominously unlucky as that was thought to be. The Elizabethan Age feared and hated hoarders and was delighted when the hoarded commodity was opened up to others. King John articulated the feelings of many when he commanded Philip the Bastard: "And ere our coming see thou shake the bags / Of hoarding abbots, imprisoned angels [gold coins] / Set at liberty. The fat ribs of peace / Must by the hungry now be fed upon" (*King John*, III.iii.7–10). Although many became wealthy during the Elizabethan era, many others endured drastic poverty, and there were recurring shortages of grain. Particularly during extreme shortages were the hoarders hated:

Latimer attacked such as 'bought corn [grain] in the markets to lay it up in store, and then sell it again', together with burgesses and farmers who had become regraters [retailers] and aldermen who profiteered in wood and coals. Lever condemned hoarders of corn whom 'neither God by blessing and cursing, neither king by proclamation and commission, neither the poor by praying and paying' could move, and pointed to the discrepancy between the price wrung from the consumer and that received by the husbandman who tilled the ground and paid the rent. (Jones 147)

Queen Elizabeth, or her ministers in her name, issued many different proclamations against those who hoarded or otherwise sought to profit from shortages or rumored shortages of grain. In the ninth year of her reign, a proclamation of "20. January" included the following:

that altogether there be no scarcity [of grain] in the Realm (thanked be almighty God) yet thereby, the covetousness of such as have either of their own store, or by unlawful bargains engrossed into their hands, great quantities of all manner of grain, will take occasions to enhance the prices therof without necessary cause, to the detriment and burden of the multitude which have lack. (*Proclamations* fol. 98)

There was another proclamation about the dearth of grain in 1587, two more in 1596, and there were still others. Shylock, of course, was not a hoarder of grain, but his hoarding miserliness would arouse distinct antipathy in a Shakespearean audience, even though they were constantly exhorted by Protestant pulpiteers to be frugal and to save. Frugality merits approval but miserly hoarding only repugnance. The Dolphin in *Henry V* expresses one typical attitude toward the foolishness of misers: "Doth like a miser spoil his coat with scanting / A little cloth"

(II.iv.47–48). Shylock, the miser, proclaims his hoarding manifesto in his "proverb never stale in a thrifty mind"—namely, "fast bind [bind tightly and securely], fast find [quickly obtain]" (II.v.54–55), but he has maintained such a skinflint lifestyle that his daughter determines to escape.

Forsaking all religious, ethical, and social considerations, Jessica elopes with a Christian, Lorenzo, taking with her as much of her father's hoarded wealth as she can carry. Shylock's virtually hysterical outcry has aroused more mockery than sympathy from the first production, no doubt, to the present:

> My daughter! O my ducats! O my daughter!
> Fled with a Christian! O my Christian ducats!
> Justice! the law! my ducats, and my daughter!
> A sealed bag, two sealed bags of ducats,
> Of double ducats, stol'n from me by my daughter!
> And jewels, two stones, two rich and precious stones,
> Stol'n by my daughter! Justice! find the girl,
> She hath the stones upon her, and the ducats. (II.viii.15–22)

That is the pain and outrage of a miser who has lost an important segment of his wealth. Most viewers despise his identification of his daughter with his material property, his ducats, jewels, and daughter all lamented in the same breath. However, marriageable children were very much a part of a man's wealth. One should never forget John Stockwood's declaration that "the children are worthily to be reckoned among the goods and substance of their fathers" (21). Ralph A. Houlbrooke, in *The English Family, 1450–1700*, points out that a daughter who is an only child, an heiress, was highly marriageable with prospects for an extremely desirable marriage settlement (66 and 75). Yet so determined is Jessica to escape the hell of her house that she abandons Judaism for Christianity, steals ducats and jewels from her father, and denies him his rightful expectation for filial obedience concerning the choice of husband and the consequent lucrative marriage arrangement for her.

As she is about to leave her home for the last time, Jessica tells her husband-to-be, Lorenzo, to whom she has already tossed a casket full of gold and jewels, "I will make fast the doors, and gild myself / With some moe ducats, and be with you straight" (II.vi.49–50). There is probably a pun intended in the word "gild." The first meaning is obvious: she will make herself still more attractive by adding a further overlay of gold. However, in those days as now, the *d* and *t* distinction, brought about by voicing the *d* with a slight hum in the larynx, was difficult to hear; the *d* often sounds like a *t*. Shakespeare probably intended for her to say what sounded like "I will gilt [guilt] myself." Gratiano's gleeful response to her statement included an intentional pun: "Now by my hood, a gentle, and no Jew" (51). He claims that Jessica has, by stealing more ducats, demonstrated that she is an excellent person, by Christian standards, just like the nobility, for "gentle" as a noun usually meant a person of honorable or noble birth, and therefore "no Jew." However, "gentle" was often spelled "gentil," and pronounced in such a way that the pun upon "gentile" was clear to all. Jessica has, indeed, become a Gentile and no Jew, for one of the deliberate contrasts of the play is the wasteful lifestyle of the Gentiles versus the miserly hoarding lifestyle of the Jews.

Like many of the "English Gentry" concerning whom Thomas Lodge worries, Bassanio has lived far beyond his means; "something too prodigal" [I.i.129] are his own words for his lifestyle. He has "great debts" (128), and Antonio is merely the chief among many other creditors. As most of the preachers against covetousness exclaim, as Stubs did, "Covetousness is a raging Sea, and a bottomless pit, never satisfied nor contented" (imprinted 74, but 72, verso), so are wasters never able to have enough. "I owe you much, and like a willful youth, / That which I owe is lost" (I.i.146–147), Bassanio admits to Antonio. The more one has, the more one spends, and debts mount up. In *Family and Fortune*, Lawrence Stone details many of the financial maneuvers of Robert Cecil, the younger son by a second wife of William Cecil, Lord Burghley. Robert Cecil, perhaps the most powerful man in the early government of King James, had enormous income for those days, much of it from more or less expected bribes and graft from public offices. Stone says, "As Lord Keynes once remarked, in some societies corruption is the simplest and most convenient method of taxation. Under certain circumstances, and practised with moderation, it is not incompatible with a devotion to the public interest" (55). It was not until the nineteenth century that civil servants began to earn a living salary from the state, for they were expected to glean compensation from those persons in the public whom they served, and occasional gifts that nowadays would be called bribes were also normal. Stone comments that modern ethical standards of professional integrity simply do not apply, for their system could not likely have existed without bribes. The fact remained that Cecil's enormous income merely made it possible for him to pile up staggering debts, and Stone records that most of the borrowed money came from twenty-one London merchants and financiers, and he specifically names Sir Baptist Hicks, the silk-merchant and Alexander Prescott, the goldsmith. The merchant/usurers of London made it possible for gentlemen like Robert Cecil to go deep into debt, despite huge incomes. Antonio, the merchant, has been making it possible for Bassanio to plunge deeply into debt.

Antonio is not a usurer; in fact, because he charges no interest of persons like Bassanio who might otherwise be forced to go to Shylock, the money-lender, Shylock hates the merchant, and also because he has been a racist Jew-baiter. Bassanio comes to Antonio for a fresh loan, hoping, as many English gentlemen did, to recoup his earlier losses by a rich marriage, but Antonio has a cash-flow problem. He has "an argosy bound to Tripolis, another to the Indies; . . . a third at Mexico, a fourth for England, and other ventures" (I.iii.18–21). However, he generously promises to make use of his own excellent credit rating to aid Bassanio, borrowing to lend. When Bassanio approaches Shylock for such a loan to Antonio, Shylock himself confesses a cash-flow problem, declaring that he will have to borrow from "Tubal, a wealthy Hebrew of my tribe . . . {to} furnish me" (I.iii.57–58). Antonio's shortage was real; Shylock's was probably fictional, intended to suggest the usual money-lender's ploy of pleading his own need to borrow in order to push the rate of interest to the highest possible level, often beyond the legal limits.

Bassanio's need for money, and Antonio's help to him, results from Bassanio's wasteful lifestyle. He represents the common plight of young gentlemen who live beyond their means. Foss speaks about the "new age of deceit and greed" resulting from capitalism. He tells of Sir Horatio Palavincino's requirement that Lord Shrewsbury convey to him valuable land and forfeit it if the interest were not paid in three months, and to pay all legal and other fees as well. Thomas Lodge indicts the merchants for enticing young gentlemen to spend on expensive imported merchandise in order to lure them into borrowing at high interest rates, so as to lay claim to their lands. The merchants thus made money both ways, on the goods they imported and on the money lent. As soon as Bassanio gets his hands on the fresh 3,000 ducats borrowed from Shylock on Antonio's credit, he plans an expensive feast, and he immediately sets about outfitting himself and his retinue in all new clothes.

Clothes were virtually an obsession for just about everyone among the middle and upper classes in Elizabethan and early Jacobean years. As merchants became rich, they could literally outbuy the nobility; proclamation after proclamation issued from Queen Elizabeth, or from her government in her name and signed by her, placed limits upon the kind and cost of clothing permitted to the different levels of the social hierarchy. In the fourth year of her reign, a proclamation that referred to an earlier one, "Anno.i.&.ii. Philip & Marie," attempted to effect

the due execution of the Statutes of Apparel, and for the reformation of the outrageous excess thereof . . . that no Tailor, Hosier, or other person whatsoever he shall be, . . . shall put any more cloth in any one pair of hose for the outside, than one yard and a half, or at the most, one yard and three quarters of a yard of kersey, or of any other cloth, leather, or any other kind of stuff above that quantity . . . or with more linings than one, and that plain and just to the legs, as is above said, neither with any Shirts having double ruffs, either at the collar or sleeves, which ruffs shall not be worn otherwise, than single, and the singleness to be used in a due and mean sort, as was orderly, and comely used before the coming in of the outrageous double ruffs, which now of late are crept in. (*Proclamations*, fol.53.54.55)

The English developed a reputation for going after outlandish styles from abroad, a fact to which Shakespeare specifically alludes in *The Merchant of Venice*. Speaking of Falconbridge, the young baron of England, Portia declares, "How oddly he is suited! I think he bought his doublet in Italy, his round hose in France, his bonnet in Germany, and his behavior every where" (I.ii.73–76). Queen Elizabeth's proclamations—also in the fourth year of her reign, and apparently as a part of the same effort to limit who could wear what—presented a chart specifying who could wear silk the color of purple ("only the King, Queen, King's Mother, Children, Brethren & sisters"); who could wear cloth of gold and silver and "tinsel satin"; who could wear velvet, furs, and many other specific details of apparel. The proclamations about "excess of Apparell" followed with great regularity: in the eighth, sixteenth, nineteenth, twenty-second, thirtieth, and thirty-ninth years of her Majesty's reign.

Phillip Stubs goes into great detail to describe the excesses of dress indulged in, despite the illegality of those indulgences. He uses the name "Ailgna" for the country about which he writes, but he clearly refers to England:

But now there is such a confused mingle mangle of apparel in Ailgna, and such preposterous excess thereof, as every one is permitted to flaunt it out, in what apparel he lusteth himself, or can get by any means. So that it is very hard to know, who is noble, who is worshipful, who is a gentleman who is not: for you shall have those, which are neither of nobility, gentility, nor yeomanry, no, nor yet any Magistrate or officer in the commonwealth, go daily in Silks, Velvets, Satins, Damasks, Taffetas, and such like: notwithstanding, that they be both base by birth, mean by estate, and servile by calling. (8, verso and 9, recto)

He criticizes hats, "great & monstrous Ruffs," shirts, doublets, hose, nether-stocks, "Corked shoes," coats, and jerkins, Cloaks, Boothose, and further items of dress—"Rapiers, Swords, and Daggers gilt . . . Scabbards and Sheaths of Velvet, or the like" (5, recto through 28, recto, but imprinted 31). He everywhere blasts away at the extreme cost of all these things. Concerning nether-stocks, for example, he cries,

And to such impudent insolency, and shameful outrage it is now grown, that every one (almost) though otherwise very poor, having scarce forty shillings of wages by the year, will not stick to have two or three pair of these Silk nether-stocks, or else of the finest Yarn that may be got, though the price of them be a ryall [a gold coin first issued by Edward IV at a value of ten shillings] or twenty shillings, or more, as commonly it is, for how can they be less: when as the very knitting of them is worth a noble [a gold coin first minted under Edward III, having a value of nearly seven shillings], or a ryall, and some much more: The time hath been, when one might have clothed all his body well, for less than a pair of these nether-stocks will cost. (24, verso)

Moreover, Lodge accuses the merchants of greedily enticing young noblemen into exactly such extravagance, such obsession with clothes, such a wasteful lifestyle: "A greedy desire of gain, is the disease that infecteth you, some terms it thriftiness . . . but in plain terms, it is usury: and that is nought else but a greedy desire of other men's goods" (19, recto). The wasteful lifestyle of Bassanio leads to the hell at the heart of this play, the threat to the life of Antonio, but the hell of Shylock's house about which Jessica originally complains is nothing compared to that to which Shylock is subjected when his own daughter becomes a wasteful "gentle [Gentile] and no Jew." Conflict about property is central to this play. Shakespeare presents the hoarders, the "Jewish" lifestyle, and the wasters, the "Christian" lifestyle, and he seems to say, as Dante does when he places hoarders and wasters on the same circle of hell in *The Divine Comedy*, that the extremes meet because both lifestyles abuse the stewardship of property. The flaws of both Jews and Christians are obvious in this play, but there are more than a few hints that Shakespeare suggests that beneath the skin, all share a common humanity, a flawed but commendable humanity.

Shylock's flaws need no highlighting, but his commendable features do. He is willing to lend the money on Antonio's own terms, interest free. Minority persons find acceptance by dominant cultures difficult to achieve. Shylock declares, and there is no reason to doubt him, "I would be friends with you, and have your love, / Forget the shames that you have stain'd me with, / Supply your present wants, and take no doit / Of usance for my moneys, and you'll not hear me" (I.iii.138–142). Some doubters think that he is angling for the devilish bond, but there is no logical reason for thinking that Shylock could possibly hope that Antonio would fail to pay his debt and thus give Shylock the opportunity to collect his "flesh." Shylock makes that clear to Bassanio: "my meaning in saying he [Antonio] is a good man is to have you understand me that he is sufficient [adequate for the ends proposed or, in this case, able to pay his debts]" (I.iii.15–17). Even when he has mentally reviewed Antonio's many commitments, and he already knows them, Shylock nevertheless concludes, "The man is notwithstanding sufficient" (25–26). Moreover,

Shylock's life, if one will accept the way Shakespeare convinces his audience that his characters have a life beyond the limits of the play, has been one of making bonds and collecting on them. It is beyond belief that, if he had any serious hope of collecting his "merry bond," he would be so careless of those very details used by Portia easily to demolish his bond and place his own life in serious jeopardy. Although there is no denying that he did not take kindly to Antonio's mistreatment of him and clearly admits his hatred of Antonio before his loss of Jessica, his vicious demand for revenge emerges only after his beloved daughter, and with her great portions of his wealth, has been stolen away by a Christian. Flawed as he unquestionably is, Shylock's futile gesture to "be friends" with Antonio merits careful attention. Moreover, Antonio's flaws, not only toward Shylock but also his self-pity and desire to be remembered for his beneficence are at least as obvious as his genuine kindness is. Beneath the skin, all share a flawed but commendable common humanity, and, therefore, since merchant and usurer are two sides of the same coin and since hoarders and wasters are extremes that meet, it is entirely appropriate for Gentile Lorenzo and Jewess Jessica to be united in a marriage that is so sweet as virtually to make it possible to hear the music of the spheres.

PROPERTY AS AN EXTENSION OF PERSON

The family fight initiated by King Lear and perpetuated by his two older daughters is about property as an extension of person. That fact may be seen in Lear's plan, in his emptiness resulting in his concern for externalities, evident in his need for retinue, together with Goneril and Regan's determination to trim that retinue, and in various allusions to clothes. An increased understanding of similar concerns in Shakespeare's England will contribute to a firmer grasp of Shakespeare's profundity in this play.

Many modern interpreters ridicule Lear's plan to divest himself of his property before his death. The plan itself is not especially unusual, however, when seen from the perspective of actual practices in early seventeenth-century England. For many years, reaching back into the Middle Ages, peasant fathers retired from working the land, handing it over to son or son-in-law provided that agreements could be reached about pension rights for both parents during their lifetimes. However, at higher levels of society, settlements upon adult children before the death of the father were also rather frequent. Ralph Houlbrooke makes several relevant comments. He describes what the seventeenth-century clergyman Ralph Josselin did: "Nearly half the resources flowing from Josselin to his surviving children in the shape of land, goods and payments for education, apprenticeship and marriage portions had already been transferred before he made his will" (228). According to Houlbrooke, the pattern of transferring property to adult children was "probably common among men of his economic standing" (228). Naturally, the younger the children were when the father died, the smaller the proportion of the estate passed on to the children before his death. "Conversely," Houlbrooke comments, "a man who reached advanced old age and saw all his children attain adulthood might have divested himself of nearly all his property beforehand" (229). William Cecil, the first Lord Burghley, held many important offices in the government of Queen Elizabeth—Master of the Court of Wards, Secretary of State, and Lord Treasurer. He was one of the most powerful men in England and regularly spoke with the Queen. Lawrence Stone has made a special study of Burghley's second son, Robert. Stone describes how Burghley arranged for the final division of his property after his death, having already made a suitable marriage for Robert. Thomas, the somewhat dull and unpromising elder son, was to receive Burghley House, the Strand town house in London, and all estates outside the home counties. He gave Robert the "gigantic palace at Theobalds . . . with the accompanying eight sub-manors, the five other manors in the same county," and many other properties. He even added more lands to Robert's portion as Robert became more useful to him in his governmental responsibilities and political maneuverings. It is clear that Shakespeare and his audience would not necessarily consider Lear's plan to divide his property before his death particularly strange or absurd, especially since there were specific arrangements about provisions for himself until his death.

Moreover, that would be particularly true in Lear's case since there is no son to whom he can pass his kingdom intact. The principle of primogeniture resulted in the development of entails, essentially making the eldest son the temporary tenant of the inherited family estate, which he, in turn, passed on to his eldest son with at least the inherited property intact. Any property settlement on younger sons should be, as it was with Burghley, property acquired beyond the original inheritance. But when there was no son to inherit, it was quite common to make an equal division among the daughters, the eldest not necessarily receiving the larger share because of her seniority. Lisa Jardine points out, "A number of factors contributed to this change of strategy away from strict male succession to one involving daughters as direct heirs; the most obvious was the dearth of male heirs amongst the nobility" (85). Inheritance practices were not the same in all parts of England; some counties, Kent, for example, more readily permitted partible inheritance, called "gavelkind." Yet when there was no son to inherit, customs nearly everywhere permitted equal partitioning of the land among the daughters. Houlbrooke observes, "Strict settlements of the seventeenth century commonly made payments of daughters' portions conditional on their compliance with parental wishes" (232), and if that were true of marriage portions, it would certainly be true of partible inheritances. The underlying principle of Lear's plan, the more or less equal division of his property among his three daughters, was not strange or unusual, and, from the cultural conventions of Shakespeare's day, even the principle of rewarding those who were obedient and compliant to parental directions was not considered wrong.

However, Lear's plan, as he conceives and executes it, is terribly absurd and wrong-headed. The basic wrong is the identification of his property with himself in a harmful manner—that is, in effect, "the more you love me, the more of my land will I give you." Probably, in nearly all human societies and cultures in all ages, one's property and one's personhood are intimately if not inseparably interrelated. Certainly, that was true in Shakespeare's lifetime in England. English culture had become intensely competitive and acquisitive. Stone's examination of the finances of Robert Cecil, Earl of Salisbury, makes that fact inescapably clear. Lord Burghley had left Robert a valuable inheritance, but from 1598 until his death in 1612, Robert engaged in almost a maniacal program of land acquisition, turning "the modest inheritance from his father into one of the greatest estates in the kingdom" (*Fortune* 32). One of the valuable properties Burghley settled on Robert was the palace of Theobalds. Lord Burghley himself had improved and extended Theobalds until it was the third largest building in England, after Westminster Palace and Hampton Court. In fact, it became so attractive that King James began to covet it, and finally Salisbury had to offer it to the King, much the way Cardinal Wolsey came to a similar realization that he had to give Hampton Court to King Henry VIII. King James gave Robert other properties in return, including Hatfield, an older and much smaller Tudor palace. Salisbury lost no time in tearing down the existing palace at Hatfield and building himself another in the newest style. The cost was astronomical, and even though Salisbury had one of the largest incomes of any in the country at that time, Stone reports that the rebuilding of Hatfield meant a "terrifying load of debt" at not less than ten percent interest. The more than 40,000 English pounds required for that project compares to the ten to fifteen pounds per year earned by unskilled manual laborers at that time. To the question of why Salisbury dared to run up such an enormous debt, Stone replies, "The answer, in brief, is that he found himself in a world of fiercely competitive conspicuous consumption that reached its apogee during his time. As a leading figure in one of the most recklessly extravagant courts in Europe, he had little option but to compete in the race" (28). Shakespeare presents property as an extension of person in *King Lear*, in part, no doubt, because his entire culture, especially the most prominent members, viewed property as a manifestation of personhood.

The identity of property with person is not necessarily harmful, but it probably was in the intensely competitive and greedily acquisitive age of Shakespeare, and would be in any age when greed simply to acquire for its own sake becomes a conscious effort to outdo real or imaginary rivals. In *Lear*, the problem is massive, especially the way Lear contrives it. The plan to divide his property before his death could have been a sensible matter, but the manner in which he does it, requiring his daughters to compete in a silly game of extravagant expressions of love for him and relating that to the size of the portion given, becomes devastatingly destructive to himself and his family. Goneril gushes out such extreme statements as to be obviously false to any rational person. Then, incredible as it seems, Regan, in essence, says, "Everything Goneril asserts, I do too, 'Only she comes too short'" (I.i.72). The fact is, Lear does not seem to hear anything either of them says. He has already decided the boundaries of the three portions, and when each of the two older daughters completes her statement, his only remarks have to do with the portion assigned to each. He has been eagerly awaiting just one statement, that of his youngest daughter Cordelia, on whom he dotes and with whom he expects to spend his final years. He set up the competition of love declarations to extract from Cordelia her assertion of love. He expects to give her the largest portion: "I lov'd her most, and thought to set my rest / On her kind nursery" (I.i.122–123). When her turn comes, he seems almost to rub his hands in anticipation, "Now, our joy / . . . what can you say to draw / A third more opulent than your sisters? Speak" (82, 85–86). The identification of love for him, or the assertion of love for him, with the size of the portion given is carrying the view of property as an extension of person to absurd and destructive lengths.

Cordelia's response conveys a key concept in the play, "Nothing, my lord" (I.i.87). She has listened with increasing dismay as her two sisters lie effusively and unconscionably. She determines to be honest, expressing her love for her father as his parenthood and parental care deserve, but frankly declaring her intention to give half her love and care to her husband when she weds. Therefore, she answers Lear's question as a question, not answering his egocentric intent. His question asks, and Shakespeare does not phrase these key passages carelessly, "what can you say to draw / A third more opulent than your sisters?" (I.i.85–86) Cordelia responds to that wording with "Nothing, my lord." Lear, utterly surprised and taken aback, can only stammer a weak echo of her key word. "Nothing?" He takes that word to refer to her love itself, not, as Cordelia intended, to describe response that would gain a larger portion than her sisters. Cordelia remains firm, "Nothing." Ever an irascible, choleric person with a hair-trigger release for his anger, he replies with an ominous threat, his anger already evident: "Nothing will come of nothing, speak again" (90). In this extended exchange where the word "nothing" occurs five times in four lines, one encounters a deliberate Shakespearean focus. Lear has reached old age as a "nothing," a zero—all exterior, hollow at the core—indeed with a wholly empty interior. He has been and here remains so utterly selfish and self-centered that he pays almost no attention to what Goneril and Regan say because he is intent upon his own objective, to extract from Cordelia a flattering statement of love, to provide him an excuse to do what he had planned to do without reference to any of them. The entire game focuses disgustingly upon his enormously inflated ego, blown up like a balloon, empty air held together by a fragile membrane.

"Nothing" recurs in this play, but Shakespeare's use of the word to describe the obsession of Lear with externalities and his ignorance of himself, not realizing how hollow he is inside, becomes explicit. The Fool has been seeking to awaken self-knowledge in Lear. He chants a rhyming ditty; Kent, disguised now as Caius, declares, "This is nothing, Fool." The Fool replies, "you gave me nothing for it," but he turns immediately to Lear, "Can *you* make no use of nothing, nuncle?" (I.iv.128, 130-131, emphasis added). Lear replies in words that hauntingly echo his threat to Cordelia, "Why, no, boy, nothing can be made out of nothing" (132). This exchange flows inescapably to the key revelation of Lear; the Fool asserts, "now thou art an O without a figure. I am better than thou art now, I am a Fool, thou art nothing" (191–193). As usual in Shakespeare, those pregnant words have an initial meaning quite natural to the immediate dramatic situation. The Fool is saying what Lear's audience has recognized from the beginning; "You are no longer king, despite the title, for you gave away your power when you gave away your property and put yourself totally at the mercy of your two older daughters." His vivid figure for Lear's vulnerability is this: "Thou mad'st thy daughters thy mothers, for . . . thou gav'st them the rod, and put'st down thine own breeches" (173–174). The Fool unquestionably loves Lear; he feels the pain of Lear's condition, the hopelessness of which he sees clearly, and consistently seeks to help Lear see and understand. However, beyond that immediate meaning, the Fool describes in those words Lear's inner condition throughout the first half of the play: empty inside, and therefore preoccupied with externalities. That is why Lear has an exaggerated view of property as an extension of himself, (property is out there for all to see) a view that most harmfully identifies personhood with those externalities.

Lear's inability to cope with Goneril and Regan's determined conspiracy to reduce his retinue results from his identification of his personhood with property. The play has much to say about clothes, as will become evident shortly, and the king's train or retinue makes up a significant form of that outward display, a part of his royal "clothing," in a sense. When he begins to see which way the wind is blowing as Goneril sets the conspiracy in motion, he asks a question that echoes pathetically, "Who is it that can tell me who I am?" (I.iv.230). More and more, it becomes clear that loss of externalities, specifically here the loss of retinue, destroys Lear's sense of personhood. It is that which drives him mad. The cruelty of Goneril and Regan in determinedly reducing Lear's sense of person contributes to Lear's plunge into madness, but much of his problem results from his own ignorance of his inner self because of his proud fixation on externalities, on the trappings of royalty.

At the beginning of the play, Goneril comments on Lear's poor judgment in his treatment of Cordelia. Regan observes, "'Tis the infirmity of his age, yet he hath ever but slenderly known himself" (I.i.291, 293–294). They determine from that point to do something to control Lear. Goneril, his first hostess, complains that his hundred knights are so "disorder'd, so debosh'd [debauched]" that her court has been turned into a "riotous inn . . . more like a tavern or a brothel / Than a grac'd palace" (I.iv.242, 245–246). She declares her remedy—"A little to disquantity [lower the number of] your train" and to retain only those most compatible with his advanced years. Predictably, Lear explodes: "Darkness and devils! . . . Degenerate bastard, I'll not trouble thee; / Yet have I left a daughter" (252, 254–255). He has no inkling of their conspiracy. Goneril writes to Regan about her action; the hour of the expected showdown with their father has come. Regan plays her part; she supports Goneril's decision to reduce his retinue to only fifty followers: "How in one house / Should many people under two commands / Hold amity?" (II.iv.241–242), and she tells Lear, "If you will come to me . . . bring but five and twenty" (246, 248). Astounded and outraged, yet already sensing his helplessness, Lear turns to Goneril, who has also arrived for the showdown, "I'll go with thee, / Thy fifty yet doth double five and twenty, / And thou art twice her love" (259–260). He pathetically still identifies personhood with property, his train, and still measures love for himself in terms of the property granted him, now the mere count of knights allowed him in his retinue. Goneril will no longer permit fifty: "What need you five and twenty? ten? five?" and Regan chimes in, "What need one?" (261, 263). Lear's reference to clothing at this point is not illogical in his mind, taken up as it is with externalities, with appearances, for clothing, although more immediate to one's person than a retinue, is after all a part of the same concept. But first, one should look again at the increasingly contested inheritance customs in the culture at large.

Although settlements were often made prior to the father's death, clear contractual details usually kept Lear's kind of problem from arising. Lear reminds his daughters that he "kept a reservation to be followed / With such a number" of knights (II.iv.252–253). His problem is unique, because he has nowhere to turn for the enforcement of the blatantly violated contract. His only recourse is to appeal to their duty as children, to their filial obedience and gratitude. "I gave you all" he exclaims in various wordings to them both. Regan coldly replies, "And in good time you gave it" (250). Adult children increasingly came to expect not only an inheritance but a settlement while still young enough to enjoy it, without waiting for the father's death. Moralizers and preachers incessantly propounded the parents' duty to be frugal, to develop an estate, to provide for their children, frequently citing 1 Timothy 5:8, and thereby branding those who did not provide an inheritance for their children as worse than infidels.

Gouge, a typical spokesman for conventional ideas, teaches, "The two particular things to be observed by parents for manifestation of their provident care over their children for the time to come, even after their departure, especially in regard of their temporal estate, are these, 1. That they will make a will. 2. That they leave their estates to their children" (570). A father should take those steps that "he may the more quietly settle himself for heavenly contemplations, and preparations for death" (571), and parents so improvident as to live up their material resources and not have any to leave their children are worse than the heathen. The Gloucester/Edgar/Edmund subplot in *King Lear* perhaps more substantively reinforces the main plot than a subplot does in any other Shakespearean play. So widespread had become the expectation of adult children to receive a settlement before the death of the father that Edmund's lying letter supposedly from Edgar to Edmund immediately convinces Gloucester: "This policy and reverence of age makes the world bitter to the best of our times; keeps our fortunes from us till our oldness cannot relish them. I begin to find an idle and fond bondage in the oppression of aged tyranny, who sways, not as it hath power, but as it is suffer'd" (I.ii.46–51). The impatience of young people to get their hands on their inheritance found many expressions. Goulart tells of a son who, in order to gain control of his father's property, accused his father of having "carnal knowledge with a beast" (344). The father was tortured on the rack and finally burned alive, but he died peacefully in the assurance of his innocence. Within a month, Goulart writes, "this execrable parricide, falling into despair, hanged himself" (345). Goneril and Regan speak for many adult children in Shakespeare's period when they remind Lear of his age, his "dotage," his weakness ("I pray you, father, being weak, seem so" [II.iv.201]), and the division of his property "in good time." Adult children who had come to expect an inheritance as a right—and their settlements before their fathers' deaths as the norm—had a reduced sense of obligation, despite all the preaching about filial duties toward parents.

Nevertheless, the culture at large still found ingratitude in children utterly repugnant and repulsive. "Ingratitude is monstrous," Shakespeare has a citizen say in *Coriolanus,* and his entire culture echoed that utterance from cottage to castle. Animal imagery permeates *King Lear,* and Albany, in an animal image, most severely rebukes Goneril for the ingratitude she and Regan demonstrate toward Lear: "Tigers, not daughters . . . Most barbarous, most degenerate, have you madded" "A father, and a gracious aged man" (IV.ii.40, 44, 41). Incessantly children were reminded of their duty to "recompense" their parents—so said Robert Allen, John Calvin, the writer of *The A.B.C. with the Catechisme,* and countless others. Typically, Gouge goes into considerable detail:

Nature hath taught thus much, not only unto heathen men, but also unto the unreasonable creatures. Among other unreasonable creatures, the example of the *Stork* is worthy to be noted: for it is recorded of that kind, that when the dams are old, the young ones feed them; and when through age, they are ready to faint in their flying, the young ones carry them on their backs. The Greek name of a *Stork* is taken from that *word,* which signifieth, *to requite a parent's kindness:* or else this word is taken from that name: they are both of the same notation. (474)

The ingratitude of Lear's older daughters rightly arouses indignation, in Shakespeare's audience as well as in Lear himself.

"What need one?" asks Regan, as she and Goneril determinedly make Lear recognize his loss of authority as they diminish his retinue. "O reason not the need!" Lear blurts out in response, "our basest beggars / Are in the poorest thing superfluous. / Allow not nature more than nature needs, / Man's life is cheap as beast's" (II.iv.264–267). Here he identifies possessions not merely with his individual personhood but with being human as distinct from being a beast. Turning for an example from retinue to actual clothing, Lear reasons, "If only to go warm were gorgeous [magnificent or splendid], / Why, nature needs not what thou gorgeous wear'st, / Which scarcely keeps thee warm" (268-270). From this point, clothes, more than retinue, become the metaphor for property as the extension of person. Clothes, as the property most immediately on display with the person wherever one goes, absorbed enormous sums of money from just about everyone who was not a frugal Puritan or hopelessly poverty-stricken.

Phillip Stubs goes to great lengths to describe "Pride of apparell" as the sin that "offendeth God more than the other two [Pride of heart and Pride of mouth]" because, he explains, it "induceth the whole man to wickedness and sin" (5, recto). Probably no sixteenth-century writer more clearly identifies clothing as that property considered as an extension of person than does Stubs. He justifies "rich attire, as Silks, Velvets, Satins, Damasks, Sarcenet, Taffeta, Chamlet [camlet] and the like" for countries that produce those goods, but the English cannot content themselves with clothing "as our own country doth afford us,"—that is, wool, kersey, frieze, and similar materials native to England. Stubs inveighs against hats, sometimes like the "shaft of a steeple, standing a quarter of a yard above the crown of their heads, some more, some less, as please the phantasies of their inconstant minds" (20, recto). He criticizes "monstrous Ruffs . . . either of Cambric, Holland, Lawn, or else of some other the finest cloth that can be got for money . . . that . . . stand a full quarter of a yard (and more) from their necks, hanging over their shoulder points" (20, verso). He rants against shirts that cost "some ten shillings, some twenty, some forty, some five pound, some twenty Nobles and (which is horrible to hear) some ten pounds a piece, yea, the meanest shirt that commonly is worn of any, doth cost a crown, or a noble at the least: and yet this is scarcely thought fine enough for the simplest person that is" (22, recto). He continues to rave:

Their doublets are no less monstrous than the rest: for now the fashion is, to have them hang down to the middle of their thighs, or at least to their privy members, being so hard quilted, stuffed, bombasted & sewed, as they can neither work, nor yet well play in them, through the excessive heat thereof: & therefore are forced to wear them loose about them for the most part, otherwise they could very hardly either stoop or decline to the ground. . . . for certain I am there was never any kind of apparel ever invented, that could more disproportion the body of man, than these doublets with great bellies hanging down beneath their Pudenda, . . . & stuffed with four, five, or six pound of Bombast [cotton wool] at the least: I say nothing of what their Doublets be made, some of Satin, Taffeta, Silk, Grograin [a coarse fabric of silk or of mohair and wool or of those materials mixed with silk and often stiffened with gum], Chamlet, gold silver, and what not? flashed, jagged, cut, carved, pinked, and laced with all kind of costly lace of divers and sundry colors. (23, recto and verso)

Yet all of this is only a small portion of Stubs' denunciation of the pride of apparel, clothing as the extension of person. Lear, in the midst of the family fight with his older daughters, addresses that point when he shifts the argument about his retinue to the very clothing Regan is wearing at the moment, worn for style, not comfort: "Which scarcely keeps thee warm" (II.iv.270). Exclaiming, "O Fool, I shall go mad!" Lear races out onto the heath, into a raging storm, accompanied only by those most devoted to him.

PROPERTY AS SOCIAL RESPONSIBILITY

There were spokespersons for social justice in Shakespeare's lifetime, but if one were to judge by the extant sermons about that subject, one would have to admit that the social conscience became dramatically more sensitive nearly a hundred years later, toward the end of the seventeenth century and thereafter. Many preachers urged care for the poor, and, both legally and as a matter of custom, some people of Shakespeare's day clearly felt responsibility for the poor and the homeless. However, their social conscience was by no means as sensitively developed as their greed for ostentatious display, property as an extension of person. According to Stone, Robert Cecil, Earl of Salisbury, spent more than 600 pounds per year for clothing and used some 400 pounds for pocket money. His taste "for exotic toys and novelties" resulted in his purchase for Hatfield House at a price of more than a thousand pounds a number of fancy items: an organ, a picture-like table of silver, a tortoise-shaped clock, a "bird of Arabia in a cage," a white parrot, and other rareties (*Fortune* 29). He spent money like water, year after year, yet his concern for the poor was virtually nonexistent. He gave alms in the amount of about sixty pounds per year and about another twenty to the church (30).

Lear's own development of a social conscience began where his development of internal content did, out on the heath in the midst of a storm of cold, pelting rain. Kent has found a hovel, no doubt intended for animals and similar in concept if not in building material to those that dot the English countryside to this day. The storm is pitiless. Lear admits, "My wits begin to turn" (III.ii.67), but then, perhaps for the first time in his entire life, recognizing that the play requires the audience to think of Lear as having a life prior to the beginning of the drama ("he hath ever but slenderly known himself"), Lear thinks of someone else before himself: "Art cold?" he asks the Fool solicitously, and only then does he confess, "I am cold myself." He turns to Kent to ask about the hovel with the straw, "Where is this straw, my fellow? / The art of our necessities is strange / And can make vild things precious" (68–71). This self-centered old man who has just been fighting with his daughters about the number of knights in his retinue and exclaiming about rich clothing has begun to realize that in certain circumstances a little ordinary straw is precious. Led by Kent to the hovel, once more Lear practices uncharacteristic unselfishness. He urges the Fool to enter the hovel first: "In, boy, go first." He stays out in the storm to pray, but his prayer must be silent and internal, for what he actually says is an apostrophe to "houseless poverty":

> Poor naked wretches, wherso'er you are,
> That bide the pelting of this pitiless storm, How shall your houseless heads and unfed sides,
> Your {loop'd} and window'd raggedness, defend you
> From seasons such as these? (III.iv.26, 28–32)

No longer concerned about gorgeous clothing, or about a hundred knights to accompany him on every progress, nor even about the magnificence of the property divided between Goneril and Regan, Lear has suddenly realized in the midst of the storm that the poor regularly suffer in "seasons such as these." "O," he exclaims, "I have ta'en / Too little care of this!" (32–33). And aroused for the first time to social responsibility, he wants others with wealth to become more sensitive to the needs of the poor. He cries: "Take physic [medicine], pomp [those capable of magnificent splendour in lifestyle and like himself obsessed with externalities], / Expose thyself to feel what wretches feel, / That thou mayst shake the superflux to them, / And show the heavens more just" (33–36).

The Fool has entered the hovel, but comes bursting out again. They have coincidentally found the very hovel where Edgar, disguised as a madman beggar, Tom o' Bedlam, has taken shelter. As Edgar scrambles out of the hovel, naked, repeatedly exclaiming, "Tom's a-cold," Lear asks, "Didst *thou* give all to thy daughters? And art thou come to this?" (50, emphasis added). Lear cannot free himself from the thought that ungrateful daughters must have reduced Tom/Edgar to his naked state: "Nothing could have subdu'd nature / To such a lowness but his unkind [unnatural as well as unmerciful] daughters. / Is it the fashion, that discarded fathers / Should have thus little mercy on their flesh?" (70–73). He calls them "pelican daughters" because it was commonly thought that pelicans fed their young with their own flesh and blood.

As the storm continues, Lear again demonstrates concern for someone other than himself: "Thou wert better in a grave," he declares to Tom/Edgar, "than to answer with thy uncover'd body this extremity of the skies" (101–102). Again, Lear's movement from emptiness or "nothing" toward internal content of genuine humanity is evident. He lists some of the wasteful extravagances that the wealthy heap upon their bodies—silks, furs, wool, perfumes—and declares that Tom/Edgar has indulged in none of those. As though he has suddenly realized for the first time what being human is, he exclaims to Tom/Edgar, "Thou art the thing itself: unaccommodated [unadorned or unornamented with externalities] man is no more but such a poor, bare, fork'd animal as thou art" (106–108), and, as if determined to join humanity at last, he cries, "Off, off, you lendings!" (108) and begins tearing off his expensive clothes. If played as Shakespeare's ideas suggest, so far as modesty on stage would permit, these two men, Tom/Edgar and Lear himself, would stand naked in the storm. Lear has begun to realize that being a person is more than the externalities of property.

Again, the Gloucester subplot substantively supports and advances the main plot. Edmund, successful in alienating Edgar from their father, resulting in Edgar's flight and disguise as Tom o' Bedlam, has also betrayed his own father. He indeed succeeds to the title of Earl of Gloucester and gains control over his father's estate during his father's lifetime. In fact, in the bloodiest scene to be depicted on stage in a Shakespearean play, Cornwall and Regan, sure that Gloucester has taken sides with Lear against them, gouge out the eyes of Gloucester, first one and then the other. His bleeding eye sockets bound up with eggwhite and flax, blind Gloucester sets out for Dover. He encounters an old man, one of his tenants, who wants to help him. He also encounters Tom/Edgar, and the old man informs him that Tom is both a madman and a beggar. Gloucester remembers, "I' th' last night's storm I such a fellow saw, / Which made me think a man a worm" (IV.i.32–33). Just as Lear, in the depths of his own need, began to feel the stirrings of social responsibility, so does Gloucester. He urges Tom/Edgar to take a purse for the supplying of his needs, and, like Lear, he cries out to the heavens:

> Let the superfluous and lust-dieted man,
> That slaves your ordinance [subverts the heavenly principle of care for the poor because of their obsession with selfish indulgence], that will not see
> Because he does not feel, feel your pow'r quickly;
> So distribution should undo excess,
> And each man have enough. (IV.i.67–71)

In the midst of their pain, both Lear and Gloucester begin the development of genuine humanity, and that fact is most clearly evident in their new-found concern for the poor and needy, concern for social justice.

Lear goes completely mad, and in his madness imagines a judgment scene where, as king, he once more metes out justice. Though mad, he addresses an identity problem that recurs in Shakespearean plays. Just as Portia asks, "Which is the merchant here? and which the Jew?" and just as Escalus asks, "Which is wiser here: Justice or Iniquity?" so in this mad judgment scene Lear asks, "Which is the justice, which is the thief?" (IV.vi.153–154). Lear, in his madness, and Shakespeare in his sanity observe that the "justice" and the "thief" are not as easily distinguished as unthinking people might believe. Mad Lear wants to sit in judgment on his daughters, but his fantastic courtroom is crowded. He exclaims: "Thou rascal beadle [the official public whipper], hold thy bloody hand! / Why dost thou lash that whore? Strip thine own back, / Thou hotly lusts to use her in that kind [manner] / For which thou whip'st her. The usurer hangs the cozener [the cunning cheater]" (160–163). The utter injustice of the conventional system of justice now presents itself to Lear's mind with complete clarity: "Thorough [through] tatter'd clothes {small} vices do appear, / Robes and furr'd gowns hide all. {Plate sin} with gold, / And the strong lance of justice hurtless breaks; / Arm it in rags, a pigmy's straw does pierce it" (164–167). Lear's development from "nothing" to "something," from emptiness to fullness of humanity, continues through the change taking place in his mind during his madness on the heath. He now has a vision of social justice, of social responsibility, a vision utterly alien to him when he was obsessed with property as the extension of person.

THE END OF THE LEAR FAMILY FIGHT

Information about Goneril and Regan's breach of contract with their father and his consequent homelessness has brought Cordelia, married dowerless to the King of France, to England with an army from France to rectify the wrongs against her father. Both Goneril and Regan put armies into the field. However, the two of them have their own covert quarrel. Regan is now a widow because a servant, so horrified by Cornwall's blinding of Gloucester, fatally wounded Cornwall. Goneril has become disgusted with Albany, accusing him of being a coward. Both Goneril and Regan lust after Edmund, their degenerate natures compatible with his, each planning to make him her consort. Lear's family has become a veritable hell. Unprincipled Goneril and Regan covertly competing with each other, with Edmund heading Regan's army, set out to war against Cordelia, seeking justice for her father. Cordelia succeeds in finding her father, and she provides medical care and fresh clothes. Lear has gained some self-knowledge: "I am a very foolish fond old man" (IV.vii.59). He has gained humility and a degree of gentleness: "Be your tears wet?" he asks Cordelia, "Yes, faith," he continues:

> . . . I pray weep not.
> If you have poison for me, I will drink it.
> I know you do not love me [still misunderstanding her "nothing"], for your sisters
> Have (as I do remember) done me wrong [but the thought no longer sends him into rage, and so he has grown in emotional maturity at last]:
> You have some cause, they have not [stated as a simple fact, without apparent bitterness or a recurrence of his violent anger]. (70–74)

Cordelia, who has ever loved her father, despite his terrible nature until this seemingly miraculous change in him during the last few days of his life, murmurs with completely loving forgiveness, "No cause, no cause" (75). Imperious Lear is so no more. He humbly asks Cordelia's forgiveness: "Pray you now forget, and forgive" (84).

Unfortunately, Cordelia's quest for justice for her father fails. Both she and her father fall captive to Edmund. Cordelia laments only for her father, "oppressed king," and asks, "Shall we not see these daughters and these sisters" (V.iii.5, 7). Lear is no longer the least interested in continuing the family fight. His reconciliation with Cordelia has brought him such joy that he cries:

> No, no, no, no! Come let's away to prison:
> We two alone will sing like birds i' th' cage;
> When thou dost ask me blessing [a ritual obedient children, even adult children, daily sought on their knees from their parents], I'll kneel down
> And ask of thee forgiveness. So we'll live,
> And pray, and sing, and tell old tales, and laugh
> At gilded butterflies, and hear poor rogues
> Talk of court news . . . who's in, who's out—
> . . . and we'll wear out,
> In a wall'd prison, packs and sects of great ones,
> That ebb and flow by th' moon. (V.iii.8–19)

So long as he can be with Cordelia, Lear can be content. No longer is property or power or prestige or any other externality of any importance to him. Lear has become a changed person, a person of content and therefore contentment.

His older daughters, however, continue their fight with each other. Goneril poisons Regan and, after Edmund falls to Edgar's sword, kills herself with a knife. Edmund had given orders for Cordelia to be hanged, and despite his death-bed effort to save her, she has already been executed. Lear himself dies hoping against hope that Cordelia is reviving. The family fight he has initiated and his two older daughters have perpetuated finally ends in the deaths of himself and his entire family. No longer do externalities matter to him or any of them.

ATTITUDES TOWARD PROPERTY: TOO SWEET AND TOO SOUR

Timon of Athens does not present a literal family conflict, since Timon has no family, in the sense of wife and/or children. He does have servants, however, considered a part of family in Shakespeare's day, and he is as disillusioned with his metaphorical family, the city of Athens, as Lear with his children. *Timon of Athens* presents many interpretive problems: the degree of Shakespeare's participation in its composition, its unfinished or very imperfectly finished condition as a work of art, and, for Shakespeare, uncharacteristically harsh and unrelieved misanthropy. Despite these problems, the central focus of the play upon property and the grasp of greed demonstrates the significance of this issue in the culture of early seventeenth-century England and the concern it raised in thinking people. Hardly any main character in Tudor and early Jacobean drama manifests such a complete flip-flop from the extreme of philanthropy to the extreme of misanthropy more painfully than does Timon, and attitudes toward property form the inescapable core of this play, accounting, as in *King Lear*, for rage against ingratitude.

Magnanimity had been an ideal from antiquity, and it certainly remained a cultural value in Renaissance England. Reciprocity was integral to the *comitatus* relationships of the warrior age and throughout the feudal period. Reciprocity, gratitude, loyalty to benefactors, and a sense of obligation to recompense as able—all these continued as articulated values, but the dramatic increase of the money economy, a diminishing of the absolute quality of "heavenly gain" by the competing importance of "earthly gain," the rise of individualism (a nineteenth-century term not yet used in England), overt opportunism, and, finally, the outright grasp of greed resulted in a social condition addressed in the unpleasant play *Timon of Athens*. The criticism of wrong attitudes toward material gain is as severe in this play as one finds in sermons and moral treatises. Timon simply cannot find the golden mean, and his sweet and sour attitudes turn out to be too sweet and too sour.

In the beginning of the play, Timon seems to be the exemplar of magnanimity; soon one sees that he is the caricature, the extreme, and the bad example of that value. W. Vaughan, in a work that had reached a second edition by 1608, *The Golden-Groue . . .* , distinguishes between magnificence and liberality: "for magnificence is a virtue that consisteth in sumptuous and great expences; whereas liberality is conversant in small things: so that the one is peculiar to Noblemen, and the other to common Gentlemen" (I 3, recto). Timon's munificence pours from his hand toward all alike, without the first three essential qualities of liberality—judicious discrimination, acceptance of limitations, and recognition of need. Vaughan makes this clear: "The first law of liberality is, to distribute unto them, who are most worthy: Otherwise, he is like a blind man, when he knoweth not to whom he giveth" (I 4, verso).

Timon's indiscriminate liberality toward simply everyone—poet,- painter, servant, jeweller, merchant, and friends including those not in need as well as one who is—finally becomes the frenetic outpouring of Vaughan's blind man. Vaughan continues, "The second circumstance [literally "that which stands around or surrounds" resulting in the meaning of "condition," here of "liberality"] is, that a man give not more, than his ability will afford, but rather he must cut out his coat in proportion according to this cloth: because *repentance followeth hasty liberality*" (I 5, recto). Timon has utterly ignored this principle until it is too late. His steward Flavius protests Timon's complaint, "You make me marvel wherefore ere this time / Had you not fully laid my state before me, / That I might so have rated [computed or calculated] my expense / As I had leave of means" (II.ii.124–127). The steward exclaims, "O my good lord, / At many times I brought you my accompts [accounts], / Laid them before you; you would throw them off" (132–134). Moreover, Timon has been so indiscriminately generous that he has violated the third essential principle of genuine liberality articulated by Vaughan: "The third, he must not give to them, which have enough already" (I 5, recto). He has been so extravagant that his various friends have taken advantage of his bounty. Two unneedy lords have been invited to another of Timon's string of feasts. One says, ". . . shall we in / And taste Lord Timon's bounty? he outgoes [exceeds] / The very heart of kindness." The second lord replies:

> He pours it out: Plutus the god of gold
> Is but his steward. No meed [deserved praise, or, perhaps service, here, in this particular context] but he repays
> Sevenfold above itself; no gift to him
> But breeds the giver a return exceeding
> All the use of quittance [here, return in excess of money put out to usury].
> (I.i.274–280)

Timon's magnanimity caricatures true liberality; it is simply too sweet to last.

Timon views his relationship with his friends as that of family. In an absurdly idealistic and unrealistic speech, Timon extols their relationship:

> O you gods, think I, what need we have any friends, if we should ne'er have need of 'em? . . . Why, I have often wish'd myself poorer, that I might come nearer to you. We are born to do benefits; and what better or properer can we call our own than the riches of our friends? O, what a precious comfort 'tis to have so many like brothers commanding one another's fortunes! (I.ii.95–96, 100–105)

The wealthy families of Renaissance England did, indeed, lend to and borrow from one another, and the same sort of borrowing and lending took place among friends. However, most were much more hard-nosed about these exchanges than idealistic Timon is. Nearly all the wealthy families studied by Stone in *Family and Fortune* engaged in borrowing and lending among themselves and their friends, although most of them went to merchant/usurers as well. Robert Ashton details a series of loans made by neighbors to their friends in the early seventeenth century, but he observes, "Some of these loans were in a real sense acts of good neighborliness on the part of the lenders, a fact which did not, of course," he adds somewhat wryly, "preclude them from charging interest at the statutory maximum rate" (37). Timon's naivete concerning fallen human nature's grasp for greed arouses sniggers of scorn both inside and outside the play. His view that humans ought to be "like brothers commanding one another's fortunes" is simply too sweet to be true in this rather selfish world.

Shakespeare, in Sonnet 94, observes: "For sweetest things turn sourest by their deeds; / Lilies that fester smell far worse than weeds" (13–14). When Timon is good, he is very, very good, but when he turns bad, he is horrid. His idealistic view of human relationships, once shattered, can find no middle ground. Too sweet turns too sour. When Timon discovers that he is bankrupt, that his lands have been mortgaged to sustain the enormous debt load piled up by his extravagant and utterly unwise liberality, and that he therefore cannot even sell his land, he almost joyfully exclaims, "I am wealthy in my friends" (II.ii.184). Predictably, they all, as with one accord, find various excuses to turn him down. Their ingratitude drives him into a kind of madness from which, unlike Lear, he learns nothing. He abandons Athens as furiously as Coriolanus abandons Rome. The corruption of Athens arises from the grasp of greed. Alcibiades articulates it as clearly as Timon:

> Banish me?
> Banish your dotage, banish usury,
> That makes the Senate ugly!
> . . . I have kept back their foes,
> While they have told [counted] their money, and let out
> Their coin upon large interest—I myself
> Rich only in hurts. All those, for this?
> Is this the balsom [healing balm] that the usuring Senate
> Pours into captains' wounds? (III.V.98–99, 105–110)

Timon abandons corrupt Athens to become a hermit—only, in digging for roots to eat, to discover gold. He uses his new wealth not to return to Athens but viciously to seek its destruction. His apostrophe to gold, "O thou sweet king-killer," prays "by thy virtue / Set them into confounding odds [destructive conflicts], that beasts / May have the world in empire! (IV.iii.381, 389–391). Timon gives gold to prostitutes to return to Athens and "give them diseases" (IV.iii.85). Their declaration, "Believ't that we'll do anything for gold," essentially sums up this second extreme view of humanity Timon now embraces. He gives gold to banditti, crying, "Cut throats, / All that you meet are thieves. To Athens go, / Break open shops; nothing can you steal / But thieves do lose it" (IV.iii.445–448). He gives gold to Alcibiades to slay utterly in Athens:

> Let not thy sword skip one.
> Pity not honor'd age for his white beard,
> He is an usurer. Strike me the counterfeit matron,
> It is her habit only that is honest,
> Herself's a bawd. Let not the virgin's cheek
> Make soft thy trenchant sword; for those milk paps,
> That through the window{-bars} bore at men's eyes,
> Are not within the leaf of pity writ [not exempt from destruction],
> But set them down horrible traitors. Spare not the babe,
> Whose dimpled smiles from fools exhaust their mercy;
> Think it a bastard. (111–121)

His rage continues; he exhorts Alcibiades: "Put armor on thine ears and on thine eyes, / Whose proof nor yells of mothers, maids, nor babes, / Nor sight of priests in holy vestments bleeding, / Shall pierce a jot. There's gold to pay thy soldiers" (124–127). Timon's sweet idealism, were it more realistic, has great worth, but "sweetest things turn sourest by their deeds; / Lilies that fester smell far worse than weeds."

Timon of Athens is a severe criticism of social conditions in London, specifically, and in England, generally. It carries a message as painful as that of William Whately in *Charitable Teares* . . . :

But England, Ah England! God's Signet, God's Jewel which he hath fostered as tenderly, and adorned as graciously, as ever he did Judea. England, the one and only Nation, almost, that doth openly and solely profess the true Religion of God: I say, England aboundeth in all these sins. . . . Much murder and bloodshed is committed, and for envy and malice, the Land aboundeth with them, whoredom and filthiness stinks in every corner; theft, oppression, usury, simony, sacrilege: where shall a man stir, but he shall meet with them? Lying, deceit, fraud and guile are become amongst the necessary ornaments of a good chapman, and one cannot live without them now-a-days. (244–245, 250)

Timon of Athens suggests that both too sweet and too sour are wrong, but it also laments the destructive power of the grasp of greed, destroying the macrocosmic family of city and nation as surely as it destroys the microcosmic nuclear family as seen in *The Merchant of Venice* and *The Tragedy of King Lear*. "Property," inseparable from "proper," "one's own" or "belonging to one's self," when grasped after greedily, plunges families, domestic and civic, into hell.

6

The Divisive Pursuit of Power:
The History Plays and *Macbeth*

The "will to power" was a well-known human characteristic long before Nietzsche wrote about it or Hitler articulated his version in *Mein Kampf*. Humans, like other higher animals, seem driven to establish a "pecking order" in their social organizations, with aggression an inherent feature in the drive for power. Freud widened his view of human motivation beyond the pleasure principle. In *Civilization and Its Discontents*, he asserts:

The element of truth behind all this, which people are so ready to disavow, is that men are not gentle creatures who want to be loved, and who at the most can defend themselves if they are attacked; they are, on the contrary, creatures among whose instinctual endowments is to be reckoned a powerful share of aggressiveness. As a result, their neighbor is for them not only a potential helper or sexual object, but also someone who tempts them to satisfy their aggressiveness on him, to exploit his capacity for work without compensation, to use him sexually without his consent, to seize his possessions, to humiliate him, to cause him pain, to torture and to kill him. *Homo homini lupus* [man, to man, is a wolf]. (58)

Even inside the family, Shakespeare makes clear in many of his plays, the will to dominate, to subjugate others, to exercise power over them aggressively asserts itself, often dividing family members against themselves and, too often, causing great harm to the fabric not only of the family but of society at large. Shakespeare's earliest plays, the three parts of *Henry VI*, manifest his concern. They were plays written in the early 1590s when many in society at large were already worrying about what sort of bloody upheaval might occur in England upon Elizabeth's death. In the *Henry VI* plays, Shakespeare portrays the internecine Wars of the Roses, the house of Plantagenet divided against itself, and the savage struggle for power, even to the killing of one's own family members. In play after play, Shakespeare deals with the divisive pursuit of power, shattering the family both microcosmic and macrocosmic.

SHAKESPEARE'S TWO TETRALOGIES

Shakespeare heard that note of concern in one of his probable major sources, Edward Hall's *The Vnion of the Two Noble and Illustre Famelies of Lancastre & Yorke*, first published in 1548:

What mischief hath insurged in realms by intestine division, what depopulacion hath ensued in countries by civil dissension, what detestable murder hath been committed in cities by separate factions, and what calamity hath ensued in famous regions by domestical discord & unnatural controversy: . . . especially this noble realm of England can apparently declare and make demonstration. (1)

The "domestical discord & unnatural controversy" of the two branches of the Plantagenet family—the Yorks, choosing the symbol of the white rose, challenging the Lancasters, who took the symbol of the red—forms the core of the first four history plays Shakespeare wrote, called the "minor tetralogy" because the second four plays, the "major tetralogy," dealing with an earlier historical period, are artistically superior. The first four history plays are the three parts of *Henry VI*, concluding with *Richard III*. The time period covered in these four plays begins with the death of Henry V in 1422 and ends with the Battle of Bosworth Field in 1485, the death of Richard III in that battle, and the consequent beginning of the Tudor line, the union of the two houses once more, for the Earl of Richmond who became Henry VII, the first Tudor monarch, declares at the end of *Richard III*, "We will unite the White Rose [Elizabeth of the house of York] and the Red [himself of the Lancaster line], / Smile heaven upon this fair conjunction" (V.v.19–20).

The second or "major" tetralogy begins with *Richard II*, in which Henry Bullingbrook, the son of John of Gaunt, Duke of Lancaster, forces the abdication of Richard II in 1399, and it includes also the two parts of *Henry IV* and concludes with *Henry V*—not with his death but with his preparations for marriage to Katherine, daughter of the mad Charles VI of France. The Chorus, presenting the Epilogue of *Henry V*, announces:

> Henry the Sixt, in infant bands crown'd King
> Of France and England, did this king succeed;

> Whose state so many had the managing,
> That they lost France, and made his England bleed;
> Which oft our stage hath shown. (V.ii.9–13)

There is little doubt about the fact that Shakespeare considered his efforts in these eight plays to form a kind of whole. Most, though not all, focus sharply upon the divisive pursuit of power within the larger royal family and the consequent civil discord in the metaphorical family of society. Most of them, therefore, address the problem "Who should rule?"—and that problem was rapidly becoming the chief national concern in Shakespeare's day as many worried about the successor to Elizabeth, the last Tudor ruler.

THE DIVISIVE PURSUIT OF POWER AMONG TUDOR KIN

Shakespeare, like the Tudor historians whose materials he transmuted into his history plays, dealt favorably with the Tudors whenever and wherever possible. He wrote two other plays presenting English history: *The Life and Death of King John*, who ruled from 1199 to 1216, and *The Famous History of the Life of Henry the Eighth*, a play that concludes with virtually a messianic "prophecy" by Cranmer about Elizabeth:

> In her days every man shall eat in safety
> Under his own vine what he plants, and sing
> The merry songs of peace to all his neighbors.
> God shall be truly known, and those about her
> From her shall read the perfect {ways} of honor,
> And by those claim their greatness, not by blood. (V.iv.33–38)

This play, however, was written approximately ten years after the death of Elizabeth, and the question of succession had been peacefully managed, not with the war that King James had threatened when he was still King James VI of Scotland, but with the skillful help of Robert Cecil, Earl of Salisbury, who probably risked his own life in corresponding with James during the last years of Elizabeth's life. James had peacefully succeeded to the English throne as King James I, uniting Scotland and England now under the same royal family, the Stuart line.

Shakespeare, of course, does not miss an opportunity to speak also very favorably about King James. In the same Cranmer "prophecy" in *Henry VIII*, he asserts:

So shall she leave her blessedness to one
(When heaven shall call her from this cloud of darkness)
Who from the sacred ashes of her honor
Shall star-like rise as great in fame as she was [a forgivable exaggeration,
     considering the political value in praising King James],
And so stand fix'd. Peace, plenty, love, truth, terror,
That were the servants to this chosen infant,
Shall then be his, and like a vine grow to him.
Where ever the bright sun of heaven shall shine,
His honor and the greatness of his name
Shall be, and make new nations. He shall flourish,
And like a mountain cedar reach his branches
To all the plants about him. Our children's children
Shall see this, and bless heaven. (43–55)

When he wrote *Henry VIII*, Shakespeare could safely write such a prophecy, but in the 1590s no one could foretell what was going to happen
when Elizabeth died, and, toward the end of her life, she strictly forbade
anyone's discussing the question of succession.

   There was plenty of evidence in common knowledge and in Shakespeare's source materials to testify to the Tudor family's own prior internal struggles, one family member against another, enough evidence
that in the 1590s Shakespeare might well worry about a bloody contest
among the various contenders for Elizabeth's throne upon her death, to
the great detriment of the nation as a whole. Henry VIII's increasingly
urgent quest for a male heir prompted not only his initial agonizing
discarding of Katherine but his disposal of other wives as well. Henry
admired Katherine and was genuinely grieved that she could not bear
him a son that lived. Shakespeare's favorable portrayal of her in Henry
VIII is no accident. However, Henry's efforts to ensure the succession of
the Tudor dynasty actually complicated things as much as they helped.
He finally had a son by Jane Seymour, Edward VI, who ruled from Henry's death in 1547 until his own in 1553. If Edward had been a healthy
heir who could have produced another male heir, the continuation of
the Tudor dynasty probably would not have been a problem.

   The transition from Henry to Edward was simple enough and tran-
quil enough, but on Edward's death in 1553, the first Tudor family fight
for power began. Richard Grafton, another of Shakespeare's probable
sources, describes the scramble in the last days of Edward's life

to declare the said Lady Jane eldest niece to king Henry the eight, and wife to
the said Lord Gilford to be rightful heir in succession to the crown of England
without respect had to the statute made in the .xxxxv. year of King Henry the
eight: The true meaning of which statute, they did impugn & overthrow by divers subtle and sinister constructions of the same, to disinherit the said king's

sisters to whom the succession of the crown of England did right appertained. (2: 532)

Grafton records, "Immediately after the death of king Edward, the aforesaid Lady Jane was proclaimed Queen of this realm by the sound of the trumpet, that is to say, the .ix. day of July, at which Proclamation were present the Lords of the Council, the Mayor of London with other" (533). However, Mary, knowing that her claim to the crown, apart from Edward's bastardizing statute, was superior to Jane's, left Honesdon in Hartfordshire and went to "her Castell of Fremingham." An army, "a power of men," was called together, at first under Jane's father, the Duke of Suffolk, but he was, upon further consideration, replaced by John Dudley, Earl of Warwick and Duke of Northumberland, Jane's father-in-law. Grafton further describes the developments:

The Lords of the council being in this mean while at London, after they understood how the better part of the realm were inclined, and hearing every day news of great assemblies, began to suspect the sequel of this enterprise: that providing for their own surety without respect of the Duke [that is, Northumberland] (who was at Bury) they fell to a new council, & lastly, by assent made proclamation at London in the name of Lady Mary [daughter of Henry VIII and Katherine], by the name of Mary Queen of England, France, and Ireland defender of the faith, and of the Churches of England and Ireland supreme head. (533)

That left Northumberland and his army high and dry. Grafton rather wryly remarks that the:

proclamation made a sudden change of minds in his army, for they that late before seemed most forward in that quarrel [between those cousins, Jane against Mary], began first to fly from him, and so every man shifting for himself, he that late before was furnished of such multitude of Soldiers, was suddenly forsaken of all saving of a few, whose perils were joined with his. (534)

As for Northumberland, he was soon arrested with three of his sons and other men in the army intended to support the right of Lady Jane Grey to the throne. Despite the fact that some of the men who sat as judges in his trial had also been involved in commissioning him, Northumberland was condemned to death and executed on the 22nd of August, approximately one month after Mary was proclaimed Queen.

Not long into the reign of Mary, there was a serious rebellion, one that had great possibilities for success. Although Elizabeth, Mary's half-sister, did not play a formative role in this uprising, there is little doubt about her benefit had the rebellion succeeded. Mary was proclaimed Queen in July 1553. In November of that year, the House of Commons asked her to marry someone within her realm. Her response made clear her decision to take Philip of Spain as husband. Mary was a staunch Roman Catholic. King Edward VI had been made into a straightlaced Protestant, and in the final days of his life, Northumberland had persuaded him to devise an order of succession declaring both Mary and Elizabeth illegitimate and willing the throne to Lady Jane Grey, a devout Protestant also. That plan having failed, the Protestants were terribly upset by Mary's choice of Philip and the imminent return of England to the Roman Catholic fold. Some of the gentry wanted Elizabeth, a Protestant albeit one more flexible than Lady Jane Grey, to marry Edward Courtenay, not much of a man, but one of royal blood, a great-grandson of Edward IV. They wanted then to place Elizabeth on the throne instead of Mary. Originally scheduled for 18 March 1554, the planned uprising became known to Mary's government in January and confirmed by "the foolish and unreliable Courtenay" on 21 January (Fletcher 79). The date for the uprising had to be moved earlier than planned. Sir James Croft, surprised by the new timing, did not even attempt to arouse support in Herefordshire. The Duke of Suffolk found only apathy in Leicester and hostility in Coventry. He "never gathered round him more than 140 men, most of whom were his own retainers" (79), and abandoning his efforts, he went into hiding only to be arrested and taken to the Tower of London. Sir Peter Carew, having too little influence to arouse support in Devon, also bailed out and fled to Normandy.

However, the greater abilities of Sir Thomas Wyatt made the Kentish segment of the conspiracy alone sufficiently strong as almost to topple Mary and to seize the throne. While Wyatt and his forces were in Rochester, Queen Mary sent a band of "White Coates" from London under the leadership of the Duke of Norfolk, but just outside Rochester,

Wyatt with all his company being in the town, the said Captains with the white Coats suddenly revolted from the said Duke, and went straight to the side of Wyatt, whereby the said Duke being thus forsaken by his unfaithful fellowship, was forced to return again to London, and so to the Court without any effect of his journey: Which repulse unto him being then an aged man, and fortunate before in all Wars, impressed such dolor of mind, that he lived but short while after. (Grafton, 2: 538–539)

Wyatt, despite that proof of support in London had he hurried, being too cautious, advanced too slowly, and by the time he reached London, he found the mood of the indecisive city now against him. He failed, and on 11 April was beheaded. Fletcher observes, "Wyatt came nearer than any other Tudor rebel to toppling a monarch from the throne"

(90). Wyatt's rebellion, as the conspiracy has come to be known, was not Elizabeth's own direct pursuit of power, but it was intended to make her Queen, and only her support in Parliament kept Mary from disinheriting her, if not something worse, as a consequence. Although Mary was personally fond of Elizabeth, having years earlier comforted her after the beheading of Anne Boleyn, Elizabeth's mother, the ever-present pressure to seek power made these half-sisters extremely wary of each other if not outright enemies.

Elizabeth succeeded the childless Mary in November 1558, without any challenge of the sort Mary had experienced from Lady Jane. Grafton describes the great joy with which the proclamation was hailed declaring "Lady Elizabeth Queen of this Realm," first in the House of Commons and then in the City of London where the proclamation was greeted "with no less universal joy, and thanksgiving to God" (2: 567). The Protestants of England had had quite enough of Mary's forcible return of the country to Roman Catholicism—hence the extreme joy and the peaceful transition to Elizabeth. However, outside of England, there was an immediate challenge to Elizabeth's succession. Henry VII, Elizabeth's grandfather, had given Margaret, Elizabeth's aunt, the oldest sister of Henry VIII, in marriage to the Scottish king. Toward the end of his reign, Henry VIII had sought to arrange a marriage between his son Edward and his niece, Mary, the young Queen of Scots. Henry's plan fell through, and Mary was instead joined in marriage to the Dauphin of France. Mary, Queen of Scots, was first cousin to Elizabeth. Thus, inside England, Elizabeth could succeed Mary without a hitch, but in France, King Henry II, proclaimed Mary Stuart, Queen of Scots and now his daughter-in-law, to be Queen of Scotland, England, and Ireland. The first year of Elizabeth's reign was fraught with fear of the power of this cousin, for soon, upon the accidental death of Henry II, Mary's Dauphin husband became King Francis II of France, and Mary, Queen of France.

The threat to Elizabeth from this cousin, Mary Queen of Scots, continued for many years. Mary and Francis II asserted her claim to the throne of England by adopting the English coat of arms into their own, and in various other ways pressed her right to the English throne in opposition to Elizabeth's. The story of Mary Queen of Scots is incredibly complex and replete with scandal. Francis II died; Mary returned to Scotland to rule, where, in time, she married Lord Darnley, a second cousin to both herself and Elizabeth. Lord Darnley's mother, Lady Margaret Douglas, Countess of Lennox, the daughter of Margaret Tudor, Elizabeth's aunt, was, therefore, another cousin of Elizabeth. Since her son, Lord Darnley, had been born in England, Lady Margaret maintained that his claim to the English throne was superior to that of Mary Queen of Scots. Certainly, the marriage of the Scottish Queen to Darnley did not weaken her own claim to Elizabeth's throne.

Mary Queen of Scots was somewhat younger than Elizabeth and far less wise in her control of her emotions. Elizabeth herself had become involved emotionally with "her Robin," Robert Dudley, son of the Duke of Northumberland. She had made Dudley Master of her Horse and, though he was a married man, took daily rides with him and, apparently, had an emotional affair of the heart, if not of the bed, with him. She intended to make Dudley a peer of the realm as Earl of Leicester, but suddenly Dudley's wife, Amy Robsard, died—of a broken neck at the bottom of a stone staircase. Was her death simply accidental, or suicidal, or homicidal? Scandalmongers tended to promote the latter, for the former two possibilities seemed much too convenient for Dudley and Elizabeth. But, after all, the latter was still less convenient, for now Elizabeth dared not join herself in marriage to such a person as Dudley under a deep cloud of suspicion. She broke off with Dudley, even though she later made him Earl of Leicester, and, for years to come, he continued to live in hope of marriage with Elizabeth.

Mary Queen of Scots had mocked Elizabeth's affair with her horse-keeper; however, Elizabeth's scandal was pallid and paltry compared to those which ultimately drove Mary from her throne, forcing her to seek refuge in England and the protection of her English cousin whose throne she had repeatedly claimed for herself. Her marriage with Darnley produced a son, James, but it turned out to be not a happy one. Mary herself became involved with her Italian secretary, David Rizzo, so much so that the scandalmongers declared "that Mary's son James [later King James VI of Scotland and James I of England] was rightly called Solomon since he was the son of David who played upon the harp [for Rizzo's first position in Mary's government was court musician]" (Read 346). Darnley supposedly found Rizzo, half undressed, in Mary's bedroom at one in the morning. Not long after, one evening when Rizzo and Mary were at dinner together, Rizzo was seized and murdered, "with Darnley egging the murderers on" (Read 349).

Then Mary became involved in another affair, this time with James Hepburn, Earl of Bothwell, who used gunpowder to blow up Darnley's house with Darnley in it. Mary herself was accused of being an accomplice in Darnley's murder. In about two months after Darnley's death, Bothwell took a band of men and seized and "raped" Mary, a story that might have been more convincing were it not for the fact that Bothwell divorced his wife and, less than a month after the pretended rape, Mary took him as her third husband. All that was too much for the Scots, who defeated the forces of Bothwell and Mary, took Mary captive to Edinburgh, forced her abdication, and replaced her on the throne with her son, King James. Mary was in serious mortal danger for an extended period, but she later escaped from her prison at Lochleven, found protection at Hamilton, and managed to gather a small army, only to be defeated. Her way to France being blocked, she fled to England and sought Elizabeth's protection. Ten years into Elizabeth's reign, Mary Queen of Scots, Elizabeth's close kinswoman who had sought Elizabeth's throne for her own, was Elizabeth's pensioner and, practically speaking, prisoner, and remained so for nearly twenty years.

About a year after Mary sought refuge in England, there was a Catholic uprising in the north. Dudley, (now Earl of Leicester), Throckmorton, and a number of others—as much desiring to oust William Cecil, Lord Burghley, from his role as leading advisor to Elizabeth as anything else—advocated the marriage of the Duke of Norfolk to Mary Queen of Scots. Mary's role in the northern rebellion was not central, but, however weakened and dependent she seemed to be, she ever remained a threat to Elizabeth. "When Mary crossed the border as a deposed queen she came expecting support in the north. . . . Among those who paid court to the exiled queen was Thomas Percy, the seventh Earl of Northumberland" (Fletcher 91). Catholics remained much more numerous in the north than in the south, with Northumberland a natural leader of them. Mary was always active in her own behalf, hoping to return to Scotland as Queen, and never completely relinquishing her claim to Elizabeth's throne, at least as successor upon Elizabeth's death. "Certainly Mary had been tireless in her letters of encouragement to all whose help she hoped for both in England and abroad" (Fletcher 92). Northumberland did not like the Norfolk-Mary marriage idea, but when Norfolk suddenly left London without permission, Elizabeth assumed it was to lead an uprising against her in the name of Mary, and she hurried to make certain Mary's secure captivity. And both the Earl of Westmoreland, Norfolk's brother-in-law, and the Earl of Northumberland assumed, as Cecil and Elizabeth did, that Norfolk's uprising was at hand. Norfolk lost his courage, sent Westmoreland a message not to rebel, and returned to London to seek Elizabeth's mercy. But the northern Catholics were already aroused, and they continued a rebellion that paralyzed the north for about two months toward the end of 1569. Fletcher remarks that the rebellion had only very limited geographic support but primarily lacked coherence and direction. Even the Earls of Westmoreland and Northumberland never mobilized their own full resources. However great the intentions of the two Earls might have been to reach and release Mary and rally around her cause, those plans had to be abandoned. Robert Crompton describes the end of the rebellion:

Did not the Earls of Northumberland and Westmoreland, with fifty Knights, Esquires and Gentlemen, besides a great number of the common sort, rebel in the North parts of this Realm, in the xi. year of her Majesty's reign, to the end to have had alteration of this Religion and most happy state. But what was the end of those Earls, were not they both attainted of treason, and was not the Earl of Northumberland beheaded at York, and did not the other fly the Realm. (B.iiii., verso and C.i., recto)

Henry Percy, the brother of Thomas and his successor as the eighth Earl of Northumberland, took no part in the 1569–70 rebellion; indeed, he had raised forces with the intent to help suppress that uprising. Nevertheless, some time thereafter, he also was involved in a plot, supposedly with Lord Paget and Throckmorton, for setting Mary free. A work without a named author tells of his indictment in the "fourteenth year of her Majesty's reign" for this further effort on behalf of Mary Queen of Scots (*A true and summarie reporte* . . . 1–2). He was committed to the Tower of London where he shot and killed himself. Thus, another plot that seemed like another power play by Elizabeth's cousin, the Scottish Queen, had come to an unhappy end.

Crompton's major reason for writing his *A shorte declaration of the ende of Traytors* was to tell of the final conspiracy of Mary Queen of Scots. The remainder of his long title reveals more of his purpose: *Wherein are also breefely touched, sundry offenses of the S. Queene, committed against the crowne of this Land, & the manner of the honorable proceding for her conuiction thereof, and also the reasons & causes alledged & allowed in Parliament, why it was thought dangerous to the state, if she should haue liued.* He refers to the plot just recounted:

Did not the Earl of Northumberland [that is Henry Percy, the eighth Earl] conspire with the Lord Paget, and Charles his Brother, with Shelley and Throgmorton [an alternative spelling for Throckmorton], to have suppressed this Religion, to have advanced the Romish Religion, and by foreign invasion into this Land, to have utterly subverted this noble state, and to have advanced to the Crown the S. Queen. In which their treason was also employed, the destruction of our most gracious sovereign Lady. . . .Was not the said Throgmorton, about two year last past executed as Traitor for that cause. Did not the said Earl, knowing himself guilty of those treasons, most miserable destroy himself with his own hand in the Tower of London, the xxvii.year of her Majesty's reign. (C.i, recto and verso)

However, Crompton has not reached his primary goal in those remarks. He continues:

And was not the said late S. Queen, privy to sundry of the said conspiracies, and treasons, was she not a principal, and better [abettor] and comforter of the said offenders therein: It is very evident . . . by how many practises the said Scottish Queen, had compassed the destruction of her highness' most royal person . . . to bring back again this noble Realm into the thraldom of Romish tyranny . . . And for asmuch as the said Queen of Scots, was the very ground and only subject, whereupon such dangerous practises and complots, had been founded against her Majesty's most royal person, and the estate of this Realm for these many years. . . . She boldly and openly professed, that it was lawful for her to move invasion upon her Majesty, . . . that she thought it lawful, for her to destroy her Majesty's sacred person. She did not think it not only lawful, but honorable also and meritorious to take her Majesty's life from her, as being all ready deprived of her Crown, by the excommunication of the holy Father. . . . it was concluded by the whole assembly of both houses, that there could not be other assured means for the preservation of her Majesty's life, continuance of God's Religion, and quiet of this state, than by the full execution of the said sentence. . . . and afterward the said Scottish Queen was executed in the Castle of Frodringham in the Country of Northhampton . . . on Wednesday, the 8, of February.1586. And the next day after, there were Bonfires, ringing of Bells, and singing of Psalms, by children and many others at the said fires, in the City of London, whereby appeareth that the people were joyful that so dangerous an enemy to this Commonwealth was taken away. (C.i., verso through D.i., recto)

And so the conflict between these cousins, Mary Queen of Scots and Queen Elizabeth, a conflict continuing from 1558 to 1586, was finally at an end. Mary's pursuit of power resulted in the ultimate division, her head from her body and herself from life.

INTRAFAMILIAL PURSUIT OF POWER, REGARDLESS OF CONSEQUENCES

Although nobody in Shakespeare's day could have used the term, since it did not enter the language until the nineteenth century, Shakespeare and his compatriots were filled with a great spirit of "nationalism," especially as a consequence of the celebrated defeat of the Spanish Armada in 1588. So in the early 1590s when Shakespeare began writing his first plays, the history plays of *Henry VI*, he was no doubt inspired by a nationalistic spirit that manifests itself in the entire eight plays of the minor and major tetralogies. However, as he read his primary source material in Holinshed's *Chronicles*, Shakespeare found family members quarrelling with and actually seeking the destruction of each other for the sake of power. His sources also told Shakespeare what he chose to highlight in these plays—namely, that these relatives often fought for self-aggrandizement, even to the hurt of national interests and to the destruction of the commonweal. Particularly, the *Henry VI* plays develop that important theme, the harm to national interests resulting from the intrafamilial pursuit of power, regardless of consequences.

Joel Hurstfield observes, "There were about a dozen people who in the 1590s could present themselves, with varying degrees of optimism, as the future occupants of Elizabeth's throne" (108). Of course, all of those claimants were, in one way or another, members of the same larger royal family, all relatives of each other. Among the various nationalistic themes Shakespeare sounded in his history plays, one solemn note that tolled through most of them was the divisive and destructive nature of the pursuit of power among family members, "unnatural controversy," to use Hall's phrase, because family members ought to help, protect, and support one another. Instead, these family members became intensely hated enemies of one another, destroyers of each other, and, in the process, the cause of serious national losses.

1 Henry VI opens with the funeral of Henry V, and early in the first scene, John, Duke of Bedford, the dead king's brother, prays to the spirit of Hal, Henry V: "Henry the Fift, thy ghost I invocate: / Prosper this realm, keep it from civil broils" (I.i.52-53). However, that very prayer is interrupted by a messenger from France with the bad news of fresh losses, "of slaughter and discomfiture: / Guienne, Champaigne, Rheims, Orleance, / Paris, Guysors, Poictiers, are all quite lost" (59–61). When Exeter asks "what treachery," the messenger replies, "No treachery, but want of men and money. / Amongst the soldiers this is muttered, / That here you maintain several factions" (68–71). Indeed, that precise theme continues through the play; for the sake of selfish pursuit of power, these relatives will undercut each other, and in so doing allow terrible slaughter of Englishmen and loss of English possessions in France.

King Henry VI, Hal's son, is a babe of only nine months when Hal dies in 1422. The babe is surrounded by power-hungry uncles and great-uncles. Since this baby cannot rule, these relatives divide the responsibilities of rule amongst themselves. Holinshed records, "The custody of this young prince was appointed to Thomas duke of Excester, & to Henry Beauford bishop of Winchester. The duke of Bedford was deputed regent of France, and the duke of Gloucester was ordained protector of England" (3: 136). Henry IV had four sons: Hal, who became Henry V; Thomas, Duke of Clarence; John, Duke of Bedford; and Humphrey, Duke of Gloucester. Thomas, had been killed in 1421; therefore, when Henry V died, the baby King Henry VI looked up into the faces of two uncles, John, Duke of Bedford, next in line to the throne after Henry VI, and Humphrey, Duke of Gloucester. However, John of Gaunt had, through his mistress Katherine who became his third wife, three other sons, half-brothers to Henry IV, uncles to Henry V and great-uncles to Henry VI. They were John, Henry, and Thomas Beauford (usually spelled Beaufort). Although these three sons were all bastard children when they were born, all the Beaufords were granted legitimacy in 1396. In *1 Henry VI*, Shakespeare presents three Beaufords, but in a different order: Thomas, Duke of Exeter; Henry, Bishop of Winchester and afterward Cardinal; and John, Earl and afterwards Duke of Somerset.

That John is a bit of a problem. John Beauford, Earl of Somerset, died in 1410. Although he had one son also called John and who later did indeed become Duke of Somerset, this person in Shakespeare's play seems rather to be actually another son of the first John Beauford, Edmund, Duke of Somerset.

In *1 Henry VI*, the first hint of internal quarrelling appears at the end of the first scene. When all alone, Henry, Bishop of Winchester, declares: "Each hath his place and function to attend: / I am left out; for me nothing remains. / But long I will not be Jack out of office" (173–175). Indeed, in the third scene of the first act, when Gloucester attempts to enter the Tower of London, his way is barred. He is told, "The Cardinal of Winchester forbids" (19). While Gloucester is threatening to break down the gates if necessary, Winchester himself enters and exclaims, "How now, ambitious {Humphrey}, what means this?" Gloucester asks if indeed Winchester had ordered him shut out, and Winchester replies, "I do, thou most ursurping proditor [that is, betrayer or traitor] / And *not* Protector, of King or realm" (31-32, emphasis added). Thus, Shakespeare portrays the first open conflict of family member against family member, this time the uncle, Winchester, against nephew, Gloucester. The conflict turns into such a hurly-burly that the Mayor of London, entering with his officers, cries out, "Fie, lords, that you, being supreme magistrates, / Thus contumeliously [insolently] should break the peace!" (57–58). Shakespeare's primary source for his history plays provides him with the information upon which he bases this first family conflict:

Somewhat before this season fell a great division in the realm of England, which of a sparkle was like to have grown to a great flame. For whether the bishop of Winchester called Henry Beaufort, son to John duke of Lancaster by his third wife, envied the authority of Humphrey duke of Gloucester, protector of the realm; or whether the duke disdained at the riches and pompous estate of the bishop: sure it is that the whole realm was troubled with them and their partakers: so that the citizens of London were fain to keep daily and nightly watches, and to shut up their shops for fear. (Holinshed, 3: 146)

The ongoing family fight between Winchester and Gloucester is one that Shakespeare declares is harmful to the commonwealth. He puts those words into the mouth of the child King Henry VI. When their quarrel breaks open in King Henry's very presence, each calling the other names and making serious charges against each other, Shakespeare's precocious child King exclaims, "Uncles of Gloucester and Winchester, / . . . Believe me, lords, my tender years can tell, / Civil dissension is a viperous worm / That gnaws the bowels of the commonwealth" (III.i.65, 71–73). However, this destructive quarrel continues, and Shakespeare's Winchester articulates such a selfish and reckless pursuit of power regardless of consequences to the nation that one can scarcely refrain from believing that it is one of Shakespeare's most serious concerns. Winchester declares:

> Now Winchester will not submit, I trow,
> Or be inferior to the proudest peer.
> Humphrey of Gloucester, thou shalt well perceive
> That neither in birth, or for authority,
> The Bishop will be overborne by thee.
> I'll either make thee stoop and bend thy knee,
> Or sack this country with a mutiny. (V.i.56–62)

As destructive as the Winchester/Gloucester or uncle/nephew quarrel is, Shakespeare's primary subject is the consequences of the Wars of the Roses, two warring segments of the same Platagenet family. This quarrel is primarily between the Duke of York and the Duke of Somerset of the Lancaster side of the family. Richard, Duke of York, is the son of another Richard, Earl of Cambridge, a man who conspired against Henry V in 1415 just before the latter was to depart for France for wars in which he won great fame, especially for the extraordinary victory at the Battle of Agincourt, the dramatic focus of Shakespeare's play *The Life of Henry the Fifth*. However, Shakespeare's Richard had been cleared of his father's taint, partly because his uncle, Edward, Duke of York, had died for Henry V in the Battle of Agincourt. Shakespeare's Richard became the Duke of York upon his uncle's death. Although Richard does not press his claim until years into the reign of King Henry VI, he actually considers himself the rightful king of England. On his father's side, he derives from Edmund of Langley, Duke of York, the fifth son of Edward III, whereas the Kings Henry—IV, V, and VI—all derive from John of Gaunt, the fourth son of Edward III. However, on his mother's side, Richard descends from the Mortimers, a name Henry IV always feared because the Mortimers sprang from Lionel, Duke of Clarence, the third son of Edward III, and, therefore, the Mortimers had a closer blood-line claim, or claim according to primogeniture, than Henry IV or his descendants after him. Richard's claim to the throne is mentioned in this play, but that particular issue does not become central until *2 Henry VI*.

In *1 Henry VI*, the conflict between the house of York, represented by Richard, and the house of Lancaster, represented by Somerset, is vague. Shakespeare refers to the conflict as simply "a case of truth." York says, "If he suppose that I have pleaded truth, / From off this brier pluck a white rose with me" (II.iv.29-30), and Somerset retorts, "Let him that is no coward nor no flatterer, / But dare maintain the party of the truth, / Pluck a red rose from off this thorn with me" (31–33). Thus, Shakespeare dramatically portrays the choosing of the dominant symbols of the Wars of the Roses, the white rose of York and the red rose of Lancaster. In Shakespeare's source, this conflict actually emerges only after the death of John, Duke of Bedford, when Richard, Duke of York, was named Regent of France. Holinshed records:

After the death of that noble prince the duke of Bedford, . . . all these mishaps could not anything abash the valiant courages of the English people: for they having no mistrust in God . . . began the war afresh, and appointed for regent in France, Richard duke of York . . . . Although the duke of York was worthy (both for birth and courage) of this honor and preferment, yet so disdained of Edmund duke of Summerset being cousin to the king, that by all means possible he sought his hindrance, as one glad of his loss, and sorry of his well doing. (3: 185).

Thus Shakespeare, picking up on the quarrel evident in Holinshed, begins to depict in *1 Henry VI* the harmful consequences of the divisive pursuit of power between two powerful branches of the Plantagenet family. Curiously, it is this Richard, Duke of York, who first makes significant use of the family name Plantagenet, and he does so to emphasize his royal blood and thereby enhance his claim to the throne. The first Plantagenet English king was Henry II, son of Maud (also spelled "Molde" or "Mawde"), daughter of Henry I, and "Geffrey Plantagenet earl of Anjou" (Holinshed, 2: 111). In *1 Henry VI*, Shakespeare repeatedly refers to Richard, Duke of York, as Plantagenet, and he is historically correct in doing so.

The quarrel between Edmund Beauford (whom Shakespeare calls John), Duke of Somerset, of the house of Lancaster and a closer relative to King Henry VI than his opponent, Richard Plantagenet, Duke of York, inspires a prophecy in Warwick: "And here I prophesy: this brawl to-day, / Grown to this faction in the Temple Garden, / Shall send between the Red Rose and the White / A thousand souls to death and deadly night" (II.iv.124–127). The child King Henry VI foresees a similar evil consequence: "Good Lord, what madness rules in brain-sick men, / When for so slight and frivolous a cause / Such factious emulations shall arise!" (IV.i.111–113). He predicts that in the English territories in France, the people will see dissension in the English ranks and rebel. He says of Somerset and York, "Both are my kinsmen, and I love them both" (IV.i.155), yet Shakespeare has him don the red rose of Lancaster, even as he seeks to reconcile these two quarrelling factions of his larger family. He abhors the scandal that will arise among foreign princes when they see that "King Henry's peers and chief nobility / Destroy'd themselves, and lost the realm of France!" (IV.i.146–147).

Although he is able to force Somerset and York into a grudging show of reconciliation, when all others have left the scene, Thomas Beauford, Duke of Exeter, articulates this Shakespearean worry about the divisive pursuit of power, here dramatized by these two warring houses of the Plantagenet family:

> . . . no simple man that sees
> This jarring discord of nobility,
> This shouldering of each other in the court,
> This factious bandying of their favorites,
> But that it doth presage some ill event.
> 'Tis much, when sceptres are in children's hands;
> But more, when envy breeds unkind [not only "ungracious" but also in the still deeper etymological sense of "not according to *kin*"] division:
> There comes the ruin, there begins confusion. (IV.i.187–194)

The major confusion and ruin in this play resulting from this "unkind division" soon occurs. York, as Regent of France, orders Somerset to send aid to heroic Talbot, engaged in deadly combat at the gates of Burdeaux. Somerset, to embarrass York by allowing the loss of Talbot, England's greatest warrior in France, delays, York says, "my promised supply / Of horsemen, that were levied for this siege! / Renowned Talbot doth expect my aid, / And I am louted [made a fool of] by a traitor villain / And cannot help the noble chevalier" (IV.iii.11–14). Lucy, on his way to Somerset to seek the promised help, observes:

> Thus while the vulture of sedition
> Feeds in the bosom of such great commanders,
> Sleeping neglection doth betray to loss
> The conquest of our scarce-cold conqueror,
> That ever-living man of memory,
> Henry the Fift. Whiles they each other cross,
> Lives, honors, lands, and all, hurry to loss. (IV.iii.47–53)

When he reaches Somerset, Lucy pleads with him, "Let not your private discord keep away / The levied succors that should lend him [Talbot] aid" (IV.iv.22–23). However, because of his intense desire to humiliate York, Somerset refuses. In this play, Shakespeare makes Talbot and his young son, John, die together, heroically but wastefully, resulting from the aggression that Freud describes hundreds of years later as the desire "to humiliate." And that will to power is, to Shakespeare, all the more horrible because it not only sets family member against family member but results in national loss. Lucy laments: "The fraud of England, not the force of France, / Hath now entrapp'd the noble-minded Talbot: / Never to England shall he bear his life, / But dies, betray'd to fortune by your strife" (IV.iv.36–39).

1 Henry VI does not end with Talbot's death but with the arrangement of a marriage for King Henry. The Duke of Suffolk seeks the hand of poverty-stricken Margaret of Anjou, according to Shakespeare, not because she is necessarily the best match for Henry but because Suffolk himself lusts after Margaret and has great ambitions for himself in his own pursuit of power. The play ends with these ominous words as Suffolk speaks aloud to himself: "Margaret shall now be Queen, and rule the King; / But I will rule both her, the King, and realm" (V.v.107–109). The unresolved and continuing quarrels within the Plantagenet family absorb so much energy as to allow such an outrageous objective to be thinkable.

In all three *Henry VI* plays, Shakespeare develops other themes, but repeatedly sounded through them all is the bass note of intrafamilial pursuit of power, resulting in great harm to the commonweal. In *2 Henry VI*, probably the first play that Shakespeare wrote, both major family fights—between Winchester and Gloucester, and between York and Somerset of the Lancasters, now supported by the Suffolk/Margaret liaison—reach new disastrous proportions. The quarrel between Winchester and Gloucester broadens, for Shakespeare portrays the Duchess of Gloucester to be ambitious for her husband, since, now that Bedford is dead and King Henry and Margaret as yet have no heir, Gloucester himself is next in line for the throne. Shakespeare has her say, "Were I a man, a duke, and next of blood, / I would remove these tedious stumblng-blocks, / And smooth my way upon their headless necks" (I.ii.63–65). Her ambition goes not unnoticed by Margaret. Margaret declares that "that proud dame, the Lord Protector's wife; / . . . sweeps it through the court with troops of ladies, / More like an empress than Duke Humphrey's wife" (I.iii.76–78). Her lover, Suffolk, counsels her:

> Although we fancy not the Cardinal [Winchester],
> Yet must we join with him and with the lords,
> Till we have brought Duke Humphrey in disgrace. . . .
> So one by one we'll weed them all at last,
> And you, yourself shall steer the happy helm. (94–96, 99–100)

Shakespeare picks up on one sentence in Holinshed: "For first this year, dame Eleanor Cobham, wife to the said duke [Gloucester], was accused of treason; for that she by sorcery and enchantment intended to destroy the king, to the intent to advance her husband unto the crown" (3: 203). Using his own imagination, Shakespeare develops a seance in which the called-up spirit foretells three key events: (1) of King Henry, "The duke yet lives that Henry shall depose; / But him out-live, and die a violent death" (I.iv.30–31), (2) of Suffolk, "By water shall he die, and take his end" (33), (3) of Somerset, "Let him shun castles" (35). But Eleanor is seized, condemned as a witch, and utterly humiliated. King Henry banishes her to the Isle of Man (II.iii.13). Moreover, incited by Margaret, King Henry requires Gloucester to give up his staff of office as Lord Protector, for, he says, "Henry will to himself / Protector be, and God shall be my hope" (II.iii.213–24). The coalition of Winchester/Suffolk/Margaret has successfully brought down Gloucester with "two pulls at once— / His lady banished, and a limb lopp'd off. / This staff of honor raught" (41-43). Not satisfied with that, the same coalition succeeds also in arresting Gloucester for treason. Suffolk says, "I do arrest you in his Highness' name, / And here commit you to my Lord Cardinal" (III.i.136–137).

Even that is not enough; they coldly plot and carry out his murder, and when King Henry asks, alarmed, "Where is our uncle?" Suffolk announces, "Dead in his bed, my lord; Gloucester is dead" (III.ii.28–29). Holinshed describes the theories concerning Gloucester's death: "Some judged him to be strangled, some affirm that an hot spit was put in his fundament, other write that he was smouldered between two feather-beds, and some have affirmed that he died of very grief" (3: 211). Shakespeare settles for Suffolk's simple, "Dead in his bed." King Henry responds to Suffolk, who ostensibly seeks to "comfort" him, "Lay not thy hands on me: forbear, I say! / Their touch affrights me as a serpent's sting" (46–47). Indeed, the uncle has murdered his nephew for the sake of power, and Henry is now fully unprotected and in the exploitative hands of Suffolk and Margaret, for Winchester soon dies a horrible death, tortured by visions of Duke Humphrey's ghost by his side.

In *2 Henry VI*, the Wars of the Roses actually begin. Somerset schemes to humiliate York by having himself named as Regent of France and having York shunted off to what he thinks is a political dead-end for him, to Ireland. York has his own plot. According to Shakespeare, he hires Jack Cade, a Kentishman who somewhat resembles the dead John Mortimer, to test the waters for Richard as to the possible claims of one whose primogeniture rights are stronger than those of the Lancasters. Historically, the Jack Cade revolt, based on just such claims, succeeded so extraordinarily well that the government of Henry was, for a time, virtually ended. However, York's commission to Ireland included a statement that would allow him to return to England should a national emergency arise, and that was exactly what he did. In the play, he privately declares to the Earl of Warwick and to Warwick's father, the Earl of Salisbury, his claim to the throne. They both kneel before him and declare, "Long live our sovereign Richard, England's king!" (II.ii.63). As York returns, he announces: "From Ireland thus comes York to claim his right, / And pluck the crown from feeble Henry's head. / Ring bells, aloud, burn bonfires clear and bright / To entertain great England's lawful king!" (V.i.1–4). In the Battle of St. Albans that follows (in life it was more of an accidental encounter between the Yorkish and Lancastrian armies than an intended battle), Shakespeare has Richard, the hunchbacked son of York and later Richard III, slay Somerset, who is identified in this play as Edmund Beauford. As Somerset dies, Richard gloats, "So lie thou there; / For underneath an alehouse' paltry sign, / The Castle in Saint Albons, Somerset / Hath made the wizard famous in his death" (V.ii.66–69). And this play comes to an end with Warwick prophesying: "Saint Albons battle won by famous York / Shall be eterniz'd in all age to come. / Sound drum and trumpets, and to London all, / And more such days as these to us befall" (V.iii.30–34).

In this second of the *Henry VI* plays, Winchester (or Suffolk with Winchester's full complicity) murders Gloucester, only to die miserably himself. Suffolk, who is a de la Pole but claims to bear "The honorable blood of Lancaster" (IV.i.51), the lover of Queen Margaret, is banished and then killed by Walter, a name that in those days was pronounced "water," thus fulfilling the prophecy concerning his end. And, finally, a York slays Somerset, under the sign of a castle, something the prophecy said he should avoid. Intrafamilial jostling for power has taken its deadly toll, but the Wars of the Roses continue.

The third part of *Henry VI* continues with events that immediately follow the Battle of St. Albans, with the humpbacked Richard displaying the head of Somerset. However, the conflict over the crown temporarily ends with a compromise that King Henry shall reign for the rest of his life but that Richard Plantagenet, Duke of York, will succeed him, and the York heirs will inherit the crown after him: "Let me for my life-time reign as king," Henry asks, and York replies, "Confirm the crown to me and to mine heirs, / And thou shalt reign in quiet while thou liv'st." Henry agrees:

> I am content: Richard Plantagenet,
> Enjoy the kingdom after my decease. . . . I here entail
> The crown to thee and to thine heirs for ever,
> Conditionally that here thou take an oath
> To cease this civil war. (I.i.171–175, 195–201)

York so swears.

Unfortunately, what seems to be the end of the Wars of the Roses merely opens a new breach, this time within King Henry's own family. Margaret, now the mother of a son, Edward (about whom Holinshed declares "the common people . . . had an opinion that the king was not able to get a child; and . . . that this was not his son . . ." [3: 236]), is outraged. Prince Edward bitterly complains, "Father, you cannot disinherit me. / If you be king, why should not I succeed?" (226–227). Margaret declares: "I here divorce myself / Both from thy table, Henry, and thy bed, / Until that act of parliament be repeal'd / Whereby my son is disinherited" (247–250). Holinshed refers to Margaret as a "manly Queene," and she certainly seems so as she orders Prince Edward, "Come, son, let's away. / Our army is ready; come we'll after them" (255-256). Warlike Margaret continues the fight. Moreover, York's own sons, Edward and Richard in particular, are equally warlike. Edward, York's eldest son, protests York's oath to Henry to cease fighting: "But for a kingdom any oath may be broken: / I would break a thousand oaths to reign one year" (I.ii.13–14). The lust for power seems to corrupt all. In history, these events cover years, but Shakespeare rigorously compresses them.

York is in Sandal Castle. The Lancastrian army, much larger than York's, appears. Some of York's men had gone out to gather food, but they were surrounded by the Lancastrians. York, heroically, but unwisely, goes to attempt their rescue—and to his own death. Holinshed records:

Some write that the duke was taken alive, and in derision caused to stand upon a molehill, on whose head they put a garland instead of a crown, which they fashioned and made of sedges or bulrushes; and having so crowned him with that garland, they kneeled down afore him (as Jews did unto Christ) in scorn, saying to him; *Hail king without rule, hail king without heritage, hail duke and prince without people or possessions.* And at length having thus scorned him with these and diverse other the like despiteful words, they struck off his head, which (as ye have heard) they presented to the queen. (3: 269)

Shakespeare uses an earlier reference in Holinshed but changes it so that Margaret herself places a paper crown on the live York's head. Then Clifford stabs first, but Margaret herself also stabs York. With York's blood on her hands, she shouts, "Off with his head, and set it on York gates, / So York may overlook the town of York" (I.iv.179–180).

Once more, one might think the Wars of the Roses over. Not so. York's sons continue. Edward, the eldest, who is the Earl of March and now the new Duke of York, with Warwick's help proclaims himself King of England. Once more Shakespeare portrays a battle, and he strikes that funeral toll of harm to the commonwealth resulting from these intestine fights. He has a son enter, dragging the body of a person whom he killed in the confusion of battle, thinking this person might have "some store of crowns [coins, worth about five shillings each]." However, as he sees his victim in the light, he cries, "O God! it is my father's face, / Whom in this conflict I, unawares, have kill'd" (II.v.61–62). Immediately thereafter, a father enters carrying a body, again hoping for gold only to discover for the first time that he has slain his own son: "Ah, no, no, no, it is mine only son!" (83). King Henry observes these horrible discoveries, and of this father, he pleads: "O, pity, pity, gentle heaven, pity! / The red rose and the white are on his face, / The fatal colors of our striving houses" (96–98). The hell of these members of the larger royal family killing off one another for the sake of power is bad enough, but Shakespeare laments the hell it brings to the other and ordinary families in his beloved country.

Shakespeare deals with many other details pertaining to the Wars of the Roses—Warwick's embarrassment when Edward marries Lady Grey (openly in Shakespeare but secretly in Holinshed) while Warwick is trying to arrange a marriage for him in France, Warwick's consequent changing of sides to join with Margaret and the Lancastrians, even taking Edward's brother George, Duke of Clarence, with him in his defection to the Lancastrians, and still other ramifications. Nevertheless, Shakespeare continues to press the theme of England's miseries when royal family members indulge in the divisive pursuit of power regardless of consequences. Margaret, before yet one more battle, laments: "Henry, your sovereign, / Is prisoner to the foe, his state usurp'd, / His realm a slaughter-house, his subjects slain, / His statutes cancell'd, and his treasure spent" (V.iv.76–80). Margaret soon has other personal reasons to grieve. The York forces prevail; Margaret's son, Prince Edward, is taken prisoner and promptly stabbed, first by King Edward, then by Richard, Duke of Gloucester, and finally, by George, Duke of Clarence, who has once more changed sides back from the Lancastrians to the Yorkists. On the walls of the Tower of London, Richard, the humpbacked Duke of Gloucester, confronts King Henry VI, who has been kept prisoner there. King Henry prophesies the suffering of old men, widows, orphans, fathers for their sons, wives for their husbands, and many others—all to be caused by Richard. Gloucester abruptly blurts, "I'll hear no more; die, prophet, in thy speech" (V.vi.57), and he stabs him.

The bloody Wars of the Roses are at last at an end, but not the deadly destruction by one family member of another—all in the endless pursuit of power.

PURSUIT OF POWER JUSTIFIED BY THE BEST-MAN THEORY

As Shakespeare and other thinking persons in the early 1590s were worrying about the possible harm to the nation upon Queen Elizabeth's death should competing contenders for the crown once more pursue power regardless of consequences, some of them also no doubt quietly discussed among themselves one solution to the question "Who should rule?"—a political idea not new in Anglo-Saxon tradition, the best-man theory. The doctrine of primogeniture, that is, the "divine right" of the eldest son of the eldest son of royal blood to rule, was not stressed as much in earlier ages in England as it was in the sixteenth and early seventeenth centuries. Among Germanic peoples, on the continent as well as in England, even when a particular bloodline had a tradition of leadership, often the "best man" of that bloodline became the leader, either by election or by sheer ability or by force, perhaps the force resulting from superior ability. Certainly, when a government was monarchical, most people wanted a leader like Edward III, a big, handsome man of great courage and fighting ability and with astuteness as a political leader as well. Monarchical systems suffer most when a child is the ostensible king, or when the king is passive or inept. In his plays, Shakespeare always deals gently and honorably with King Henry VI, but the madness of Charles II of France was apparently transmitted through the genes of Katherine whom Henry V took as wife, the event Shakespeare celebrates at the end of *Henry V*. Henry VI was not usually a vigorous leader even in his saner periods. It is only natural, therefore, that having completed the *Henry VI* plays in the early 1590s, Shakespeare might turn to another facet of the question "Who should rule?" as he wrote his second and major tetralogy of history plays. Once more these plays are complex, treating many important issues, but one major issue running through *Richard II*, *1* and *2 Henry IV*, and culminating with the model magistrate portrayed in *Henry V* was the tantalizing debate about the "divine right" theory versus the "best man" theory as the answer to the question "Who should rule?"

The material for probing into this debate was readily at hand in the account of Richard II found in Holinshed and earlier Tudor historians. Richard's great-grandfather, Edward II, was so inept that he was forced to abdicate and later killed. Even as early as 1327, a precedent had been established for removing an inadequate king. However, that precedent did not establish the "best man" concept, for the son of Edward II, Edward III, was placed on the throne when he was "but fourteen years of age" and with "his father yet living" (Holinshed, 2: 589). More quickly than anyone expected, Edward III became an effective king, at age eighteen convicting and executing Roger Mortimer for killing Edward II. Determined to win back disputed French possessions, Edward III launched war in France in 1337, winning celebrated victories at Crecy in 1346 and Poitiers in 1356. Edward III became, therefore, a great English hero, and his first son, Edward, the Black Prince, also became a celebrated hero for his victories in France, particularly at Poitiers. Other sons of Edward were born after this eldest: William of Hatfield, who did not survive; Lionel, Duke of Clarence; John of Gaunt, Duke of Lancaster;

Edmund of Langley, Duke of York; Thomas of Woodstock, Duke of Gloucester; and one more who did not survive, William of Windsor. When Edward III died in 1377, Edward the Black Prince was already dead, having died the preceding year. Once more England had a child king, "Richard, the second of that name, and son to prince Edward, called the black prince, the son of king Edward the third, a child of the age of eleven years" (Holinshed, 2: 711).

When the eleven-year-old Richard became King Richard II in 1377, he was surrounded by three powerful royal uncles. Since Lionel, Duke of Clarence, had died in 1368, the eldest surviving uncle was John of Gaunt, Duke of Lancaster, the richest and most powerful man in England at the close of the fourteenth century. However, John was a firm supporter of Richard's right to England's throne; his own monarchal ambitions focused on his trying to become King of Castile, and, especially from 1384, he spent many years on the continent. Edmund of Langley, Duke of York, was not particularly ambitious politically, but the youngest of the royal uncles, Thomas of Woodstock, Duke of Gloucester, was. When Richard gathered around him a coterie of friends and counselors and sought to rule in his own right, in 1386, Gloucester, believing himself to be the intended victim of a murder plot hatched by Richard and his newly elevated "earl of Suffolk," Michael de la Pole (whom Richard had also advanced as lord chancellor), convinced Parliament to dismiss Suffolk as Lord Chancellor and to name thirteen lords to have the oversight of the kingdom. Parliament charged Suffolk and other appointees of Richard's with additional wrongs: "the king's treasure had been embezzled, lewdly wasted, & prodigally spent, nothing to his profit" (2: 776).

Gloucester's actions actually meant that the powers of kingship were in his own hands. By 1388, Richard had once more gathered around him his own favorites: "Alexander archb. of York, Robert Veer duke of Ireland, Michael de la Pole earl of Suffolk, Robert Trisilian, & his fellows" (781). Gloucester countered, forcing Richard to make a proclamation clearing the names of "Thomas duke of Glocester, Richard earl of Arundel, & Thomas earl of Warwick . . . defamed of treason . . . [by] Alexander archbishop of York, sir Robert Veer duke of Ireland, Michael de la Pole earl of Suffolk, Robert Trisilian lord chief justice, and sir Nicholas Brambre of London knight" (788). And later that same year, "in the beginning of this parliament, there were openly called Robert Veer duke of Ireland, Alexander Neville archbishop of York, Michael de la Pole earl of Suffolk, sir Robert Trisilian lord chief justice of England to answer Thomas of Woodstock duke of Glocester, Richard earl of Arundel, Henry earl of Derby, and Thomas earl of Nottingham, upon certain articles of high treason, which these lords did charge them with" (793). Thus, in one combination or another, the chief "Lords Appellant," so called because the word "appeal" meant "to accuse of a crime," were Gloucester, Warwick, Arundel, Derby (Henry Bullingbrook, son of John of Gaunt and later Duke of Herford), and Nottingham (Thomas Mowbray, later Duke of Norfolk). This much background to *Richard II* helps one begin to understand how the play opens and some of what happens in it.

Richard was at last able to become king in his own right in late 1389, when John of Gaunt had returned from the continent. He ruled with increasing dynamism for approximately eight years. Two of the five Lords Appellant had become his own close friends and supporters, Bullingbrook and Mowbray. Richard, however, had not forgotten the humiliation he had suffered under his power-hungry uncle Thomas, Duke of Gloucester. By this time, Richard had new favorites around him: John Bushy, William Bagot, and Thomas Green (according to Holinshed, 2: 840 and elsewhere, but Shakespeare chooses Henry Green, mentioned in Holinshed, 2: 852 and also elsewhere), and others. In 1397, a fresh quarrel broke out between Richard and Gloucester. Richard had "by evil counsel" sold Brest to the Duke of Brittany. At a dinner, Gloucester openly rebuked Richard for selling possessions gained "with great adventure by the manhood and policy of your noble progenitors" (835) instead of going out and fighting and gaining new possessions for England.

Richard had had enough. Later in 1397, he had Arundel and Warwick seized and charged with treason. Arundel, despite his declarations of innocence, was convicted and beheaded. Warwick confessed, bringing Richard so much relief of mind that he exclaimed, "By saint John Baptist, Thomas of Warwick, this confession that thou hast made, is unto me more available [that is, beneficial or profitable] than all the duke of Glocester's and the earl of Warwick's lands" (842). Warwick was exiled to the Isle of Man. Grafton provides more details than does Holinshed about the arrest of Gloucester. Richard took 15,000 men with him and asked Gloucester to go with him. Gloucester went cheerfully, for only a short time earlier the king had so honored him with gifts and "lordships" that everyone thought Gloucester to be the one man in England most in the king's favor. Richard had the popular Gloucester taken to Calais, and, for fear of Gloucester's popular support, never brought open charges against him, but, according to Grafton, ordered Thomas Mowbray, Earl Marshall and the officer in charge of Calais, to have Gloucester privately killed. Mowbray hesitated, but, Grafton says, Richard in effect told Mowbray that he must take Gloucester's life or Richard would take Mowbray's. At that, Mowbray killed Gloucester at midnight, casting featherbeds upon him and smothering him.

By this time, Richard was acting so peremptorily, if not tyrannically, as to cause concern even among his friends. He issued a general pardon "for all offenses to all the king's subjects (fifty only excepted) whose names he would not by any means express, but reserved them to his own knowledge, but when any of the nobility offended him, he might at his pleasure name him to be one of the number excepted, and so keep them still within his danger" (Holinshed, 2: 844). Richard spent so much money that he constantly kept seizing property of those thus accused, and still he raised taxes right and left. Holinshed does not provide many details about the quarrel between Bullingbrook and Mowbray with which *Richard II* opens, but Grafton provides more. According to Grafton, Bullingbrook was genuinely grieved over Richard's tyrannical behavior, especially Richard's charges against various nobles, supposedly of that mysterious fifty, resulting in the deaths of some and the banishments of others and the loss of their properties thereby. The common people were also grumbling against Richard's severity. Knowing how close Mowbray was to Richard, Bullingbrook asked him to urge Richard to reflect upon his behavior, "to turn the leaf," and to "use a better way." Mowbray heard all that and reckoned, Grafton says, he had gotten himself information through which he would receive great favor of the king. Grafton says that Mowbray sought to aggravate the offense and make it greater by adding words that Bullingbrook never used. Bullingbrook was called to an account, but he then brought charges against Mowbray, and at this point Shakespeare makes use of the material Holinshed provides. And topping all of Bullingbrook's charges was the accusation that Mowbray had murdered the uncle of both Richard and Bullingbrook, the Duke of Gloucester. Bullingbrook declared that he would "prove this with his body against the body of the said duke of Norfolk [Mowbray] within lists" (Holinshed, 2: 845). At that, "The king . . . waxed angry" (845).

In *Richard II*, Shakespeare presents a sharp contrast between the imperious, tyrannical, unjust, wasteful, politically inept, poetically wordy but practically ineffective King Richard and his first cousin, Henry Bullingbrook, Duke of Herford, politically astute, "humble" before commoners, essentially fair-minded, comparatively taciturn, and practically efficient and able to take decisive action. In short, Richard represents the "divine right" king who does not deserve to be king because of his character flaws and ineptness and also for both wrong and foolish actions, and Henry the "best man," the capable leader. Shakespeare never definitively decides for his thinking audience which is better, but he does portray Richard's weaknesses so vividly as to make Henry's guilt in overthrowing the divine-right king almost necessary, even though, at the same time, he subtly makes that guilt even more treasonous than it initially in fact was.

Shakespeare finds most of Richard's flaws very evident in Holinshed and the other Tudor histories. Richard allows the charges and counter-charges between Mowbray and Bullingbrook to go to trial by combat, and despite the heavy costs of setting up such a tourney, Richard permits all to continue until the two opponents are actually ready to charge at each other before he dramatically, yet peremptorily, stops the tourney. The disparity between the two sentences—life for Mowbray and ten years for Henry—remains a mystery. Among the most probable factors were (1) that Henry was a royal duke and Mowbray was not, 2) that Mowbray had indeed murdered Gloucester at Richard's behest and now Richard could be free of him forever, and (3) that John of Gaunt, Henry's father, had always supported Richard. Holinshed gives no charge against Henry, but against Mowbray Holinshed records this reason for his banishment: "because he had sown sedition in the realm by his words" (2: 847). Shakespeare's Richard gives such a muddled set of reasons as to be virtually incomprehensible, grammatically or logically, and, of course, that dramatic portrayal of Richard is precisely the effect that Shakespeare wanted. The absurdity that Richard would allow things to come to this is proof, in both real history and Shakespeare's dramatic version, of Richard's love for histrionics, despite the financial waste of it all, and of his political ineptness.

Shakespeare, following material found in Tudor histories, makes Richard guilty of Gloucester's death, even though Shakespeare's scene between Gaunt and Gloucester's widow seems wholly imaginary. The scene underscores the favorite Tudor doctrine of passive obedience, articulated by Gaunt in I.ii.1–8 and 37–41. Gaunt's deathbed charges against Richard in his desire to see Richard correct his wrongs are all to be found in one form or another in Shakespeare's sources. Dramatically, all of that is an exposition of Richard's divine right to be king but also of his disqualifying characteristics. Shakespeare makes Richard callously indifferent to Gaunt's illness, angry as a spoiled brat at Gaunt's effort to bring him to his senses, and foolishly short-sighted in his illegal seizure of Gaunt's vast properties. Holinshed has this to say about the latter act:

The death of the duke [of Lancaster] gave occasion of increasing more hatred in the people of this realm toward the king [Richard], for he seized into his hands all the goods that belonged to him, and also received all the rents and revenues of his lands which ought to have descended unto the duke of Hereford by lawful inheritance, in revoking letters patents, which he had granted to him [that is, to Henry] before, by virtue wherof he might make his attorneys general to sue livery for him, by any manner of inheritances or possessions that might from thenceforth fall unto him, and that his homage might be respited, with making reasonable fine: whereby it was evident, that the king meant his [Henry's] utter undoing. (2: 849)

York's protest at Richard's wrongdoing appears in Holinshed, but is not at all as eloquent and as cogent there as it is in Shakespeare's play. However, Holinshed has this effective figure of speech concerning Richard's illegal and incredibly unwise seizure of the Lancastrian properties: "such an unadvised captain, as with a leaden sword would cut his own throat" (849).

Richard's stupidities mount up, but Henry, as popular as he really was, appears in Shakespeare guilty in a more culpable way than he does in Holinshed. Holinshed records Henry's departure from England after his banishment:

The duke of Hereford took his leave of the king at Eltham, who there released four years of his banishment [originally ten, as in Shakespeare]: . . . A wonder it was to see what number of people ran after him in every town and street where he came, before he took the sea, lamenting and bewailing his departure, as who would say, that when he was departed, the only shield, defense and comfort of the commonwealth was vaded [departed] and gone. (2: 848)

Shakespeare embellishes that departure with Henry's doffing his "bonnet to an oyster-wench" and the "tribute of his supple knee" to a brace of draymen (I.iv.31–33). But according to Shakespeare, when Richard seizes all of Gaunt's property, in the very room where that act took place and without ever leaving the room, Northumberland reveals to Willoughby and Ross that Henry with an army has already departed France and will shortly "touch our northern shore" (II.i.277–298). That means that Shakespeare makes Henry guilty of treason without, as yet, having any possible way of knowing of Richard's illegal seizure of his property. Moreover, in Holinshed, Henry not only knows of Richard's wrongdoings against him, but also

many of the magistrates and rulers of the cities, towns, and communalties, here in England, perceiving daily how the realm drew to utter ruin, not like to be recovered to the former state of wealth, whilest king Richard lived and reigned (as they took it) devised with great deliberation, and considerate advise, to send and signify by letters unto duke Henry, whom they now called (as he was indeed) duke of Lancaster and Hereford, requiring him with all convenient speed to convey himself into England, promising him all their aid, power and assistance, if he expelling K. Richard, as a man not meet for the office he bear, would take upon him the scepter, rule, diadem of his native land and region. (2: 852)

It is clear that Shakespeare chose not to provide Henry with such powerful underpinnings for his return to England. Seldom, if ever, seeing reality in terms of simple blacks and whites, Shakespeare presents the argument for the "best man" as justification for the seizure of power from an inept "divine right" king in far more subtle and complex ways than his primary source does.

For example, in *1 Henry IV*, Shakespeare goes far beyond anything he found in his sources in creating Hal as a playboy prince, indulging in pranks and practical jokes, and keeping company with the likes of Falstaff. In the mind of Shakespeare's Henry IV, there is a sharp and unfavorable contrast between the apparently irresponsible Hal and the hardworking Hotspur, who, in Hal's own words, "kills me some six or seven dozens of Scots at a breakfast, washes his hands, and says to his wife, 'Fie upon this quiet life! I want [lack] work'" (II.iv.102–104). Among Henry's various fears, one of the greatest is worry about Hal, whose irresponsibility of lifestyle Shakespeare had already begun to create in *Richard II*: "Can no man tell me of my unthrifty [wasteful or extravagant, having overtones of prodigality] son? . . . Inquire at London, 'mongst the taverns there, / For there, they say, he daily doth frequent, / With unrestrained loose companions" (V.iii.1–7). In *1 Henry IV*, Shakespeare even makes Henry long for someone to assure him "That some night-tripping fairy had exchang'd / In cradle-clothes our children where they lay, / And call'd mine Percy, his Plantagenet! / Then would I have his Harry and he mine" (I.i.87–90). All of this is entirely out of Shakespeare's imagination, focusing sharply upon the issue of "best man" versus "divine right." Richard had been deposed as one unworthy to be king, with thirty-three "solemne articles" against him, including the first, that he "wastefully spent the treasure of the realm," and the second, that he murdered Gloucester, and many others, including doing things "contrary to law" (Holinshed, 2: 859 and 861). Now Shakespeare creates a prodigal and wasteful Hal who also breaks the law, not by robbing the travellers but by robbing the robbers, just for the joke of it, and yet is an accomplice in the original robbery. At least in Henry's mind, Hal is irresponsible, and Henry seeks to teach Hal how deliberately and carefully he played the political game to become, in the eyes of the people of England, the "best man" in contrast to irresponsible Richard (III.ii.29–91).

The fact is, as Hal points out early in *1 Henry IV*, that Hal also knows how to be political. He makes his own method clear in I.ii.195–217, and he promises his father, as he seeks to reassure him of his integrity, "That I shall make this northern youth [Hotspur] exchange / His glorious deeds for my indignities" (III.ii.145–146). All of this contrast between Hal and Hotspur, this searching of what responsibility is in contrast to irresponsibility, is Shakespeare's imaginative creation as he explores the issues in the debate of the "best man" theory versus "divine right." Moreover, Shakespeare has Hal prove true to his word; he does achieve heroic deeds in the Battle of Shrewsbury and there kills Hotspur, the rebel. Some of Hal's heroism appears in Holinshed:

The prince that day holp his father like a lusty young gentleman: for although he was hurt in the face with an arrow, so that diverse noble men that were about him, would have conveyed him forth out of the field, yet he would not suffer them so to do, lest his departure from amongst his men might happily [perhaps] have stricken some fear into their hearts: and so without regard of his hurt, he continued with his men, & never ceased, either to fight where the battle was most hot, or to encourage his men where it seemed most need. (3: 26)

The rest is Shakespeare's justification of Hal as a true "best man" as surely as his father was. Ironically, Shakespeare's audience might infer that if irresponsible Hal could prove to be responsible and effective, if given more time, irresponsible Richard might have too.

In the major tetralogy, Shakespeare presents one member of the larger royal family subjugating another—in this case, one cousin, Henry, subjugating another cousin, the "divine right" king, Richard—and justifying that power grab in the name of being the "best man," although no one uses that term per se in any of these plays. In *Richard II*, when Henry returns to England, he justifies his acts to York, who accuses Henry of being a traitor, in these words: "Will you permit that I shall stand condemn'd / A wandering vagabond, my rights and royalties / Pluck'd from my arms perforce—and given away / To upstart unthrifts [wastrels]?" (II.iii.119–122). Nevertheless, no justification is, after all, adequate to clear Henry of guilt, not in Holinshed and not in Shakespeare. Holinshed's indictment of Henry is much more severe than Shakespeare's:

The duke of Gloucester chief instrument of this mischief, to what end he came ye have heard. And although his nephew the duke of Hereford took upon him to revenge his death, yet wanted he [lacked he] moderation and loyalty in his doings, for the which both he himself and his lineal race were scourged afterwards, as a due punishment unto rebellious subjects; so as deserved vengeance seemed not to stay long for his ambitious cruelty, that thought it not enough to drive king Richard to resign his crown and regal dignity over unto him, except he should also take from him his guiltless life. What unnaturalness, or rather what tigerlike cruelty was this, not to be content with his principality? not to be content with his treasure? not to be content with his deprivation? not to be content with his imprisonment? but being so nearly knit in consanguinity, which ought to have moved them like lambs to have loved each other, wolfishly to lie in wait for the distressed creatures life, and ravenously to thirst after his blood, the spilling whereof should have touched his conscience so, as that death ought rather to have been adventured for his safety, than so savagely to have sought his life after the loss of his royalty. (2: 869)

Thus, Holinshed waxes rhetorically florid in inveighing against the "domestical discord & unnatural controversy" resulting from one kinsman's abuse of another in the savage drive for power, regardless of any justification or rationalization with which he might seek to color it.

Shakespeare is not as abusive as Holinshed is, but he distinctly daubs Henry's guilt black. Even at the end of *Richard II*, Henry already experiences deep-dyed guilt:

> Lords, I protest my soul is full of woe
> That blood should sprinkle me to make me grow.
> Come mourn with me for what I do lament,
> And put on sullen black incontinent [without delay].
> I'll make a voyage to the Holy Land,
> To wash this blood off from my guilty hand. (V.vi.45–50)

Similarly, *1 Henry IV* begins with his plans to make a crusade of penance to the Holy Land. Yet even more ominously, his guilt manifests itself in "civil butchery" that once more forces the postponement of the visit to "those holy fields, / Over whose acres walk'd those blessed feet" (I.i.13, 24–25). The slaughter inside the macrocosmic family results from his pursuit of power, the fulfillment of the prophecy of Carlisle in *Richard II*:

> My Lord of Herford here, whom you call king,
> Is a foul traitor to proud Herford's king,
> And if you crown him, let me prophesy,
> The blood of English shall manure the ground,
> And future ages groan for this foul act. (IV.i.134–138)

All the bloodshed, not only during his own lifetime but also throughout the long Wars of the Roses, flows from Henry's seizure of power from Richard—so says Carlisle, and, in a sense, so says Shakespeare.

In *2 Henry IV*, Henry cannot sleep; even in a storm, a ship-boy can sleep, but Henry cannot sleep in the most luxurious chamber of a king. "Uneasy lies the head that wears a crown" (III.i.31) he mourns, especially a crown gained as his was. He continues to lament the "rank diseases" that grow in "the body of our kingdom." He must continue to worry over Hal's apparent profligacy, a "grief" that

> Stretches itself beyond the hour of death.
> . . . For when his headstrong riot hath no curb,
> When rage and hot blood are his counsellors [as they
> were for Richard II, rendering him, according to the best-man theory,
> unworthy],
> What means and lavish manners meet together,
> O, with what wings shall his affections fly
> Towards fronting peril and oppos'd decay [consequent ruin].
> (IV.iv.56–66)

To Hal, Henry confesses, "God knows, my son, / By what by-paths and indirect [lawless] crook'd ways / I met this crown, and I myself know well / How troublesome it sate upon my head" (IV.v.183–186). Henry's guilt drove him repeatedly to seek a pilgrimage to the Holy Land, but constant civil broils in England always prevented his going. At last, while "making his prayers at saint Edwards shrine" (Holinshed, 3: 58), he found his illness taking a severe turn for the worse. He was taken into a chamber belonging to the abbot of Westminster. Henry roused up enough to ask what the chamber was called, for rooms were often given names in those days. He was told "Jerusalem." Henry, who never made it to the Holy Land because of the consequences of his guilt, sighed, *"Lauds be given to the father of heaven, for now I know that I shall die here in this chamber, according to the prophesy of me declared, that I should depart this life in Jerusalem"* (58).

In his major tetralogy, Shakespeare makes the best-man theory the outward justification of the divisive pursuit of power within the royal family, but he never fully places his own approval upon that pursuit. Holinshed says of Richard that "he was given to follow evil counsel, and used such inconvenient ways and meanes, through insolent misgovernance, and youthful outrage," that "he was prodigal, ambitious, and much given to the pleasure of the body" (2: 868), and, therefore, Richard was obviously a bad king, but he also had good qualities, and Henry had no right, despite his rationalization, to wrest the crown from him. Shakespeare never makes the case as distinctly open-and-shut as that. He examines the debate from various angles and forces his thinking audience to consider many different ramifications of the debate, but, since facts are facts, he passes on to *Henry V*, and there he presents the exemplary king, one who has a measure of "divine right," since he inherited his throne from a ruling king, and most especially one who is clearly the "best man."

MACHIAVELLIAN MONSTERS AND THE PURSUIT OF POWER

Shakespeare makes one more momentous turn of the screw as he considers the hell of families savagely shredded by the lust for power. He portrays two Machiavellian monsters, one who is already a monster and the other who becomes one—the former, Richard III, and the latter, Macbeth. Machiavelli had been known in England for many years before Shakespeare began writing. It is possible that Shakespeare himself did not have firsthand knowledge of Machiavelli's *The Prince*, the most notorious of his writings in England. *Notorious* is the correct word, for the English were distinctly influenced in their view of Machiavelli by the French, who "originated" the "popular legend of Machiavelli, the wicked politician" (Praz 3). One of the most influential works spreading the French anti-machiavellianism was *Contre-Machiavel* by Gentillet, published in 1576, circulated first in England in Latin, and going through three editions during Shakespeare's lifetime. In 1602, Simon Patericke published his English translation, one made in 1577 when the Gentillet work was still quite new (Praz 6). By the time Shakespeare was writing his plays, the myth of the evil "Machiavel," the atheistic and utterly unscrupulous grasper after political power, was common knowledge in England.

It is not surprising, therefore, that Shakespeare, as he is foreshadowing the evil character of Richard III, the hunchbacked epitome of Vice, has Richard himself declare in *3 Henry VI*, "I can add colors to the chameleon, / Change shapes with Proteus for advantages, / And set the murtherous Machevil to school" (III.ii.191–193). *Richard III* depicts the fulfillment of that declaration. *Macbeth* is a more subtle play, with more dreadful implications, and nowhere is there a reference to Machiavelli in it, but it was written just after the 1605 Gunpowder Plot, and there are distinct references to equivocation, as Praz says, "a perfect counterpart of Machiavellian dissimulation. Equivocation became a byword in England since Henry Garnet, superior of the Jesuits in England, used it during his trial for complicity in the Gunpowder Plot" (39). There is little doubt that Shakespeare and many other people in England associated the goals of Machiavelli with their understanding of the goals of the Jesuits. As Praz points out:

Domination was in both cases the chief aim: everything else was degraded to the rank of tool, to be laid aside when its function had been fulfilled. In both cases all scruples had to be disregarded, whenever a certain action was conducive to the aim, which in Machiavelli's case was the glory of the country, in that of the Jesuits the glory of God. (39)

If hypocrisy in *Richard III* and equivocation in *Macbeth* be justly paralleled, then one may term both central characters in these two plays distinctly different Machiavellian monsters. Both Richard III and Macbeth murder kinsmen for the sake of power.

One might say that Richard is the born Machiavel and Macbeth, willingly led astray by Machiavellian deceit, the self-made monster. In *3 Henry VI*, Richard already schemes against his close relatives with a "cold premeditation for my purpose" (III.ii.133), because he declares:

> . . . love forswore me in my mother's womb;
> . . . To shrink mine arm up like a wither'd shrub,
> To make an envious mountain on my back,

> Where sits deformity to mock my body;
> To shape my legs of unequal size,
> To disproportion me in every part. (153–160)

He determines to seek his joys where they may be found by such a monster:

> Then since this earth affords no joy to me
> But to command, to check [that is, curb or control]
> to o'erbear such
> As are of better person than myself,
> I'll make my heaven to dream upon the crown,
> And whiles I live, t' account this world but hell,
> Until my misshap'd trunk that bears this head
> Be round impaled with a glorious crown. (165–171)

He recognizes a serious problem: there are many lives between himself and his home, the objective he has set for himself, the crown. He determines his course: "Why, I can smile, and murther whiles I smile" (182), and it is in that context that he declares that he can even "set the murtherous Machevil to school" (193).

In *Richard III*, Shakespeare loses no time in reestablishing that concept of the Machiavel of popular myth. "Plots have I laid," Richard declares to himself alone, "inductions [beginnings] dangerous, / By drunken prophecies, libels, and dreams, / To set my brother Clarence and the King / In deadly hate the one against the other" (I.i.32–35). Clarence and King Edward are his brothers. The Wars of the Roses are at an end; both Henry VI and his son, Edward, are dead; the eldest son of Richard Plantagenet, Duke of York, now reigns as Edward IV. George, Duke of Clarence, is older than Richard, Duke of Gloucester. After the two sons of Edward IV—Edward, Prince of Wales, and Richard, Duke of York—Clarence is next in line to the throne. Richard realizes that he must murder at least those three kinsmen between him and Edward IV in order to succeed Edward IV to the throne, but he is "determined to prove a villain" (30), and so as Clarence approaches, Richard becomes a Machiavellian hypocrite.

George has already been arrested as a result of Richard's plot; Richard has revived an old wives' tale. Holinshed, as he often does, quotes Hall (or quotes Grafton who quotes Hall):

Some have reported, that the cause of this noble man's death [that is, the death of George, Duke of Clarence] rose of a foolish prophecy, which was, that after K. Edward one should reign, whose first letter of his name should be G. Wherewith the king and queen were sore troubled and began to conceive a grievous grudge against this duke, and could not be quiet till they had brought him to his end. (3: 346)

Holinshed does not suggest that Richard promoted this prophecy; that is Shakespeare's idea. As guards take Clarence to the Tower of London, Richard equivocates, "I will deliver you, or else lie for you" (I.i.115). An equivocation is a form of doublespeak; derived from "equi-" or equal and "vox" or voice, the word even in Shakespeare's day meant to use a word in more than one application or sense, to use a word so that it has double meanings. The word "lie" in Richard's promise is an equivocation; outwardly to Clarence, he implies that he will enter prison and replace Clarence there, if his imprisonment is long, but inwardly to himself, his Machiavellian or Jesuitical meaning is that he will literally "tell a lie" about Clarence to worsen his plight. He convinces his brother that he will help him, but all the while he is planning his murder.

According to Gentillet, Machiavelli taught that a prince should not worry about perjuring himself but rather must learn how to deceive and dissemble, for those who can be deceived deserve to be deceived. Certainly, Richard approaches all persons with just such disdain. Lady Anne, the widow of Edward, the dead son of Henry VI and Margaret, is following the corpse of Henry VI, recently murdered by Richard, for burial. Richard, a royal duke with power, orders the procession to halt. In possibly the most bizarre courtship scene in all of literature, Shakespeare portrays Richard to be so persuasive that he can admit to killing her father-in-law Henry VI and her husband Edward and still convince Anne that he has done both because of her beauty and because of his love for her. Before the scene ends, he has won her. Anne abandons her father-in-law's corpse and goes to prepare to marry Richard. This Anne is Anne Neville, the daughter of the Earl of Warwick. Warwick had arranged the marriage of Anne with Edward as a part of his deal with the Lancastrians when he joined them against Edward IV. After Richard has won Anne, he gloats:

> Was ever woman in this humor woo'd?
> Was ever woman in this humor won?
> I'll have her, but I will not keep her long.
> What? I, that kill'd her husband and his father,
> To take her in her heart's extremest hate,
> With curses in her mouth, tears in her eyes,
> The bleeding witness of my hatred by,
> Having God, her conscience, and these bars against me,
> And I no friends to back my suit {at all}

> But the plain devil and dissembling looks?
> (I.ii.227–236)

Precisely! He is a dissembling Machiavellian devil, the embodiment of the popular English myth of a Machiavel.

The greatest deceiver is one who can convince others that he is utterly incapable of deceit. Another Shakespearean Machiavel, Iago, is so clever that nearly all the other characters in *Othello* call him "Honest Iago." Richard declares to Hastings, "Because I cannot flatter and look fair, / Smile in men's faces, smooth, deceive, and cog [cheat or dissemble], / . . . I must be held a rancorous enemy" (I.iii.47–50). He calls himself a plain man, incapable of abusing the simple truth as others do. After Edward IV's death, Richard has Buckingham spread the word that Edward's two children are bastards. Edward IV, like Edward III many years before, was a big and handsome man, and like many a great man in England in those days, an unabashed womanizer. Richard urges Buckingham to

> . . . urge his hateful luxury [one of the seven deadly
> sins, lasciviousness or wanton lust]
> And bestial appetite in change of lust,
> Which stretch'd unto their servants, daughters, wives,
> Even where his raging eye or savage heart,
> Without control, lusted to make a prey. (III.v.80–84)

That sort of evil report about Edward IV would be easy to believe. As for Richard himself, he plays the Machiavel. Gentillet argues that Machiavelli taught that because the world looks always on the exterior of things, it is sufficient for the Prince merely to appear outwardly religious and devout, even though he is not the least bit truly religious. Gentillet comments:

This Maxime is a precept, whereby this Atheist *Machiavel* teacheth the Prince to be a true contemner of God and of Religion, and only to make a show and a fair countenance outwardly before the world, to be esteemed religious and devout, although he is not. For divine punishment, for such hypocrisy and dissimulation, *Machiavell* fears not, because he believes not there is a God. (92)

Therefore, Richard appears before the Mayor of London and other citizens, between two bishops, prayer book in his hand, all the utmost hypocrisy, a mere Machiavellian outward display of religion. All of Richard's protestations about not wanting the cares of kingship, implying that all he wants is to devote himself to the worship of God, simply compound his hypocrisy.

Richard is also murderous. Gentillet propounds that Machiavelli teaches a prince to kill, but to "color it with some just color." Richard provided an excuse to have Clarence imprisoned, and once there, he has him murdered. He has Rivers, Grey, and Vaughan, all relatives and close supporters of the Queen, killed. He suddenly accuses Hastings of being a traitor, of protecting those who have bewitched Richard, causing his deformities, even though he was born in that condition; he demands that Hastings be beheaded, and even declares that he will not eat until that beheading has been accomplished. Shakespeare does not make it completely clear that Richard murders Anne, but her sudden illness seems most suspicious, especially since he earlier says, "I will not keep her long," and now declares, even while she yet lives, "I must be married to my brother's daughter, / Or else my kingdom stands on brittle glass" (IV.ii.612–62). After using Buckingham to help him gain the throne, when Buckingham hesitates to fulfill Richard's demands to kill the two princes, Richard abandons Buckingham as a friend. Buckingham forsakes Richard but has the bad luck to be captured; Richard promptly has him beheaded. Most painful of all, Richard has his two young nephews, the precocious young princes, murdered. In the beginning, Richard covers his killings with a touch of color, but by the end, he is a murderous monster who simply slaughters any and all who might be the slightest threat to him in his mad lust for power.

In sharp contrast to the exaggerated deformities of Richard, both in body and mind, Macbeth, at the beginning of the play devoted to him, is a genuinely noble and good man. Richard was a born monster, but Macbeth made himself into one, and not without considerable effort. Early in *Macbeth*, others refer to him as "brave Macbeth," "valiant cousin, worthy gentleman," "noble Macbeth," "worthiest cousin," and his wife says his nature is "too full o' the milk of human kindness / To catch the nearest way [to the throne]" (I.i.16, 24, 67; iv.14; v.17–18). Macbeth is of the royal family, a near kinsman to King Duncan, and when the Witches greet him as Thane of Glamis, a title he already has, and Thane of Cawdor, a title soon bestowed upon him, and then "that shall be King hereafter!" (I.ii.48–50), both Macbeth and Banquo begin to wonder. Macbeth reveals his natural goodness by the breathless and heart-pounding response he has to an evil thought. He recognizes the equivocal nature of the prophecies of the Witches: "This supernatural soliciting / Cannot be ill; cannot be good" (I.iii.130–131). He reasons that if the prophecies are bad (false), why was he so immediately awarded the title of Thane of Cawdor, a title Rosse has already innocently said is "an earnest of a greater honor" (104). But, then, he asks himself, the hair on the back of his neck lifting with fearful excitement, "If good, why do I *yield* to that suggestion / Whose horrid image [one he soon identifies with murder] doth unfix my hair / And make my seated heart knock at my ribs, / Against the use of nature?" (134–137, emphasis added). Only the genuinely good have a horror of evil; Richard III never demonstrates that sort of recognition of evil. Even after the parade of ghosts appears to him in his sleep, Richard awakens with no sense of horror of evil, but only of the isolation and sense of condemnation that his wrongs deserve. Richard says, "I am a villain; yet I lie, I am not" (V.iii.191), a rather arrogant attitude towards evil, even in the midst of his most aroused sensitivity to his wickedness. But Macbeth is a good man, with a good man's horror of evil, and the play makes clear why Shakespeare thinks good people ought to fear evil—it dehumanizes them and turns them into monsters.

Macbeth has to learn deceit. Lady Macbeth, knowing Macbeth to be one who desires to achieve "holily" and "not play false" (I.v.21), invokes evil spirits to "unsex" her, to fill her "from the crown to the toe topful / Of direst cruelty!" (41–43). As soon as Macbeth and Lady Macbeth meet upon his return to their castle, they greet each other lovingly. Macbeth says, "My dearest love," and there is every reason to believe that these two young people really do very much love one another in Shakespeare's depiction of them for his audience. They know that Duncan has honored them by spending the night at their castle in Inverness, and thus he is in their power. They have said very little to each other, but Macbeth and his wife know, without words, what they are both thinking. Lady Macbeth, helped perhaps by those evil spirits, if her prayer has been heard, warns Macbeth, "Your face, my thane, is as a book, where men / May read strange matters." She becomes his teacher: "To beguile [that is, to entangle with guile or to deceive] the time, / Look like the time; bear welcome in your eye, / Your hand, your tongue; look like the innocent flower, / But be the serpent under't" (I.v.63–66).

However, goodness cannot be easily overcome. Perhaps Shakespeare remembers the contrast of the "fruits of the spirit" and the "works of the flesh" described in Paul's Galatian letter. It takes work to convert this good man into an evil one.

Macbeth, upon further reflection, decides against harming Duncan. He has many reasons, the first of which is the fact that "I am his kinsman." He enumerates all the additional compelling reasons why they must not murder Duncan. He is Macbeth's king, to whom Macbeth owes allegiance. He is Macbeth's guest, and as host Macbeth "should against his murtherer shut the door, / Not bear the knife myself" (I.vii.13–15). He meditates upon Duncan's own goodness, his meekness, his integrity in office, and his other virtues. As for himself, he sees clearly, for his eye is not yet evil, that only "vaulting ambition" drives him into this pursuit of power. His meditations are interrupted by the return of his wife, but he has already reached a firm decision. "We will proceed no further in this business" (I.vii.31), he declares to her, since the man, the "head" of his wife, according to the preachers and moralists, should make the important decisions for the family.

However, Lady Macbeth is no longer, if she ever was, a meek submissive wife. She fiercely attacks his manhood: "Art thou afeared . . . Wouldst thou . . . live a coward in thine own esteem" (39, 43). Macbeth, already backpedaling from this ferocious attack, protests, "I dare do all that may become a man; / Who dares {do} more is none" (46–47). Exactly! Under Lady Macbeth's merciless prodding, he ultimately dares do more, and thereby unmans himself, turns himself into a monster. But what is a man is a matter of interpretation, according to his now tigerish wife. Then, she says, he was not a man but a "beast" when he first broached the subject of becoming king. No, she argues, he is less than a man now and will truly become a man only when he becomes king: "And to be more than what you were," she continues, "you would / Be so much *more* the man" (50–51, emphasis added). The parallel of that argument with the satanic deception of Eve in the Genesis account is striking—"Eat this," Satan says in effect, "and you will become *more* than you were; you will be like God." Macbeth has one last weak defense: "If we should fail?" (59). Lady Macbeth has won, and she knows it, but just to be sure, she viciously strikes once more at his manhood: "But screw your courage to the sticking place, / And we'll not fail" (60–61). So mannish does she seem, so much more the "man," on her terms, than he is, that Macbeth yields himself to her domination with the admiring exclamation, "Bring forth men-children only! / For thy undaunted mettle should compose / Nothing but males" (72-73). Although short in duration, the labor to unman Macbeth has been intense, and, although only the audience sees it, he is, at the end of this scene, already less of a man than he was when it began.

Shakespeare demonstrates how yielding to evil unmans Macbeth and turns him, little by little, into a monster. In the beginning, Macbeth is the victim of Machiavellian deceit, but he gradually becomes hardened into a conscienceless deceiver and tyrant; bitten and infected by Machiavellian evil, he finally becomes such a monster himself. The process makes exciting and even satisfying drama because it is not actually happening to oneself, but the horror of seeing a good man become a monster is far more terrifying than to see a born monster succeed as well as Richard III does until his death in the Battle of Bosworth Field. Macbeth must labor to overcome other obstacles standing between him as a good man and his ultimate monstrous condition. The shocking vision of the dagger pointing toward Duncan could have been a deterrent, but with utter dread, he allows himself to interpret it as marshalling him to the act. Suddenly, the dagger runs with "gouts" or streams of blood. That flowing blood, horrifying as it is, should have turned him back, yet he fearfully but doggedly presses on. The bell startles and yet "invites" him to stop, to go now to get the drink ready for him, but he drives himself forward: "Hear it not, Duncan, for it is a knell, / That summons thee to heaven or to hell" (II.i.63–64). There is no adequate textual justification for doing so, but because of the psychological horror of this last moment of decision, some have changed the line to have Macbeth say, "Hear it not, Duncan, for it is a knell, / That summons thee to heaven, *me* to hell."

"If it were done, when 'tis done" (I.vii.1), Macbeth reasons with himself earlier, but that is just the point that Shakespeare makes. Evil that turns good people into monsters is not finished when the evil deed is done; it has only begun. Macbeth returns from the murder of Duncan with white face and red hands, jumping with terror at every slight sound. When one of Duncan's party sleepily murmured "God bless us!" another said, "Amen!" but Macbeth found himself unable to utter "Amen." "But wherefore could I not pronounce 'Amen'?" he plaintively asks his wife, almost like a small boy asking his mother; "I had most need of blessing, and 'Amen' / Stuck in my throat" (II.ii.24–26, 28–30). Moreover, the mind of Macbeth, one of a good man who has with great effort forced himself to do something utterly repugnant to his nature, hears a voice, just as he murders his kinsman Duncan: "Sleep no more! / Macbeth does murther sleep" (32–33). Macbeth realizes he shall know the deep, restful sleep of the innocent no more. Only a good man who now knows something of the consequences of wrongdoing would have such a thought, or of his next one—that all the waters of the oceans cannot wash the blood from his hands, for in a moral universe, the universe of good people, the blood of guilt would sooner turn the waters of the world's oceans red than be washed clean by them. And then, in what is surely one of the most dramatic stage notes in Shakespeare, Macbeth hears a "knock *within*," suggesting that he hears his own telltale heart, so that he exclaims with a voice choked with fear, "Whence is that knocking?" (54, emphasis added). There is a real knocking, but it is a knock without, at the south entry. Lady Macbeth, already far more hardened to evil than her husband, utters one of the greatest understatements of all literature: "A little water clears us of this deed" (64). Evil is not done when it is done, Shakespeare clearly demonstrates in this play about a good man with great effort making himself into a monster, and even Lady Macbeth, who invoked evil spirits to unsex her, discovers that a little water will not clear them, not even her, of this deed.

The insistent knocking at the south gate finally awakens the drunken porter, and Shakespeare's matured artistry enables him to present successfully and simultaneously both comic relief and serious thematic advancement. In the opening thirty-five lines of this scene, "equivocate" or "equivocator" appears five times. Perhaps no word more succinctly summarizes the theme of this play than "equivocation," the doublespeak of evil. The word achieved great notoriety during the proceedings

against those charged with the Gunpowder Plot. Few events so completely outraged the nation. The indictment against the conspirators
rings repeatedly with "traitor(s)," often "false traitors"—seven times;
"treason(s)," often "horrible treasons"—fourteen times; "traitorous"—
sixteen times; and the favorite word most frequently ding-donging
throughout, "traitorously"—thirty-three times. The case for the prosecution, recorded in *A trve and perfect relation of the whole proceedings
against the late most barbarous Traitors*, articulates the core concern: "Their
Dissimulation appeareth out of the doctrine of Equivocation" (T 2,
recto). The prosecution speaker explains:

And whereas the *Jesuits* ask why we convict and condemn them not for heresy;
it is for that they will equivocate, and so cannot that way be tried or judged
according to their words. Now for the antiquity of Equivocation, it is indeed
very old, within little more than 300.years after Christ, used by *Arius* the heretic,
who having in general Council been condemned, and then by the commandment
of *Constantine* the Emperor sent into Exile, was by the said Emperor upon instant
intercession for him, and promise of his future conformity to the *Nicene* faith,
recalled again: who returning home, and having before craftily set down in
writing his heretical belief, and put it into his bosom, when he came into the
presence of the Emperor, and had the *Nicene* faith propounded unto him, and
was thereupon asked, whether he then did indeed, and so constantly would hold
that faith; he (clapping his hand upon his bosom where the paper of his heresy
lay) meaning fraudulently (by the way of Equivocation) that faith of his own,
which he had written and carried in his bosom. For these *Jesuits*, they indeed
make no vow of speaking truth, and yet even this Equivocating, and lying is a
kind of unchastity. (T 2, recto and verso)

The speaker now applies this to the actual charge against Francis
Tresham, who when so ill as about to die—as indeed he did before
the trial ended—swore on his deathbed that he had not seen Henry
Garnet, the superior of the Jesuits in England and the leading figure in
the trial, for sixteen years. When Garnet had been presented irrefutable
evidence that he and Tresham had met frequently over the last two years
and many times before that and when Garnet was asked about Tresham's
sworn deathbed testimony, Garnet "answered only this, I think he meant
to Equivocate" (T 3, verso). As he stood at the foot of the ladder leading
to his gallows, Garnet was asked if he knew anything further of danger
to the King or State. He replied, "It is no time now to Equivocate: how
it [that is, equivocation] was lawful, and when, he had showed his mind
elsewhere. But saith he, I do not now Equivocate, and more than I have
confessed, I do not know" (Fff 3, recto).

Macbeth becomes simultaneously unmanned and a monster, as a
victim of equivocation, the chief satanic weapon used against Adam

and Eve, and now against Macbeth. The equivocal doublespeak of the Witches leads him to believe that he can become king as easily and as effortlessly as he became the Thane of Cawdor. He learns that he must work hard to become a monster, but he succeeds only too well. He has Banquo murdered; he seeks to murder Macduff and, frustrated in that, monstrously has Macduff's innocent family slaughtered; he lays waste right and left until the whole country is terrified of him. When his wife commits suicide, he responds to the statement, "The Queen, my lord, is dead," with a petulant, "She should have died hereafter," and he follows that with one of the most shudderingly nihilistic utterances in human language, revealing an inner being no longer animated by a sensitive conscience but lifeless and dead. Seeking reassurance from the Witches, he receives what he thinks is the promise of total invincibility, that "none of woman born / Shall harm Macbeth" (IV.i.80–81). Yet, when he learns that Macduff was not normally born, but "untimely ripp'd" from his mother's womb, Macbeth at last realizes what an utter dupe of equivocation he has been: "And be these juggling [deceiving by conjuring or cheating through deception] fiends no more believ'd, / That palter [babble confusingly] with us in a *double sense*, / That keep the word of promise to our ear, / And break it to our hope" (V.viii.19–22, emphasis added).

Shakespeare presents the spectacle of family member killing off family member in the savage struggle for power, often to the great harm of the entire nation. Throughout the history plays he warns his thinking audience of what happens when the pursuit of power among various contenders for the throne seek self-aggrandizement, regardless of consequences. Even the justification of best man versus divine right cannot save one from the ravages of guilt, when, as Shakespeare's primary source, Holinshed, observes, "consaquinity . . . ought to have moved them like lambs to have loved each other" (2: 869). And Shakespeare portrays two Machiavellian monsters, a born one who can teach even the murderous Machiavel himself a few things, and one who, as a victim of dissimulation or equivocation, the primary tool of Machiavellians, including that original one, the devil himself, makes himself into a monster. The pursuit of power plunges the family, both microcosmic and macrocosmic, into hell.

7

From Sibling Rivalry to Education and a Suggested Solution for Family Conflict: *As You Like It* and *The Tempest*

According to the Judeo-Christian tradition, family conflict arising from sibling rivalry began with the first human family. Regardless of culture, possibly every human family with more than one child has experienced strife between or among siblings. Among the landed classes in England during and for a considerable period after Shakespeare's lifetime, primogeniture heaped most of the family's wealth upon the eldest son, leaving the younger brothers and sisters virtually disinherited. Inevitably, the natural rivalry among siblings heightened into serious conflicts in some instances and, at the least, into considerable ill feeling among many younger siblings toward the elder brother. However, Shakespeare is not unaware of the fact that the "Cain syndrome" meant that the elder brother envied, to the point of hating, the younger brother. Often, the most that younger brothers could hope for was an education—to become a minister in the church, or a schoolteacher while waiting for a ministerial opening, or a lawyer with prospects, perhaps, of some government appointment. Usually, the most the sisters could hope for was a marriage portion or minimal support in the elder brother's home during spinsterhood. However, even the sisters could expect to receive some education, primarily from their mothers, for the Christian humanists so emphasized education that only the lowest classes were seriously neglected educationally—and even they tended to be given enough to participate in the religious life of the nation.

As the entire nation became more sophisticated and as enclosures forced people out of the country and into increasingly crowded and competitive life in cities, among many of the educated who knew of the earlier pastoral and chivalric traditions emerged literary articulations of nostalgia for ideals of the past. The flood of pastoral literature toward the end of the sixteenth century continued into the next, and one might consider Milton's *Paradise Lost* the last magnificent pastoral of the English Renaissance. Inescapably, explicit in some of the pastorals and implicit in most was the question of the relationship between Nature and Nurture or Nature and Art. Shakespeare, too, demonstrates interest in the conflict between the natural and the artificial, between the blessings of education rightly used and its absurdities when not, between the virtues of the country and the values of the court. Finally, after presenting family upon family in conflict within, often seriously disrupting the larger family without, Shakespeare suggests, despite the tempestuous struggle perhaps necessary to achieve it, a solution to family strife.

SIBLING RIVALRY: A TWO-WAY CONFLICT

In both *As You Like It* and *The Tempest*, Shakespeare portrays conflicts between younger brothers and their older brothers. In the former, Duke Senior has lost his dukedom to his younger brother, Duke Frederick; in the latter, Antonio has usurped the dukedom of his older brother, Prospero. These plays have many realistic features, but *The Tempest* is a romance, and *As You Like It* contains elements of romance. Although the conflict between brothers in Shakespeare's day was doubtless quite real, the manifestation of that conflict in usurpation was a conventional literary device. Nevertheless, the conflict between brothers takes on realistic proportions in both plays. The intensity of feeling on the part of younger brothers about the unfairness of a system that tended to give all the family wealth to the eldest brother may be sensed by the fact that some fifty to sixty years after Shakespeare wrote these plays, the conflict was still unresolved.

In 1655, in an effort to get Parliament to pass laws giving more favorable inheritance treatment to younger brothers, one author with the pseudonym of Champianus Northonus, wrote *The younger Brothers Advocate: Or a line or two for Younger Brothers*. He exhorts younger brothers:

In which design let us not be discouraged, nor discountenanced, nothwithstanding, our elder brothers are advanced in power and authority above us, but let us be rather animated that our cause is just, and our determiners we hope not unjust, we shall not be unreasonable, let us not despair, for greater things have been effected: let younger brothers likewise consider, the misery, the disesteem, this use, this vast difference bringeth on them, the Elder enjoying large possessions, the younger having not sufficient maintenance, the Elder gentlemen, the Younger beggars, as if they were bastards, and no sons, servants and no children, this is so usually practised, that the very name of a younger brother is a word of contempt, and an expression of want and slender means, and amongst other Nations reckoned as one of the poor companies, some commiserating their poor condition and maintenance, that the Elder and Younger being brethren by birth of so near relation, of the same flesh and blood, should be so severed, so disjoined, and so far off in fortunes; some again deriding at the ill policy of our Kingdom, and carelessness of some Parents in bringing them up as their children, but not maintaining them as their sons, in giving them a generous breeding, but leaving them a slender allowance for the continuance of it, dealing with them as *Pharaoh* dealt with the children of *Israel*, that would have them make brick, but would give them no straw, that would have them Gentlemen, but will give them little or nothing for the support and maintenance of it. (3–4)

The same writer declares that younger brothers are so denied lawful ways to maintain themselves according to their breeding that they turn to shameful means, that "many are driven to beg, cheat, steal, and many times hanged for theft; then what can be more ignominious, more disgraceful to the Family, the sons discredit must needs be the fathers disgrace, and what can be more offensive to the quietness of a nation" (4–5). The conflict, he declares, is intense within the microcosmic family but spills out into the larger macrocosmic family as well. He reasons that "there is a priority, a precedency of place, a civil respect due to the Elder from the younger; And before the Law, a blessing and special privilege and prerogative annexed to their Birth," but he emphatically denies their right "to detain all the inheritance from the younger (much less ought they now to do so)" (10). He admits that some elder brothers have been generous with their younger brothers, but he unqualifiedly declares that "examples in that kind are rare, generally this Sanctuary proveth but a weak privilege, a slender refuge, feeding them like a bird in a Cage; and too often making them by their unnatural imperiousness, to live in an uncomfortable condition, most unlike their own brethren" (12). Moreover, he asserts, "The younger brothers idleness arising more for want of means and due Education, which being rectified, they cannot, they will not be idle; let not their sufferings be counted a fault, however their idleness may be prevented at first by the discretion and policy of Parents" (13).

Not only are younger brothers unfairly treated in the division of the inheritance, but Shakespeare suggests that the eldest brother sometimes cheats and abuses a younger brother as well. *As You Like It* opens with Orlando complaining of the treatment he receives from his eldest brother, Oliver. The thousand crowns left for Orlando's education by his father Oliver has kept, permitting the middle brother, Jaques, to be educated but denying Orlando even that much of his rightful patrimony. "For my part," Orlando complains, "he keeps me rustically at home, or (to speak more properly) stays me [makes me stay] here at home unkept [untended or uncared for]" (I.i.7–9). Orlando charges that he is no more than a stalled ox, that even Oliver's horses not only are better fed and cared for but are also educated, "taught their manage," a blessing utterly denied to him. The matter of education is a central one in both *As You Like It* and *The Tempest*, and Orlando complains bitterly of being denied a proper education and of the detrimental effects of the wrong kind of education to which he is subjected: "He lets me feed with his hinds [peasants], bars me the place of a brother, and as much as in him lies, mines [destroys] my gentility with my education" (19–21).

When Oliver enters, the emotional conflict between these two brothers soon bursts open into a physical one. Oliver rebukingly asks Orlando, "Now, sir, what make you here [that is, what have you to do here]?" Orlando replies with a deliberate use of another meaning for "make": "Nothing. I am not taught to make any thing" (29, 30). He is even denied as much of an education as a shoemaker's apprentice receives. Since Orlando uses "make" in the sense of "create" or "beget," Oliver uses its antonym, "mar." Oliver asks, sarcastically, "What mar you then, sir?" Again, Orlando complains of the idleness thrust upon him by denying him proper education, "I am helping you to mar that which God made, a poor unworthy brother of yours, with idleness" (31–34). This evil and destructive idleness, Orlando makes clear, does not result from his father's total neglect, for his father had left a thousand crowns "to breed me well," for his upbringing, his nurture, his education. When Oliver seeks to dismiss him with further sarcasm, Orlando protests, "Shall I keep your hogs and eat husks with them? What prodigal portion have I spent," obviously referring to the biblical parable of the prodigal son, "that I should come to such penury?" (37–39). Oliver now seeks to stand on ceremony, asking questions that implicitly accuse Orlando of lack of respect towards his elder, "Know you where you are, sir? . . . Know you before whom, sir?" (40, 42). Orlando replies, "The courtesy of nations allows you my better, in that you are the first born, but the same tradition takes not away my blood, were there twenty brothers betwixt us" (46–49). No longer able to restrain his own animosity, Oliver strikes Orlando, and Orlando counters by collaring Oliver. Sibling rivalry in this family, the sense of injustice felt by the younger toward the older and the hatred of the older toward the younger, has advanced from prolonged heated emotional conflict to actual physical violence.

This sort of sibling rivalry was apparently intense in Shakespeare's day, and the emotional energy generated by such conflict was by no means dissipated even by 1671 when another would-be champion for the rights of younger brothers writes, using simply the initials "F. A.," *The Yovnger Brother His Apologie*:

For some Elder Brothers are found to spend more in a year idly, then would prefer or maintain a whole Family Nobly: and to suffer their Brothers and Sisters to shift, which as these Times shape, is oftentimes to live either lewdly or most miserably: being forced either to forget their good Education, or to lay aside all Badges of Gentry; who otherwise with some reasonable helps, might do God, their Country, and Family much Honor. (20, original italicized)

The heat of the indignation felt by this writer emerges in several places in his work, despite his articulated desire to be reasonable and relatively low-keyed:

For who sees not, in these our Times, many unbridled youths [he is speaking specifically of elder brothers] so violently carried away with the humor of spending, that they neglect Brother and Sister; yea, bring to extreme misery their Natural Mothers after their Father's Death, by their unthriftiness. What help for this hath Law left unto us? No means to bridle these unruly Colts, if they become Heirs according to the custom of our Time? No truly. For some starting-hole will be found, to untie the Knot which a Father's care once tied. How then? Must many a hopeful and welldeserving Brother and Sister, be left to the Mercy of this Whirlwind? (15–16)

The conflict between Oliver and Orlando becomes more vicious. It is a two-way conflict, both of the younger toward the elder and of the older toward the younger. Not only does Orlando resent his mistreatment at Oliver's hands, but Oliver himself is deeply immersed in the Cain syndrome—the envy of the older brother toward his younger, as Cain was jealous of Abel. Oliver tells Charles, the wrastler, "I had as lief [I should as much like] thou didst break his neck as his finger" (146–147). To stimulate Charles to his most aggressive wrestling against Orlando, Oliver lies that Orlando will try to poison or otherwise treacherously kill Charles. The envy Oliver feels toward Orlando closely parallels that of Cain toward Abel. Oliver says of Orlando, "I hope I shall see an end of him; for my soul (yet I know not why) hates nothing more than he. Yet he's gentle, never school'd and yet learned, full of noble device [manner of thinking], of all sorts enchantingly belov'd, and indeed so much in the heart of the world, and especially of my own people, who best know him, that I am altogether mispris'd [undervalued]" (164-172). He hates Orlando not because Orlando has done wrong but because he has always acted so honorably that he is approved by all who know him, and, by contrast, Oliver feels undervalued to the point of feeling disapproved.

This hatred without cause has theological overtones, the mystery of iniquity, reminding one not only of Cain's envy toward Abel but also of what Jesus said, "They hated me without a cause" (John 15:25). And just as the envious enemies of Christ decided to kill him, Oliver plans to murder Orlando after the latter's victory over Charles. "Your brother," Adam warns Orlando,

> Hath heard your praises, and this night he means
> To burn the lodging where you lie,
> And you within it. If he fail of that,
> He will have other means to cut you off;
> I overheard him, and his practices [strategems or schemes].
> This is no place, this house is now a butchery [slaughter-house];
> Abhor it, fear it, do not enter it. (II.iii.19–28)

Shakespeare does not merely settle for the sibling rivalry most widely felt in his day, that of the younger brother feeling unfairly treated by the elder, but—picking up on the envy of Cain toward Abel and of the elder brother toward the prodigal younger son and of darkness toward light, as expressed in the hatred of Christ without cause—he complicates the sibling rivalry in *As You Like It* with the elder brother becoming a murderer of the younger, in intent if not in actuality.

EDUCATION: MORE THAN AN ALTERNATIVE

During the Tudor and Stuart eras, education was the usual alternative provided the younger brother to enable him to make his own way in the world. However, during the same periods, the enthusiasm of the Christian humanists for education began to make education more than merely an alternative for younger sons. Education, they declared, was central to the formation of character and so was of utmost importance to the entire commonwealth. The impact of Juan Luis Vives, the Spanish humanist, and most especially that of the great Dutch humanist, Desiderius Erasmus, upon the development of education in England during the sixteenth century is almost beyond measure. Moreover, leading English humanists—like John Colet, who founded and shaped St. Paul's very much along the lines suggested by Erasmus; William Lily, appointed the first high master of St. Paul's; Sir Thomas More, whose *Utopia* was written under the influence of Erasmus, and many others—were, like Erasmus himself, profoundly Christian and yet dedicated to the importance and value of education as a chief means of shaping human character and preparing persons for important service in this world as the best stewardship to give an account of in the next. Education before the Renaissance was entirely in the hands of the church, and its purpose, like all of life, was to prepare souls for the afterlife. Christian humanists certainly did not denigrate the importance of the afterlife, but they shared some views with the more ardent spokesmen for the

Reformation—for example, that all callings were sacred, not simply the call to become a minister in the church. They opposed the supremacy of Aquinas and, especially in the case of Erasmus, that of Duns Scotus in dominating the theological thinking of the church. They strongly recommended, instead, a return to a reading of the Bible, preferably in the original languages, particularly the writings of Paul, and they much preferred Augustine over Aquinas. They abhorred the educational methods of Scholasticism, and they introduced literary studies as also having great merit in preparing a person to serve God and sovereign in this life as most compatible with preparation for the next. The kind of education they advocated would primarily develop a noble and virtuous person who had achieved an authentic inner nobility through the liberal arts that was far superior to a mere external nobility represented on escutcheons by coats of arms.

Education of the sort that Shakespeare himself would have received began at the age of five in a "petty" school. There the child began to learn the ABCs, probably from a hornbook, then the Catechism, and progressed to the primer. Much of this had to do with the child's religious training as well as the beginning of reading and writing. Sir Thomas Elyot comments on beginning a child's education at such an early age:

Some old authors hold opinion, that before the age of seven years, a child should not be instructed in letters, but those writers were either greeks or latins: among whom all doctrine and sciences were in their maternal tongues, by reason wherof they saved all that long time, which at this days is spent in understanding perfectly the greek or latin. Wherefore it requireth now a longer time to the understanding of both. Therfore that infelicity of our time and country compelleth us to encroach somewhat upon the years of children. (15, recto)

The chief activity, all agreed, was ultimately to learn Latin, primarily, and, in many of the grammar schools, also Greek. Elyot urges that each nobleman's son

in his infancy, have with him continually, only such, as may accustom him by little and little to speak pure and elegant latin. Semblably the nurses and other women about him, if it be possible, to do the same: or at the least way, that they speak none english, but that, which is clean, polite perfectly, and articulately pronounced, omitting no letter or syllable, as foolish women often times do of a wantonness. (16, verso)

Latin was considered a living language, and the fluent speaking and writing of Latin was as important as the reading of it.

Since the study of Latin—and in some schools Greek, and in still others even some Hebrew as well as Latin and Greek—was the basic activity, the schools were correctly called grammar schools. The normal age for entering grammar school was seven. The humanists wanted education to be as pleasant as possible, and, above all, they wanted the students to read for the sake of developing moral virtues. Elyot says,

After that the child hath been pleasantly trained and induced to know the parts of speech, and can separate one of them from another, in his own language, It shall then be time, that his tutor or governor do make diligent search for such a master: as is excellently learned both in greek and latin, and therewithal is of sober and virtuous disposition, specially chaste of living, and of much affability and patience: lest by any unclean example the tender mind of the child may be infected, hard afterwards to be recovered. (21, recto)

Since virtue was the chief end of education, certainly the master himself must exemplify the virtuous life.

Both Elyot and Roger Ascham urge that the study of grammar not be an end in itself, as it too frequently was both before and during their time, but always focused upon the goal of reading the best authors. Elyot explains:

Grammar, being but an introduction to the understanding of authors, if it be made too long or exquisite to the learner, it in a manner mortifieth his courage: And by that time he cometh to the most sweet and pleasant reading of old authors, the sparks of fervent desire of learning is extinct, with the burden of grammar, like as a little fire is soon quenched with a great heap of small sticks: so that it can never come to the principal logs, where it should long burn in a great pleasant fire. (25, verso)

He cites the "sweetness and fruit" Alexander found in reading Homer, so much that he kept a copy of Homer under his pillow and often awakened himself to read more of Homer during the night, for from reading Homer "he gathered courage and strength against his enemies, wisdom and eloquence for consultations and persuasions to his people and army" (26, verso). Clearly, the lessons learned from the classical writers were to be applied to activities in this life.

The reading of classical authors would be both practical and pleasant, an unceasing delight, Elyot reasons, and equally edifying in virtue. A child could learn from Virgil's Georgics "divers grains, herbs, and flowers, that be there described, that reading therein, it seemeth to a man to be in a delectable garden or paradise" (28, recto). A child could learn about horses, very practical things about their breeding and keep.

A child could learn about hunting, wrestling, running, and other exercises. A child would learn to "abhor tyranny, fraud, and avarice, when he doth see the pains of duke Theseus, Sisiphus, and such other, tormented for their dissolute and vicious living" (28, recto). Then, in contrast, "How glad soon after shall he be, when he shall behold the pleasant fields of Elisius, the souls of noble princes and captains, which for their virtue and labors, in advancing the public weals of their countries, do live eternally in pleasure inexplicable?" (28, recto). The study of Demosthenes and Tully would greatly benefit the child—"Of which two orators may be attained, not only eloquence excellent and perfect, but also precepts of wisdom and gentle manners: with most commodious examples of noble virtues and policy" (31, recto). Elyot gives reasons, with examples, why the study of history and cosmography are valuable and practically useful for those who are to fill leadership roles in the commonwealth. When the youth has reached the age of seventeen and his courage is "bridled with reasons," he is ready to study philosophy. Elyot recommends Aristotle's *Ethica Nicomachea* and Cicero's *De officiis*, but he especially urges the reading of Plato:

Lord god, what incomparable sweetness of words and matter shall he find in the said works of Plato and Cicero, wherein is joined gravity with delectation, excellent wisdom with divine eloquence, absolute virtue with pleasure incredible, and every place is so enforced with profitable counsel, joined with honesty, that those three books be almost sufficient to make a perfect and excellent governor. (35, recto)

One should not conclude that the ideas of Elyot and Ascham and the example of St. Paul's were universally followed by all the grammar schools in England. Far from it. However, the influence of the humanists became pervasive, and ultimately, in one form or another, the curriculum and texts recommended and chosen by Erasmus pretty much prevailed in most of the grammar schools, even though some of the teachers no doubt deserved the fun-poking Shakespeare gives them in his depiction of Holofernes in *Love's Labor's Lost* and of Sir Hugh Evans in *The Merry Wives of Windsor*. That is, as the humanists stressed, education became such an important matter that elder sons, simply because they were to inherit wealth and enjoy a life of comparative ease, must not be denied an excellent educational experience. Indeed, a major thrust of Elyot's work is that no longer should education be left only for those who have to get an education in order to advance themselves but be neglected by those whose inheritances assure them of lives of ease. Elyot argues that noblemen must lead the way. "And it is not a reproach to a noble man," Elyot reasons, "to instruct his own children, or at the least ways, to examine them by the way of daliance or solace, considering that the emperor Octavius Augustus, disdained not to read the works of Cicero and Virgil, to his children and nephews" (16, recto).

In fact, education became important even for girls and young ladies, although they were expected to learn at home. By modern standards, Vives is hopelessly sexist, but in the sixteenth century he was remarkable for his advocacy of the education of women. Admittedly, he recommended that a girl learn all the domestic skills of sewing and embroidery, of spinning and weaving, of cooking and household management, but he also recommended that she be taught to read and that those girls who demonstrated an aptitude in learning be allowed to gain a full education. One main reason is that education develops character and the virtuous person. Women must be virtuous. "A woman shall learn the virtues of her kind all together out of books," Vives argues in *A very frvtefvl and pleasant booke, called the Instruction of a christen woman*, and "it becometh every woman to be endued with all kind of virtue, but some be necessary for her: as all vice is shameful, and some abominable and cursed, and some virtues be for wives, some for widows, some for religious women, but I will speak of such as belong unto the whole kind of women" (I.iiii, verso). As Grafton and Jardine point out, however, women paid a price for becoming educated. Isotta Nogarola, about whom they write as an example of an educated woman humanist, was libelously accused of incestuous sexual deviancy. They observe, "When a woman becomes socially visible—visible within the power structure—Renaissance literary convention makes her a sexual predator" (41). However, it is not surprising that not only are both Rosalind and Celia in *As You Like It* capable readers, but that Rosalind in particular demonstrates remarkable rhetorical skills as well. In view of the extraordinary humanistic emphasis placed upon the value of education, it is also not surprising that education plays a prominent part in both *As You Like It* and *The Tempest*. Rosalind becomes an effective teacher, and in *The Tempest*, Prospero's chief role is that of a teacher—primarily of Miranda but also of Caliban before the ship arrives and of all after the ship's passengers reach the island.

IDEALS FROM THE PAST REALISTICALLY EXAMINED

In these two plays, Shakespeare rather realistically reexamines two sets of ideals from earlier ages: the courtly love ideal embedded in the chivalric past, and the pastoral ideal continuing from antiquity. Both sets of ideals had enjoyed a literary revival in sixteenth-century England. Petrarchan love sonnets celebrating elements of the courtly love tradition blossomed as numerous as daffodils, Edmund Spenser's *Amoretti* and Sir

Philip Sidney's *Astrophel and Stella* being but two of the more famous of the sonnet sequences, not to mention countless courtly love sonnets not fashioned into sequences. The pastoral was perhaps even more fully revived, evident in Spenser's *Shepherd's Calendar* and Sidney's *Arcadia* as only two famous examples of an extremely prolific genre. Characteristically, Shakespeare has his own ideas about such matters, and in these two plays a part of the educational process to which characters are subjected for their edification and benefit results largely from the teaching of Rosalind in the one play and of Prospero in the other.

Rosalind's role as a teacher of sorts appears in a number of minor ways apart from her assumption of that role in a major way. When Celia observes that Fortune gives some women beauty but indifferent chastity to go with it and that those she makes chaste she simultaneously makes ugly, Rosalind rather pedantically remarks, "Nay, now thou goest from Fortune's office to Nature's. Fortune reigns in gifts of the world, not in the lineaments of Nature" (I.ii.40–42). Duke Frederick, afflicted as Oliver is with the mystery of iniquity, has come to hate Rosalind not because she has done something wrong but because she has not, because "the people praise her for her virtues / And pity her for her good father's sake" (I.ii.280–281). He arbitrarily banishes her from his court, referring to her as a traitor. Rosalind displays what come to be characteristic schoolteacherly tendencies. Duke Frederick declares to her, "Let it suffice thee that I trust thee not," and Rosalind promptly retorts, "Yet your mistrust cannot make me a traitor" (I.iii.55–56). The Duke persists, "Thou art thy father's daughter, there's enough," but Rosalind, almost like a teacher correcting a child with an obvious truth, responds, "Treason is not inherited, my lord" (58, 61). She treats Jaques with similar schoolteacherliness. When he says his melancholy derives from contemplating what he has seen and experienced on his travels, Rosalind replies, "I fear you have sold your own lands to see other men's; then to have seen much, and to have nothing, is to have rich eyes and poor hands" (IV.i.22-25). Her "know yourself" exhortation to Phebe is one that schoolteachers often used: "But, mistress, know yourself, down on your knees, / And thank heaven, fasting, for a good man's love" (III.v.57–58). Rosalind does not hesitate anywhere in the play to correct others and exhort them to better behavior.

However, Rosalind's major role as teacher is her playful, yet serious, attempt to enable Orlando to understand his love and its relationship to life more realistically than his initial articulations indicate. That is a difficult task, for Rosalind herself is as utterly smitten by love as Orlando is. For both, it is love at first sight. As soon as Orlando defeats Charles in the wrestling match, Rosalind gives Orlando a chain from her own neck, apparently one of her last valuable possessions. Orlando confesses that he has turned into a tilting post, "a mere liveless block" (I.ii.251).

Rosalind, a take-charge person, or as one insightful person terms her, "a managerial woman," turns back to give Orlando a strong hint of her response to him, "Sir, you have wrastled well, and overthrown / More than your enemies" (254-255). She does not assume the teacher role until Orlando suddenly appears in the forest where she and Celia have gone as a result of the banishment of Rosalind. Orlando, like the love-struck courtier of the courtly love tradition, writes poetry to hang on the trees as he carves the bark "on every tree / The fair, the chaste, the unexpressive she" (III.ii.9–10). Both Rosalind and Celia find different samples of Orlando's "tedious" homilies of love, lines that often "had more feet than the verses would bear" (165–166). When Rosalind learns from Celia that Orlando is in the forest, that he is the one "berhyming" Rosalind's name and carving it all over the forest, she is momentarily stunned, at a loss what to do, caught as she is, dressed in masculine clothes with the assumed identity of Ganymed. Quick-witted Rosalind, however, almost immediately turns that condition to her advantage. She convinces Orlando that she can teach him how to handle his struggle in the throes of love. She offers to cure his love; Orlando admits, "I would not be cur'd, youth" (III.ii.425), but he is still willing to submit himself to her tutelage. Rosalind's impromptu solution is a stroke of brilliance. She now has reason to spend extended periods of time with Orlando, to have him call her "Rosalind" and tell of his love for "Rosalind," while, under the cover of "Ganymed," she does not have to unveil her true identity to him. She can test the nature of his love and make him think about unpleasant real features of human nature and human life to help balance the extremities of his exaggerated expressions.

How much the uneducated Orlando already knows about the courtly love conventions is unclear. Rosalind certainly knows them, and her first ploy is to measure Orlando's condition against them. Knowingly or unknowingly, he has manifested one behavior of the courtly lover, writing poetry in exaggerated praise of his beloved:

> From the east to western Inde,
> No jewel is like Rosalind.
> Her worth, being mounted on the wind,
> Through all the world bears Rosalind.
> All the pictures fairest lin'd [sketched]
> Are but black to Rosalind.
> Let no face be kept in mind
> But the fair of Rosalind. (III.ii.88–95)

This conventional courtly love behavior became so prevalent during Shakespeare's day that it often was not only patently absurd but also hollow and false, the farthest extreme from any meaningful expression of genuine love. In imitation of Petrarch, Elizabethan writers of courtly love poetry praised the beauties of their various "beloveds" in outlandish figures, extolling their eyes, their skin, their cheeks, their lips, their arms and hands, even, as Jaques says elsewhere in the play, "And then the lover, / Sighing like furnace, with a woeful ballad / Made to his mistress' eyebrow" (II.vii.147–149). Shakespeare regularly holds the courtly love conventions up to scorn as absurdly unrealistic and not true to real love. Sonnet 130 is one of his "anti-Petrarchan" protests: "My mistress' eyes are nothing like the sun; / Coral is far more red than her lips' red; / . . . And yet, by heaven, I think my love as rare [excellent or praiseworthy] / As any she belied with false compare" (1–2, 13–14). Rosalind, as a clear-thinking, level-headed Shakespearean creation, rightly wants to test the exaggerations of Orlando's protestations of love.

Her first ploy is to point out to him his lack of many other conventional "marks" of courtly lovers—a neglected beard, ungartered hose, sleeves unbuttoned, shoe untied—and still more. Some of those features of the conventional courtly lover Hamlet manifests, according to Ophelia: "his doublet all unbrac'd, / No hat upon his head, his stockins fouled, / Ungart'red, and down-gyved to his ankle, / Pale as his shirt, his knees knocking each other" (II.i.75–78). Polonius is easily convinced: "This is the very ecstasy [madness] of love" (99). One of Shakespeare's remarkable achievements is the initial portrayal of Romeo as a conventional courtly lover of another "Rosaline" only to demonstrate how shallow and false that empty obsession is in contrast to the vivid reality of his love for Juliet, whom he praises in terms as extravagant as those of the empty bombast of conventional courtly lovers, and yet Romeo's poetry has the freshness, the living power of genuine love.

And so Rosalind accuses Orlando of lacking the marks of a courtly lover. Orlando protests, "Fair youth, I would I could make thee believe I love" (III.ii.386). Rosalind cleverly responds, with an undercurrent of serious intent, "Me believe it? You may as soon make her that you love believe it, which I warrant she is apter to do than to confess she does" (387–389). Orlando exclaims, "Neither rhyme nor reason can express how much" (396, 398–399). Rosalind teases that she has cured one such lover by playing the role of the beloved and becoming so changeable in moods, so capricious, so inconstant, so shallow, so "full of smiles; for every passion something, and for no passion truly anything" that she succeeded in driving out the "mad humor of love" by driving the lover into actual "living" madness. She declares that women "are for the most part cattle of this color [domestic beasts of this sort]" (414–415). One of Rosalind's objectives with Orlando is to keep reminding him that real women are not like the absurd creatures portrayed in the exaggerated expressions of courtly lovers. In attempting to reach that objective, she fights fire with fire; she exaggerates in the opposite direction, very much the way Malcolm in *Macbeth* exaggerates his own vices to Macduff to test the genuineness of Macduff's intent. Real women, like real rulers, are not absolutely flawless.

Similarly, she seeks to balance Orlando's overstatements with realism. When he says that if Rosalind rejects him he will die, Ganymed/Rosalind reminds him of famous lovers of years past, Troilus and Leander, that neither of them actually died of love, but "Troilus had his brains dash'd out with a Grecian club" and Leander, on a "hot midsummer night . . . went forth to wash him in the Hellespont, and being taken with a cramp was drown'd" (IV.i.98, 102–104). No, Ganymed/Rosalind declares to Orlando, all "the foolish chroniclers" of the past merely lied: "But these are all lies; men have died from time to time, and worms have eaten them [with emphatic attention to realistic and anti-Petrarchan detail], but not for love" (106-108). When Ganymed/Rosalind asks Orlando how long he expects to have his Rosalind after he has married her, he replies, "For ever and a day" (145). Again, Rosalind tries to correct his extremities with extreme statements of her own, and yet there is an undercurrent of realistic truth about the behavior of many wives, whether or not Rosalind herself would actually behave that way after marriage. She responds to his "For ever and a day" with:

Say "a day," without the "ever." No, no, Orlando . . . I will be more jealous of thee than a Barbary cock-pigeon over his hen, . . . more new-fangled [obsessed with foppish love of fashionable finery] than an ape, more giddy in my desires than a monkey. I will weep for nothing, like Diana in the fountain, and I will do that when you are dispos'd to be merry. I will laugh like a hyen, and that when thou are inclin'd to sleep. (146–156)

Married life, Rosalind tries to teach him, is not unmitigated and uninterrupted bliss, even though lovers tend to think so, and one reason is that wives, and husbands too, although she does not here mention them, are flawed creatures who actually live lives far below the idealistic extremes about which lovers dream. Orlando is getting an education, and a rather serious one despite the "fun and games" spirit in which it is being conducted. Like Macduff as Malcolm sifts his real motives, since Macbeth has previously used various tricks to try to deceive Malcolm into his power, Orlando ultimately passes Rosalind's various tests, and she accepts his love as genuine, of greater worth than his poor poetry would suggest.

Although the courtly love elements in *The Tempest* are fewer than in *As You Like It*, once more the teacher, Prospero, must sift the deeper motives of the professed love, and again an educational process takes place.

Like that of Orlando and Rosalind, the love of Ferdinand and Miranda happens at first sight. First-sight love is itself a courtly love convention, love striking irresistibly when the beauty of the beloved enters the eyes and smites the heart. The moment Miranda sees Ferdinand, he seems to her something out of this world: "What, is't a spirit? . . . I might call him / A thing divine, for nothing natural / I ever saw so noble" (I.ii.410, 418–419). Similarly, Ferdinand exclaims upon his first sight of Miranda, "Most sure, the goddess / On whom these airs attend!" (422–423). Prospero wants them to fall in love with each other, but he does not want them to plunge into the depths of their emotional love too quickly and proceed too easily: "They are both in eithers pow'rs; but this swift business / I must uneasy make, lest too light winning / Make the prize light" (451–453). Indeed, the idea that love too easily won breeds contempt is another courtly love concept. Prospero puts Ferdinand, the royal prince of Naples, to the menial task of moving "Some thousand of these logs," but Ferdinand, watched over by his beloved Miranda, who "Weeps when she sees me work," is so buoyed up by love that her presence "makes my labors pleasures" (III.i.10, 12, 7).

When Ferdinand has sufficiently passed the hard-work test, he still must be educated further about a most important matter. Prospero explains, "All thy vexations / Were but my trials of thy love, and thou / Hast strangely [extraordinarily successfully] stood the test" (IV.-i.5–6). Prospero will now allow Ferdinand to stop work, and he permits them to consider themselves engaged to be married, but he strictly warns:

> But
> If thou dost break her virgin-knot before
> All sanctimonious [holy, that is, those expressing sanctity] ceremonies may
> With full and holy rite be minist'red,
> No sweet aspersion [sprinkling of dew or rain] shall the heavens let fall
> To make this contract grow; but barren hate,
> Sour-eye'd disdain, and discord shall bestrew
> The union of your bed with weeds [not the flowers usually used] so loathly
> That you shall hate it both. (14–23)

Nowadays, premarital sex occurs so commonly that young people might consider Prospero an old fuddy-duddy, but there is a serious note of reality running through what he says. The fact that Shakespeare's first child, Suzanna, was born only six months into the marriage of the eighteen-year-old Shakespeare and his twenty-six-year-old wife, Anne Hathaway Shakespeare, might or might not have something to do with the talk about "Sour-eye'd disdain, and discord . . . [and] barren hate." Many present-day young people who simply cannot tolerate the thought of deferred gratification of any sort discover that those indulged gratifications often result in extremely destructive consequences. The courtly love tradition against which Shakespeare rather regularly reacts negatively had two distinct streams. One was the pure stream of the sort found in Dante's *Vita Nuova* and even, in a sense, in the guidance Beatrice gives the traveller in the "Paradise" section of *The Divine Comedy* resulting in his beatific vision of God. One finds the pure strain argued for in *The Courtier*. However, by far the wider, longer, and deeper stream was the muddy one of lust indulged. Certainly, in Ovid's *Ars Amatoria* from which this stream of courtly love derives, love is furtive because illegitimate and has as its primary goal the physical satisfaction of that passion. The stories of courtly lovers who indulged in illicit sex are too numerous to list, but Chaucer's *Troilus and Criseyde*, and the medieval stories about Tristan and Isolde and about Lancelot and Guinevere are but three sets of famous lovers who indulged in sexual passion.

Prospero extracts a vow from Ferdinand to protect Miranda's virginity until their marriage has been fully and properly solemnized. Ferdinand declares:

> . . . As I hope
> For quiet days, fair issue, and long life,
> With such love as 'tis now, the murkiest den,
> The most opportune place, the strong'st suggestion
> Our worser genius can, shall never melt
> Mine honor into lust, to take away
> The edge of that day's celebration,
> When I shall think or Phoebus' steeds are founder'd
> Or Night keeps chain'd below. (IV.i.23–31)

Ferdinand declares his conviction that premarital sex is dishonorable and that gratification rightly deferred until that time when sex can indeed be a sacrament becomes immeasurably intensified. Even though Ferdinand has just asserted that the "most opportune place" and strongest urgings of their "worser genius" cannot "melt . . . honor into lust," Prospero realistically warns, "do not give dalliance [wanton play or, in modern terms, "making out"] / Too much the rein. The strong-est oaths are straw / To th' fire i' th' blood. Be more abstenious, / Or else good night your vow!" (51–54). Prospero's teaching of Ferdinand is both direct and indirect.

After straightforward warnings, Prospero now provides both Ferdinand and Miranda audio-visual aids to reinforce the lessons with which he seeks to educate them about marriage. He has Ariel call up Iris, Ceres, and Juno to teach them further. Ceres, the goddess of fecundity, especially in agriculture, is invited by Iris, the rainbow goddess and messenger of Juno, "A contract of true love to celebrate, / And some donation freely to estate [to settle a possession] / On the bless'd lovers" (IV.i.84–86). Ceres considers Venus and Cupid to be her enemies, but Iris assures her, "Here *thought* they to have done / Some wanton charm upon this man and maid, / Whose vows are, that no bed-right shall be paid / Till Hymen's torch be lighted [the wedding properly completed]; but in vain" (94–97, emphasis added). Moreover, Juno promises, "Honor, riches," long life, and "Hourly joys" ever increasing upon the two for their faithful keeping of their marriage vows, while Ceres promises abundant harvests and that "Scarcity and want shall shun you" because they remain true to each other and free from infection by "Mar's hot minion," for Venus was Mar's lustful mistress, and "Her waspish-headed [irritable] son," for Cupid often did spiteful things, encouraging destructive lechery. In the midst of all the fun of both these plays, the self-appointed educators, Rosalind and Prospero, both teach virtue, and their teaching has a strongly serious strain running through it.

Neither Prospero nor Rosalind has much to say directly in teaching realistic truths to balance the extremes of the pastoral ideals. Nevertheless, both plays establish realistic forces to counterbalance the ideals usually portrayed in pastorals. One way Shakespeare does this is to examine the usual contest between the natural and the artificial, Nature versus Nurture, in terms of education wrongly as well as rightly used. In the nostalgia for the simple, uncluttered life of unlettered and wholesomely virtuous shepherds singing innocent songs to wholly virtuous brown-limbed maidens, some pastorals portrayed a never-never world, a kind of golden age, where all of nature was beneficent and all humans dwelt in sinless bliss. The crowded filth of cities, together with the poverty and the harsh and often viciously competitive struggle for survival in them, made such pastorals as the idyls of Theocritus and the eclogues of Virgil not only pleasant pastimes but models for numerous literary longings for a return to a golden age.

London had become the collecting place for persons dislocated by enclosures and other economic upheavals. By the end of the sixteenth century, London had an estimated 12,000 beggars, and, in his *Notable Discovery of Coosnage* and other *Coony-Catching* tracts, Robert Greene wrote about the thievery and cheating that went on in the underworld of London. Interestingly, Shakespeare, whom Greene blasted as "an upstart crow, beautified with our feathers," gave special meaning to those words some eighteen years after Greene's death by borrowing heavily from the plot of Greene's romance, *Pandosto*, and tied those borrowings to delightful pastoral elements in *The Winter's Tale*. Greene attended Cambridge and completed a Master of Arts degree there in

1583; even Oxford granted him a degree, enabling him to boast himself as "Master of Arts in Both Universities." Shakespeare, of course, never had more than petty school and grammar school education which he probably took at the Kynges Newe Scole of Stratford vpon Avon, both of which T. W. Baldwin writes about extensively in his *William Shakespere's Petty School* and in his two-volume work *William Shakespeare's Small Latine & Lesse Greeke*.

In contrast to the university wits, like Greene, and especially in their eyes, Shakespeare himself was something of an uneducated bumpkin, so it is not particularly surprising that he has somewhat caustic things to say about the right and wrong uses of education, especially about those who boast a pseudo-sophistication but lack true virtue in contrast to genuine virtues evident in many unsophisticated and uneducated persons. One example of the wrong sort of education is that of Jaques whose protestations are revealed to be hypocritical, pompous posturings. Concerning Jaques' behavior, a lord reports to Duke Senior:

> Thus most invectively [railingly or abusively] he pierceth through
> The body of {the} country, city, court,
> Yea, and of this our life, swearing that we
> Are mere usurpers, tyrants, and what's worse [that is, whatever one can think of that is worse]
> To fright the animals and to kill them up
> In their assign'd and native dwelling-place. (II.i.58–63)

Jaques is the self-appointed critic and reformer of the world. He returns from his melancholy stroll through the forest crowing about his droll experience with Touchstone, the clown, the fool who accompanied Rosalind and Celia to the forest. "O worthy fool!" Jaques exclaims about Touchstone, "One that hath been a courtier," a detail one should remember about Touchstone. "O that I were a fool!" Jaques continues, for, he explains concerning his sudden ambition to become a jester:

> . . . I must have liberty
> Withal, as large a charter [freedom or license] as the wind,
> To blow on whom I please, for so fools have;
> . . . Invest me in my motley; give me leave
> To speak my mind, and I will through and through
> Cleanse the foul body of th' infected world,
> If they will patiently receive my medicine.
> (III.vii.36, 42–43, 47–49, 58–61)

Duke Senior rebukes him for his corrupt hypocrisy:

Most mischievous foul sin, in chiding sin;
For thou thyself hast been a libertine,
As sensual as the brutish sting itself,
And all th' embossed sores, and headed evils,
That thou with license of free foot hast caught,
Wouldst thou disgorge into the general world. (64–69)

Jaques has boasted of his travels, considered the crowning experience of a good education, but he epitomizes the sort of traveler to Italy that Roger Ascham denounces:

But I am afraid, that over many of our travelers into Italy, do not eschew [avoid or shun] the way to Circes Court [the enchantress in Homer's *Odyssey* who turned men into pigs]: but go, and ride, and run, and fly thither, they make great haste to come to her: they make great suit to serve her: yea, I could point out some with my finger, that never had gone out of England, but only to serve Circes in Italy. Vanity and vice, and any license to ill living in England was counted stale and rude unto them. And so, being Mules and Horses before they went, return very Swine and Asses home again: yet every where very Foxes with subtle and busy heads: and where they may, very Wolves, with cruel malicious hearts. A marvelous monster, which, for filthiness of living, for dullnes to learning himself, for wiliness in dealing with others, for malice in hurting without cause, should carry at once in one body, the belly of a Swine, the head of an Ass, the brain of a Fox, the womb of a Wolf. (26, recto)

Shakespeare sets *As You Like It* in France and *The Tempest* on an island in the Mediterranean, but like all his plays, they remain indelibly English. Jaques is one of Shakespeare's many portrayals of the Italianate Englishman who has traveled to Italy and returned corrupted by his travels, a pretentious, ostentatious libertine, more degenerate than those embodying the evils of the world against which he hypocritically inveighs. He represents one extremely wrong sort of education.

The contrast between Jaques' wrong sort of Nurture, on the one hand, and Nature, virtue uncorrupted by vile institutions, on the other, emerges in his contest of wits with uneducated Orlando. It is a contest Jaques initiates: "I thank you for your company, but, good faith, I had as lief [I should have liked as much] have been myself alone" (III.ii.253–254). Orlando quickly retorts, "And so had I; but yet for fashion sake [merely pro forma] I thank you too for your society" (255–256). When Jaques insults him, Orlando at least equals him in wit. To Jaques' "God buy you [a contraction for God be with you], let's meet as little as we can," Orlando responds, "I do desire that we may be better strangers" (257–258). Thus, untutored Orlando, quickened only by Nature, easily matches wits with one whose wrong education has soured his disposition towards others. After further exchanges, Jaques realizes that he cannot win and so seeks to join: "Will you sit down with me?" he asks Orlando, "and we two will rail against our mistress the world, and all our misery." Orlando, more virtuous than that by Nature, replies, "I will chide [rebuke or scold—the very activity in which Jaques indulges himself constantly] no breather [one who lives] in the world but myself, against whom I know most faults" (277–279, 280–281). Orlando, without Nurture, already has more of the most essential knowledge, self-knowledge, than Jaques, whose pseudo-education has only enabled him to deceive himself more fully than before. Jaques simply cannot win this contest. He tries one last lunge: "By my troth, I was seeking for a fool when I found you," he virtually snarls at Orlando, only to hear Orlando reply, "He is drown'd in the brook; look but in, and you shall see him." That Shakespeare deliberately intends for Orlando to carry away the victory in this contest is evident from his turning Jaques into the straight man who utters an obvious "set up" line, "There I shall see mine own figure." Orlando clinches the triumph: "Which I take to be either a fool or a cipher [that is, since Jaques used the term "figure," Orlando shifts away from Jaques' original meaning of form, shape, or image, to that of a number, in this case zero]" (285–290). Shakespeare is assuredly not anti-education, but he depicts in Jaques one who has been corrupted by his education and consequently falls far below the wholesomeness of unlettered Orlando. Nature wins this contest over the wrong sort of Nurture.

Touchstone also represents the wrong sort of Nurture. He is the court jester, but jesters were usually extraordinarily intelligent people. Children of the royal family often became very close to court jesters, as Hamlet says he was with Yorick—"He hath bore me on his back a thousand times . . . Here hung those lips that I have kiss'd I know not how oft" (*Hamlet*, V.i.185-186, 188–189). Touchstone, with obvious mixed feelings, accompanies Celia, who says of him, "He'll go along o'er the wide world with me" (I.iii.132). Touchstone, in the forest, makes much of the fact that he is a cultured, a nurtured, person. Jaques says Touchstone is "One that hath been a courtier," and, even though that probably means nothing more than the fact that the motley-dressed Touchstone has spent much time in the Duke's court, Touchstone himself boasts of his role as a courtier in the larger sense. He says, "I broke my sword upon a stone," out of love for Jane Smile. He reveals his detailed knowledge of the rules of dueling, or, more precisely in his case, of how a courtly coward can pretend to be a true courtier without ever having to fight a duel. He declares of that procedure, "O sir, we quarrel in print, by the book—as you have books for good manners" (V.iv.90–91). Through Touchstone Shakespeare is spoofing those who made much use of the multitude of courtesy books popular in the sixteenth century, some so detailed as to give the very words one should use in a particular situation. Touchstone not only represents the wrong sort of education but also the wrong use of the possibilities afforded by education.

Touchstone, as corrupted Nurture, has his own contests with untutored Nature, the first with Corin, a simple yet virtuous shepherd of the forest. Corin is the quintessential gentle ungentle, the true gentleman of the lower classes who has nothing that the landed gentry prizes but has genuine integrity. He politely asks how Touchstone likes "this shepherd's life" only to hear the loquacious jester puff and spout essentially rhetorical nonsense. Touchstone concludes his verbose response with, "Hast any philosophy in thee, shepherd?" (III.ii.21–22). Corin responds with simple truisms about the natural life, concluding with "that he, that hath learn'd no wit [understanding] by nature, nor art [acquired by learning in contrast to nature], may complain of good breeding [lament the lack of a good education], or comes of very dull kindred [family or hereditary genes not especially contributing to intelligence]" (28–31).

Touchstone terms Corin "a natural philosopher," but he immediately plans to put this rustic down. "Wast ever in court, shepherd?" he asks Corin, and when Corin replies, "No, truly," Touchstone begins a sophistical attack upon him. "Then thou art damn'd," he flatly declares to Corin. His intent is to confuse this good, simple man with sophistical equivocation, a constant shifting from one possible meaning for a term to another:

Why, if thou was never at court, thou never saw'st good manners [meaning accepted etiquette]; if thou never saw'st good manners, then thy manners [behavior] must be wicked [the moralistic antonym for good], and wickedness is a sin, and sin is damnation. Thou art in a parlous state [a perilous or alarmingly fearful state, a phrase often used by Puritans to warn people of impending hellfire for the damned], shepherd. (40–44)

Unawed by this display of spurious sophistication and ridiculous sophistry, Corin advances commonsensical cultural relativism: "Those that are good manners at the court are as ridiculous in the country as the behavior of the country is mockable at court" (45-48). Touchstone continues with increasingly absurd sophistry and finally resorts to name-calling: "Most shallow man! thou worm's-meat" (65). Puffing himself up like a toad trying to become the size of a cow, Touchstone exclaims, "Learn of the wise, and perpend [reflect or more precisely "look at it"]" (66–67). Corin, the true gentleman, politely gives in, "You have too courtly a wit [a phrase surely loaded with double meaning for Shakespeare in this contest, although not necessarily so for Corin] for me, I'll rest" (70).

Not satisfied with that much of an apparent win, Touchstone begins to reveal his bawdy nature, the moral corruption he has brought with him from the court into the country. He accuses Corin of being a pimp because he breeds sheep. Corin does not have to respond to this fresh absurdity because Ganymed/Rosalind enters, but Touchstone's lust, hinted at in his lasciviously corrupt view of the natural reproduction of sheep, becomes explicit in his treatment of another simple yet wholesome rustic, Audrey. He has taken her into the woods, hoping to seduce her into a fling under the bushes. He complains, "Truly, I would the gods had made thee poetical" (III.iii.15–16). Audrey does not know the term "poetical." She asks, innocently, "Is it honest [probably here meaning simply "upright" or "proper"] in deed and word? Is it a true thing?" (17–18). Touchstone begins his point, "No, truly; for the truest poetry is the most feigning [inventive or imaginative, but strongly implying "lying"]" (19–20). And when Audrey repeats Touchstone's wish in the form of a question, "Do you wish then that the gods had made me poetical?" Touchstone reveals to Shakespeare's audience, though not to simple Audrey, his lustful intent: "I do, truly; for thou swear'st to me thou art honest [pure or chaste]. Now if thou wert a poet, I might have some hope thou didst feign [here almost certainly meaning simply "lie"]" (23–27). Audrey, perhaps beginning ever so slightly to understand, asks directly, "Would you not have me honest?" (28), and Touchstone replies truthfully, "*No*" (29, emphasis added). So elaborate are Touchstone's plans for seduction that he has arranged for a bumbling country minister, Sir Oliver Martext, to meet them in the woods for a pseudo-wedding, without the benefit of which he did not think he could complete his seduction of honest Audrey. In an aside, Touchstone makes that quite clear, "for he is not like to marry me well [it is unlikely that the wedding he performs will be binding]; and not being well married, it will be a good excuse for me hereafter to leave my wife" (90–94). Probably, only because Jaques discovers himself to them and because his presence as a witness spoils Touchstone's plans, the bogus wedding does not take place. Touchstone takes Audrey away with his lust still burning, "We must be married, or we must live in bawdry" (97). Touchstone is another example of false education, of pseudo-Nurture defeated by the simple purity of Nature.

The natural intelligence and gentility of those who know only Nature, uncorrupted by the vile institutions of the court, is the stuff on which pastorals flourished. But Shakespeare balances those traditional features of the pastoral with realism in both plays. In *The Tempest*, Caliban, admittedly of very bad "kindred," the son of the evil witch Sycorax, unquestionably represents a product of Nature that is, after all, unnatural, and all the loveliness of the island has not turned him into a good creature. Even in *As You Like It*, good-natured as they are, William and Audrey and Phebe are not terribly attractive persons. They are too uncomfortably realistic to make one want to be like them. Shakespeare clearly does not expect the return to Nature to solve human conflicts and human problems, even though in both these plays the changes take place for the better in the country and not in the court. The proof that the mere return to Nature is not the permanent answer is evident in the fact that it is too simpleminded, too idealistic, and in both plays, the characters, by and large—except for the "converted" Duke Frederick, who plans to become a hermit, and the unconverted excentric Jaques, who continues his contradictions, and Caliban, who has no real place off the island—all expect to return to court.

Yet in *The Tempest*, Shakespeare portrays a different kind of problem pertaining to education—namely, education as a dead end, as an "ivory tower," as an end in itself. It is exactly Prospero's "ivory tower" absorption in education, cut off from real life, that makes Antonio's usurpation of his dukedom possible. Prospero explains to Miranda:

> And Prospero, the prime duke, being so reputed
> In dignity, and for the liberal arts
> Without a parallel; those being all my study,
> The government I cast upon my brother,
> And to my state grew stranger, being transported
> And rapt in secret studies. (I.ii.72–77)

In his complete absorption with his studies, he provided Antonio all the opportunity he needed to usurp the dukedom. Prospero further describes his preoccupation and its consequent evil effects on Antonio:

> I, thus neglecting worldy ends, all dedicated
> To closeness and the bettering of my mind
> With that which, but by being so retir'd,
> O'er-priz'd all popular rate in my false brother
> Awak'd an evil nature. (89–93)

On the island, Prospero has come to recognize the wrong-headedness of his "ivory tower" approach to education. Curiously, that is exactly the point that the Christian humanists had made all along, that education was to have significant practical application to life in this world: "This, then, is the true end of all studies, Vives affirms, 'this is the goal. Having acquired our knowledge we must turn it to usefulness, and employ it to the common good' " (Simon 120). Repeatedly, the Christian humanists insisted that "All learning is empty unless applied to use" (Simon

118). Prospero's recognition that education is not an end in itself, that it fulfills its purpose only when put to practical use for the improvement of society, is one key point Shakespeare makes about education in *The Tempest*. On the island, blessed by Nature, Prospero learns that most important lesson, applies education to valuable ends, and then lays aside the extraordinary powers of magic to return to the court wholesomely to apply the benefits of Nurture to the ruling of Milan.

A SOLUTION FOR FAMILY, AND HUMAN, CONFLICT

Shakespeare's dramatic families, almost without exception, are in deep conflict. Oliver hates, mistreats, and attempts to murder Orlando. Duke Frederick usurps the dukedom of Duke Senior and then banishes his niece, Rosalind, without any cause other than that people praise her for her virtues, resulting in Celia's going into banishment with Rosalind for friendship's sake. Antonio usurps the dukedom of Prospero and persuades Sebastian to kill, or to attempt to kill, his brother, Alonso, the King of Naples. Family conflicts set both plays in motion. Nowhere does Shakespeare come as close to suggesting a solution for family—and, by extension, human—conflict as he does in *The Tempest*.

Pastorals tended to imply or openly teach that the solution for human problems requires a return to nature, an abandonment of corrupt human institutions, but pastorals were, for the most part, escape literature in the sixteenth century, a nostalgic imaginary return to the simpler past. Probably very few, if any, took the key ideas of pastorals as a serious solution until Rousseau in the eighteenth century and, in England, from Blake on through the Romantics in the late eighteenth and early nineteenth centuries. Shakespeare, through Duke Senior, celebrates the wholesome benefits of the country, a life "more sweet / Than that of painted pomp," a life where one "Finds tongues in trees, books in the running brooks, / Sermons in stones, and good in every thing" (II.i.2–3, 16–17). Moreover, it is on the island that Prospero comes to himself and recognizes the right uses of education. However, despite the fact that almost everyone in both plays who gets out of the court and comes to the country benefits from the experience, the solution suggested by Shakespeare is more than the pastoral return-to-nature motif.

It seems a little too facile to say that *As You Like It* is a love play and therefore that love is the solution. Shakespeare's portrayal of love in *As You Like It* is too subtle and complex to permit such a solution, despite the excellent examples of love in the play. *As You Like It* presents many different kinds of love. Old Adam so loves Orlando that he is willing to give up his life's savings, thriftily put aside to sustain him in his old age, to help Orlando escape Oliver's murderous wrath, willing, the aches of age notwithstanding, to go into the wild unknown with Orlando. Orlando so loves Adam that he is willing, single-handedly, to fight an entire party of men to try to get food for Adam, and willing, weak from hunger and fatigue himself, to carry old Adam to the place of nourishment. Certainly, Jaques' cynical description of old age as being "sans everything" does not pertain when devoted love such as that of Adam and Orlando for each other prevails.

One of the most interesting examples of love is that of Celia and Rosalind for each other. The code of friendship was a noble concept extending from antiquity. The eloquent and learned Jeremy Taylor wrote, in 1657, "Fraternity is but a cognation [a relationship of persons descending from a common ancestor], but friendship is an union of souls which are confederated by more noble ligatures" (63). Taylor echoes ideas found in the classical past. Cicero says, "Now friendship is just this and nothing else: complete sympathy in all matters of importance, plus good will and affection, and I am inclined to think that with the exception of wisdom, the gods have given nothing finer to men than this" (54-55). According to the code of classical friendship, friends experience deep rapport; each is virtually the alter ego of the other. Each would willingly die for the other, and neither would hesitate to give less than life itself, provided the purpose was honorable and virtuous, for dishonorable and ignoble purposes would harm one's friend and not help. Taylor says, "He only is fit to be chosen for a friend who can give me counsel, or defend my cause, or guide me right, or relieve my need, or can and will, when I need it, do me good; only this add: into the heap of doing good, I will reckon, *loving me*, for it is a pleasure to be loved" (41). One should not be taken aback by the seeming selfishness of that statement; friends may both say that, for reciprocity is at the heart of true friendship. Cicero asserts, "For the man who keeps his eye on a true friend, keeps it, so to speak, on a model of himself. For this reason, friends are together when they are separated, they are rich when they are poor, strong when they are weak, and—a thing even harder to ex- plain—they live on after they have died . . . " (56). Yet what is unique about Shakespeare's portrayal of Celia and Rosalind is that they are women. The classical ideal of friendship was limited to men. As late as 1657, Jeremy Taylor felt it necessary to write:

But by the way, madam [writing to Mrs. Katherine Philips], you may see how much I differ from the morosity [moroseness, the peevishness] of those cynics who would not admit your sex into the Communities of noble friendship. I can- not say that women are capable of all those excellencies by which men can oblige the world . . . but a woman can . . . die for her friend as well as the bravest Ro- man knight. (72, 73–74)

Most people would say that *As You Like It* is Rosalind's play, for she is the dominant figure, the prime mover in most instances, but Celia could not be a true friend if she were not essentially equally capable. The idea of going to the forest is Celia's, and when Rosalind expresses alarm over the dangers that two beautiful young ladies would encounter, Celia has an initial solution upon which Rosalind merely elaborates. It is Celia who declares to her father, "We still have slept together, / Rose at an instant, learn'd, play'd, eat together, / And wheresoe'er we went, like Juno's swans, Still we went coupled and inseparable" (I.iii.73-76). If Duke Senior could see "good in every thing," there are modern critics who see homosexuality in everything. Unquestionably, homosexuality existed in Shakespeare's day. Lisa Jardine has argued well that boys who play girls who then assume the role of boys, as Rosalind soon does, become hermaphroditic figures, and that hermaphroditism was associated in the minds of some Elizabethans with pederasty. As MacCary says, "there is a traceable pattern among the Elizabethans, as among the fifth century Athenians, to seek 'masculine potential' in all objects of desire" (61). However, those who try to see homosexuality in the friendship of Antonio and Bassanio in *The Merchant of Venice* and in the friendship of Celia and Rosalind in *As You Like It* possibly need to refresh themselves in the tradition of the classical code of friendship. These young ladies seem clearly heterosexual. Rather, Shakespeare, without a sexist caveat such as that used by Jeremy Taylor, boldly presents two young ladies fully capable of achieving the noble status of alter-ego friendship as wholesomely as the noblest male examples one might recall, that of Damon and Pythias (more precisely Damon and Phintias), perhaps. The true love of alter-ego friends is hardly a solution for family, and human, conflict simply because the very nature of it is too restrictive. Family members could establish such a friendship, as these two cousins do, but that fact alone does not resolve family problems. In fact, in Celia's case, it resulted in division within her nuclear family; she abandons her own father to stick with Rosalind.

The "solutions" to family conflict in *As You Like It* are, on the whole, too facile to be seriously helpful. Orlando, noble person that he is, willingly risks his very life to save Oliver, even though Oliver has pursued him into the forest to kill him. That kind of love for a brother, even for one who murderously hates as Oliver does, is Christ-like, and, Oliver, moved by Orlando's sacrifice, experiences a "conversion." However, Shakespeare hardly develops that point enough for one to say that Orlando is a "Christ figure" with the solution to family conflict. The direction is right, but the development is lacking. Duke Frederick's "conversion" is too miraculous to be a meaningful part of the play. The audience learns of it only at the very end, and that by hearsay. The middle son of the de Boys family, Jaques, suddenly appears just as the quadruple marriages end to announce to all:

> Duke Frederick, hearing how that every day
> Men of great worth resorted to this forest,
> Address'd [made ready] a mighty power, which were on foot
> In his own conduct [under his own leadership], purposely to take
> His brother here, and put him to the sword;
> And to the skirts of this wild wood he came,
> When, meeting with an old religious man,
> After some question with him, was converted
> Both from his enterprise and from the world,
> His crown bequeathing to his banish'd brother,
> And all their lands restor'd to {them} again
> That were with him exil'd. (V.iv.154–165)

So astounding is the news, so utterly untrue to life as it is usually experienced, so mysterious as to what happened to that "mighty power," that one can almost see Shakespeare smile as he has Jaques de Boys add: "This to be true, / I do engage my life" (165-166). For all the many wholesome kinds of love one can find in *As You Like It*, Shakespeare does not there present any developed solution to family conflict.

In *The Tempest*, he does, and it is a solution true to human nature, one not reached without difficulty, and one that will work. One solution to family conflict is the right use of education, education that achieves practical results, education that results in virtuous behavior. Prospero from the outset is the educator, unfortunately sometimes evincing some of the worst habits of schoolteachers: inadequate reading of feedback, irritable impatience, and lack of confidence in his own educational accomplishments. He has been teaching Miranda ever since the two of them arrived on the island. Now, with his enemies within his power, the time has come for him to reveal to Miranda for the first time the story of Antonio's usurpation and their consequent arrival on the island. "The hour's now come," he announces to her, "The very minute bids thee ope thine ear, / Obey, and be attentive" (I.ii.36–38). That this is no ordinary day and not just another lesson, Miranda, who has just witnessed the wreck of a ship in the midst of a raging tempest, very well knows. Having that sort of exhortation laid upon her from the outset—to say nothing of the absolutely spellbinding nature of the story of their past in Milan, which she is hearing for the first time—would surely be sufficient to keep this bright, intelligent, wide-awake, eager girl of fifteen years totally alert and attentive every single moment, her wide-eyed gaze fixed upon her father's face. Yet Shakespeare has Prospero irritably break into his account on five different occasions to rebuke her for inattention or to exhort her to concentrate: "I pray thee mark me" (67); "Dost thou attend me? (78); "Thou attend'st not!" (87); "I pray thee mark me" (88); "Dost thou hear?" (106).

One can say that Shakespeare has a dramatic problem—to wit, he has a great deal of exposition to handle with little dramatic conflict—and so he creates the conflict between father and daughter, or more precisely the irritation of father toward daughter, to break up the expository material into segments. That alone is not a very satisfactory explanation. The fact is, Shakespeare always has a keen eye for realistic detail. How many students have felt unjustly accused of inattention when the real problem lay within the schoolteacher? Unfortunately, too frequently schoolteachers inadequately or improperly read the feedback students give; the inattention is perhaps more within the teacher than the pupil. Shakespeare makes Prospero uncomfortably like a real schoolteacher. His irritable impatience continues all day: he is irritable with the most cooperative Ariel, irritable with recalcitrant Caliban, irritable with Ferdinand, causing Miranda to explain apologetically, "Never till this day / Saw I him touch'd with anger, so distemper'd" (IV.i.144–145). The power teachers have over students becomes a form of tyranny when they exercise that power with constant irritability. Prospero, unfortunately, exhibits some of the bad habits of some schoolteachers, but perhaps the worst is his lack of confidence in his own achievements as an educator. He exclaims, in his rage, of Caliban:

> A devil, a born devil, on whose nature
> Nurture can never stick; on whom my pains,
> Humanely taken, all, all lost, quite lost;
> And as with his age his body uglier grows,
> So his mind cankers. (IV.i.188–192)

Fortunately, Prospero proves a better educator than he knows.

And now, no longer selfishly and narcissistically isolated within his studies as an end in themselves, Prospero has become the humanist educator, profoundly engaged in seeking to effect practical results, the development of virtue. His education of Ferdinand concerning honorable premarital behavior is but one of his educational goals. He seeks to educate the drunken trio—Stephano, Trinculo, and Caliban—concerning the grossness of their drunken behavior by taking them through a "filthy-mantled pool" so that they come out smelling "all horse-piss," and concerning the shallowness of their quest for glory by easily distracting them with gaudy clothing. But most of all he seeks to educate the group made up of Alonso and Sebastian, Antonio and Gonzalo, Adrian and Francisco, most particularly the first three, for the latter three, as lesser nobility, have to experience what their superiors experience. One device is the spread banquet, inviting them to eat, only to defile it through Ariel as a harpy and whisk it away, for their attempt to satisfy themselves with earthly goodies is a contaminated feast and as ephemeral as their grasping for the empty dukedoms and kingdoms of this world. In short, all the manipulated audio-visual aids used by Prospero through Ariel are intended to effect inner changes in his students.

The solution to family conflict presented in *The Tempest* is a two-way process of education resulting in essential change in the educator as well as in the educated. Conflict inevitably means that two or more parties are involved, and the solution must affect all the family members embroiled. Prospero admits to Miranda his own wrong approach to education that had contributed to the revolt of Antonio and the seizure of the dukedom. He has himself abandoned his ivory tower and has taken his learning into the practical world, but that is by no means enough. The tempest of winds and waves that swamps the ship is but the outward manifestation of the raging tempest taking place inside Prospero throughout this eventful day of his life. He recognizes "Providence divine" (I.ii.159) at work in the protection that he and Miranda experienced in surviving their abandonment to the open sea in the "rotten carcass of a butt [cask]" (146). He implies a similar operation of providence in the fact that his enemies have been brought near enough to the island for his powers, learned from his secret studies, to operate upon them:

> . . . By accident most strange, bountiful Fortune
> . . . hath mine enemies
> Brought to this shore; and by my prescience [foreknowledge]
> I find my zenith doth depend upon
> A most auspicious star, whose influence
> If now I court not, but omit [neglect], my fortunes
> Will ever after droop. (178–184)

A recognition of the limitation of his powers, a fundamental dependence upon providence, and yet the utmost need to seize the opportunity provided him to act decisively underlie his condition on this special day. More than that, the "fury" that rages in him against his "enemies," his ravishing desire for "vengeance" is the most turbulent tempest in this play. Prospero at last has his enemies in his power; revenge is sweet, so the common wisdom declares. Now let him make them squirm, suffer, die! That is his desire, just as every wronged person finds a similar tempest within crying out for revenge. The profoundest lesson Prospero himself must learn on this very day is not to indulge himself in sweet revenge but to bring that inner raging tempest under the control of his "nobler reason."

Ariel, that bright spirit who has helped him in his educative endeavors, now helps Prospero at the most critical and decisive moment of the play. He has his enemies imprisoned in a grove of lime trees, utterly at his mercy. Now what shall he do? Ariel gently pleads, "Your charm so strongly works 'em / That if you now beheld them, your affections [your inflamed emotions bent on revenge] / Would become tender" (V.i.17–19). "Dost think so, spirit?" Prospero asks at his moment of decision. "Mine would, sir, were I human," Ariel replies. Prospero makes perhaps the most momentous decision made in all of Shakespeare's plays. He will abandon revenge; he will forgive!

> And mine shall.
> Hast thou, which art but air [as he says elsewhere so also humans ultimately are], a touch, a feeling
> Of their afflictions, and shall not myself,
> One of their kind, that relish all as sharply
> Passion as they, be kindlier mov'd than thou art?
> Though with their high wrongs I am strook to th' quick,
> Yet, with my nobler reason, 'gainst my fury
> Do I take part. The rarer [not only the most uncommon, but here especially the most excellent] action is
> In virtue than in vengeance. (20–30)

Prospero brings them before him. He reminds them of their wrongs and of the remorse they feel. To Sebastian, who absurdly planned to kill his brother Alonso to become in his stead King of Naples when there was absolutely no hope of their getting off the island so far as Sebastian knew, Prospero says, "I do forgive thee, / Unnatural though thou art" (78–79). To Antonio, Prospero turns: "For you, most wicked sir, whom to call brother / Would even infect my mouth, I do forgive / Thy rankest fault—all of them" (131–132). Easy to say, most difficult to achieve, nevertheless the conquering of fury and its accompanying lust for vengeance through "nobler reason," the sympathetic entering into the inner condition of those who have done wrong, and, finally and most significantly, the full and free forgiveness of their wrongs is a solution to family and human conflict. It has worked, and it does and will work. This part of the solution is not magic, for it can only be achieved through the anguish of stilling the inner tempest.

Prospero lays aside his robe and wand; he no longer needs that part of education. Even his worst-case student, Caliban, is not without hope. When he first arrived on the island, Prospero took Caliban into his home as a son and had taught him alongside Miranda. He had, as schoolmasters in England in Shakespeare's day were wont to do, set his better student, Miranda, to tutoring the weaker one.

Miranda says, "I pitied thee, / Took pains to make thee speak, taught thee each hour / One thing or other" (I.ii.353-355). However, Caliban experienced lust and sought to rape Miranda to people "This isle with Calibans" (350). That sort of outrageous behavior had to be punished. Even Ascham, who wrote *The Scholemaster* in response to a request from Lord Burghley—who had been perturbed by the fact that some Eton boys had run away to escape being beaten—with a major objective of expounding how to make education so enjoyable and profitable that beatings would not be necessary, declares that sometimes a beating might be necessary, "to have every vice severally corrected" (4, recto). Ascham warns that "when a schoolmaster is angry with some other matter, then will he soonest fall to beat his scholar: and though he himself should be punished for his folly, yet must he beat some scholar for his pleasure: though there be no cause for him to do so, nor yet fault in the scholar to deserve so" (4, recto and verso). Of course, Caliban for his moral delinquency deserves punishment and is made, therefore, to carry wood and water, much as the Gibeonite deceivers of Joshua had been turned into servants, into hewers of wood and drawers of water. Caliban does indeed seem incorrigible. He has learned language; he uses it to curse his benefactors. He plans murderous rebellion. He seems like a hopeless case, so much so that Prospero, exasperated, declares that Nurture can never stick to him and that the educative efforts are "all, all lost, quite lost." However, Prospero underestimates the effectiveness of his educational achievements. Possibly the most powerful impact upon Caliban resulted from witnessing Prospero forgive his enemies. Prospero urges Caliban, "As you look / To have my pardon, trim it [make clean and neat Prospero's cell] handsomely" (V.i.293–294). Prospero was probably surprised to hear Caliban's response: "Ay, that I will; and I'll be wise hereafter, / And seek for grace. What a thrice-double ass / Was I to take this drunkard for a god, / And worship this dull fool!" (295–298). There is hope for Caliban, after all. Prospero has been a better educator than he has given himself credit for.

And with his educational goals reached, most powerfully within himself first and then in reconciliation with those changed persons of the former conflicts, he lays aside robe and wand, for he will now return to the practical real world of Milan where they can all practice together the virtues resulting from that education. There is a solution for family fights. It lies in humility and forgiveness. Just in case his audience might not yet fully grasp that point, like a good educator himself, Shakespeare has Prospero sum up and repeat the primary lesson learned. In the epilogue, Prospero declares that he has now abandoned all "charms," that only his natural human strength remains "Which is most faint" (Epilogue 3). He reminds them that he has "pardon'd the deceiver," but he pleads with his audience to pray for him. He no longer has the help of Ariel, whom he has freed, nor "art to enchant." In fact, he declares,

> . . . my ending is despair,
> Unless I be reliev'd by prayer,
> Which pierces so, that it assaults
> Mercy itself, and *frees all faults*,
> As you from crimes would pardon'd be,
> Let your indulgence set me free. (15–20, emphasis added)

One can take that as nothing more than the conventional plea of an actor in the epilogue for the audience to applaud, and that element surely is present. Rosalind argues in her epilogue that even though some say "a good play needs no epilogue," still "good plays prove the better by the help of good epilogues" (4–6). Yet in view of the tempestuous struggle of Prospero to reach his solution for family conflict, his epilogue seems to have a deliberate echo of the prayer taught by Jesus to his disciples, the Lord's Prayer, "Forgive us our trespasses as we forgive those who trespass against us." Prospero seems to say, as Jesus did, "For if ye do forgive men their trespasses, your heavenly Father will also forgive you. But if ye do not forgive men their trespasses, no more will your Father forgive [you] your trespasses" (Matthew 6:14–15, Geneva Bible). Prospero urges, "As you from crimes [heavy offences, not necessarily limited to the breaches of law as the word nowaday means, and so here probably means "trespasses" or "sins"] would pardon'd be / Let your indulgence set me free." Troubled families who can learn to grow into self-knowledge as Prospero did and can learn to forgive, despite the struggle that it requires, will probably benefit from Shakespeare's own long-lasting examination of houses plunged into hell, houses divided against themselves, family members—who most ought to love one another—fighting, hating, even killing each other. The solution suggested by Shakespeare in *The Tempest* might not result in heaven on earth, but it will quite possibly diminish the sense that "Our house is hell."

Works Cited

Allen, Robert. *A Treasvrie of Catechisme, or Christian Instruction*. London, 1600.

Ascham, Roger. *The Scholemaster: Or plaine and perfite way of teaching children* . . . . London, 1571.

Ashton, Robert. *Reformation and Revolution 1558–1660*. London: Granada, 1984.

———. "Usury and High Finance in the Age of Shakespeare and Jonson." *Renaissance and Modern Studies* 37 (1960):14–43.

Barber, C. L. "The Family in Shakespeare's Development: Tragedy and Sacredness." In Murray M. Schwartz and Coppélia Kahn, eds. *Representing Shakespeare: New Psychoanalytic Essays*. Baltimore: Johns Hopkins University Press, 1980.

Beattie, J. M. "The Pattern of Crime in England 1660–1800." *Past and Present* 62 (1974):47–95.

Beecher, Marguerite and Willard. *The Mark of Cain: An Anatomy of Jealousy*. New York: Harper, 1971.

Benedict, Ruth. *Patterns of Culture*. Boston: Houghton Mifflin, 1961.

Bergeron, David M. *Shakespeare's Romances and the Royal Family*. Lawrence, Kans.: University Press of Kansas, 1985.

A Booke Containing All Svch Proclamations, as were pvblished dvring the Raigne of the late Queene Elizabeth. Collected by Humfrey Dyson. London, 1618.

Bronstein, Herbert. "Why Did Shakespeare Make Shylock a Jew?" *Jewish Digest* 11 (1966):33–40.

Campbell, Oscar James. *Shakespeare's Satire*. Hamden, Conn.: Archon Books, 1963 (an unaltered and unabridged reprint of the 1943 Oxford University Press publication).

Castilione, Baldassare. *The Book of the Courtier*. Translated by Sir Thomas Hoby. London: J. M. Dent, 1956.

Cathcart, Mary. *The City of London: A History*. New York: David McKay, 1978.

[Cawdry, Robert] R.C. *A Codly [sic] Form of Hovseholde Gouernement.* . . . London, 1598.

Champianus Northonus. *The younger Brothers Advocate: Or a line or two for Younger Brothers.* London, 1655.

Cicero, Marcus Tullus. *On Old Age and On Friendship.* Translated by Frank O. Copley. Ann Arbor: University of Michigan Press, 1967.

Cleland, James. *The Institution of a Young Noble Man.* Oxford, 1607.

Cobbett, Thomas. *A Fruitfull and Usefull Discourse touching on the Honour due from Children to Parents, and the duty of Parents toward their Children.* London, 1656.

Collis, Maurice. *British Merchant Adventurers.* London: W. Collins, 1942.

A courtlie controuersie of Cupids Cautels. . . . Trans. H. VV. London, 1578.

Crompton, Richard. *A short declaration of the ende of Traytors.* London, 1587.

Cvpper, William. *Certaine Sermons Concerning Gods Late visitation in the citie of London.* . . . London, 1592.

Dash, Irene G. *Wooing, Wedding, and Power: Women in Shakespeare's Plays.* New York: Columbia Univ. Press, 1981.

A Defence of priestes mariages. . . . London, 1567.

Dillingham, Francis. *Christian Oeconomy or Hovshold Government.* London, 1609.

Dod, John. *A Plaine and Familiar Exposition of the Ten Commandements, with a Methodicall short Catechisme.* London, 1607.

Eccles, Mark. *Shakespeare in Warwickshire.* Madison: University of Wisconsin Press, 1961.

Elyot, syr Thomas. *The Boke Named the Gouernour.* London, 1544.

Erasmus, Desiderius. *The comparation of a vyrgin and a martyr.* London, 1537.

F.A. *The Yovnger Brother His Apologie or A Fathers Free Power.* . . . Oxford, 1671.

Flandrin, Jean-Louis. *Families in Former Times: Kinship, Household and Sexuality in Early Modern France.* Translated by Richard Southern. Cambridge: Cambridge University Press, 1979.

Fletcher, Anthony. *Tudor Rebellions.* 2nd ed. London: Longman, 1973.

Foss, Michael. *Tudor Portraits: Success and Failure of an Age.* London: Harrap, 1973.

Freud, Sigmund. *Civilization and Its Discontents.* Translated and edited by James Strachey. New York: Norton, 1961.

Geneva Bible. *The Bible.* Translated according to the Ebrew and Greeke, and conferred with the best translations in diuers languages. London, 1583.

[Gentillet]. *A Discovrse vpon the Manes of vvel Governing and Maintaining in Good Peace, A Kingdome, or other Principalitie.* Translated by Simon Patericke. London, 1602.

Given, James Buchanan. *Society and Homicide in Thirteenth-Century England.* Stanford, Calif.: Stanford University Press, 1977.

Goldberg, Jonathan. *James I and the Politics of Literature: Jonson, Shakespeare, Donne, and Their Contemporaries.* Baltimore: Johns Hopkins University Press, 1983.

Gouge, William. *Of Domesticall Dvties: Eight Treatises.* London, 1622.

Goulart, I. *Admirable and Memorable Histories Containing the Wunders of Time Collected Into French out of the Best Authors and Out of French into English by Ed. Grimeston.* London, 1607.

Grafton, Anthony, and Lisa Jardine. *From Humanism to the Humanities*. Cambridge, Mass.: Harvard University Press, 1986.

Grafton, Richard. *A Chronicle at Large, and Meere History. Grafton's Chronicle; or, History of England. To Which is added his Table of the Bailiffs, Sheriffs, and Mayors, of the City of London. From the Year 1189, to 1558, Inclusive*. 2 vols. London, 1809.

Hall, Edward. *The Vnion of the Two Noble and Illustre Famelies of Lancastre & Yorke. Hall's Chronicle: Containing the History of England. During the Reign of Henry the Fourth and the Succeeding Monarchs, to the End of the Reign of Henry the Eighth*. . . . Carefully Collated With the Editions of 1548 and 1550. London, 1809.

Hanawalt, Barbara A. *The Ties That Bound Families in Medieval England*. New York: Oxford University Press, 1986.

Helgerson, Richard. *The Elizabethan Prodigals*. Berkeley: University of California Press, 1976.

Hergest, William. *The Right Rvle of Christian Chastitie*. London, 1580.

Herlihy, David. *Medieval Households*. Cambridge, Mass.: Harvard University Press, 1985.

Holinshed's Chronicles of England, Scotland, and Ireland. 6 vols. London, 1808.

Honor: Military, and Ciuill, contained in foure Bookes. . . . London, 1602.

Houlbrooke, Ralph A. *The English Family, 1450–1700*. London: Longman, 1984.

Hurstfield, Joel. *Freedom, Corruption and Government in Elizabethan England*. London: Jonathan Cape, 1973.

Jardine, Lisa. *Still Harping on Daughters: Women and Drama in the Age of Shakespeare*. Sussex: Harvester Press, 1983.

Jones, Whitney R. D. *The Tudor Commonwealth, 1529–1559*. London: Athlone, 1970.

Kahn, Coppélia. *Man's Estate: Masculine Identity in Shakespeare*. Berkeley: University of California Press, 1981.

Levin, Harry. *Shakespeare and the Revolution of the Times: Perspectives and Commentaries*. Oxford: Oxford University Press, 1976.

Lodge, Thomas. *An Alarum against Vsurers*. London, 1584.

MacCary, W. Thomas. *Friends and Lovers: The Phenomenology of Desire in Shakespearean Comedy*. New York: Columbia University Press, 1985.

Markham, Francis. *The Booke of Honour*. London, 1625.

The Memoirs of Anne, Lady Halkett and Anne, Lady Fanshawe. Edited by John Loftis. Oxford: Clarendon, 1979.

Patricius, Franciscus. *A moral Methode of Ciuile Policie*. . . . Translated by Richard Robinson. London, 1576.

Pinchbeck, Ivy, and Margaret Hewitt. *Children in English Society*. 2 vols. London: Routledge & Kegan Paul, 1969.

Praz, Mario. *Machiavelli and the Elizabethans*. London: Humphrey Milford, 1928.

Read, Conyers. *Mr. Secretary Cecil and Queen Elizabeth*. London: Jonathan Cape, 1955.

Rowse, A. L. *Sex and Society in Shakespeare's Age: Simon Forman the Astrologer*. New York: Charles Scribner's, 1974.

Saviolo, Vincentio. *His Practice in Two Bookes The First intreating of the Use of the*

Rapier and Dagger. The Second, of Honor and honorable Quarrels. London, 1595.

Sharp, Buchanan. *In Contempt of All Authority.* Berkeley: University of California Press, 1980.

Simon, Jean. *Education and Society in Tudor England.* Cambridge: Cambridge University Press, 1967.

Smith, Henry. *The Sermons of Henry Smith Gathered into One Volume.* London, 1599.

Smith, Steven R. "The London Apprentices as Seventeenth-Century Adolescents." *Past and Present* 61 (1973):149–161.

Smith, Thomas. *The Common-vvelth of England and Maner of Gouernment Thereof.* London, 1589.

Stockwood, John. *A Bartholomew Fairing for Parentes. . . .* London, 1589.

Stone, Lawrence. *The Crisis of the Aristocracy 1558–1641.* Oxford: Clarendon, 1965.

———. *Family and Fortune: Studies in Aristocratic Finance in the Sixteenth and Seventeenth Centuries.* Oxford: Clarendon, 1973.

———. *The Family, Sex and Marriage in England 1500–1800.* New York: Harper, 1977.

———. "The Rise of the Nuclear Family." In Charles E. Rosenberg, ed. *The Family in History.* Philadelphia: University of Pennsylvania Press, 1975.

Stubs, Phillip. *The Anatomie of Abuses. . . .* London, 1584.

Taylor, Jeremy. *A Discourse of Friendship.* Cedar Rapids, IA: privately printed [150 copies], 1913.

A Trve and perfect relation of the whole proceedings against the late most barbarous Traitors, Garnet a Iesuite, and his Confederate. London, 1606.

A true and summarie reporte of the declaration of some part of the Earle of Northumberlande Treasons. London, 1585.

Vaughan, W. *The Golden-Groue, Moralized in Three Bookes. . . .* London, 1608.

Vives, Lewes [Juan Luis]. *A very frvtefvl and pleasant booke called the Instruction of a christen woman.* Translated by Rycharde Hyrde. London, 1557.

Whately, William. *A Bride-Bvsh: or, A Direction for Married Persons.* London, 1619.

———. *Charitable Teares or A Sermon shewing how needfvll a thing it is for euery godly man to lament the common sinnes of our countrie.* Bound together with *A Care-Cloth.* London, 1624.

Williamson, Marilyn L. *The Patriarchy of Shakespeare's Comedies.* Detroit: Wayne State University Press, 1986.

Index

About the Author

MAX H. JAMES is Professor of English at Northern Arizona University, Flagstaff. He is currently at work on his second book, the first of a series, *Shakespeare's Plays as Tales Retold: Strong Bridges to the Originals.*